P9-DEE-401

It isn't often that an author's name becomes synonymous with the title of a book, but that is exactly what happened with David Wilkerson and his bestselling book *The Cross and the Switchblade*. Its message defined his effective and life-changing ministry to the gangs in New York and surrounding communities, later moving his outreach to young people around the world. These pages tell the story of conflict and courage in the face of danger. "The man who believed" came to know the secret of the Christian life when he said, "I do not want a visitation from the Lord … I want a habitation." As you read about David Wilkerson's fascinating life, may your heart burn with the same desire to know Christ in the fullness of his glory.

FRANKLIN GRAHAM, President and CEO,
Billy Graham Evangelistic Association, Samaritan's Purse

Fifty years ago I sat on a couch, sick and withdrawing from drugs, at the New York Teen Challenge Home that David Wilkerson opened to reach the gangs and drug addicts. My life was eternally impacted, and he inspired me to spend my life reaching the broken. Gary has effectively portrayed the legacy of his father, a man who has impacted the world with his message of hope and transformation. This is a must-read that will encourage you and stir your faith to believe God for the impossible!

— PASTOR VICTOR M. TORRES, founder and pastor,
New Life for Youth and New Life Outreach Intl. Church,
Richmond, VA

I met David Wilkerson in the early days of his ministry on the streets of New York. God used him to touch my life. I am living proof that miracles still happen.

— PASTOR SONNY ARGUINZONI SR., founder,
Victory Outreach International

Every believer in Christ understands the truth that "the Father is best made known through the Son." How appropriate that Gary has undertaken to write the story of the father he intimately knew and we all loved. David Wilkerson believed, as he preached, that God is able to use any willing vessel for his glory. This book will encourage you and bring gladness to your heart.

— CARTER CONLON, senior pastor, Times Square Church

DAVID WILKERSON

DAVID WILKERSON

THE CROSS,
THE SWITCHBLADE,
AND THE MAN
WHO BELIEVED

GARY WILKERSON

WITH R. S. B. SAWYER

 ZONDERVAN®

ZONDERVAN

David Wilkerson
Copyright © 2014 by World Challenge, Inc.

This title is also available as a Zondervan ebook. Visit www.zondervan.com/ebooks.

Requests for information should be addressed to:
Zondervan, 3900 *Sparks Dr. SE, Grand Rapids, Michigan 49546*

ISBN 978-0-310-32627-4 (hardcover)

All Scripture quotations, unless otherwise indicated, are taken from the King James Version of the Bible. Scripture also taken from the Holy Bible, New Living Translation, copyright © 1996, 2004. Used by permission of Tyndale House Publishers, Inc., Wheaton, Illinois. All rights reserved.

Any Internet addresses (websites, blogs, etc.) and telephone numbers in this book are offered as a resource. They are not intended in any way to be or imply an endorsement by Zondervan, nor does Zondervan vouch for the content of these sites and numbers for the life of this book.

All rights reserved. No part of this publication may be reproduced, stored in a retrieval system, or transmitted in any form or by any means — electronic, mechanical, photocopy, recording, or any other — except for brief quotations in printed reviews, without the prior permission of the publisher.

Unless otherwise noted, all photos used with permission of World Challenge, Inc.

Cover design: Brand Navigation
Cover photo: Jeff Calenberg
Insert background photo: naphtalina / iStockphoto®
Interior design: Katherine Lloyd, The DESK

First Printing July 2014 / Printed in the United States of America

This book looks into what God has done through one man of unshakable faith. I dedicate it to those whose faith is just now beginning to shape the course of a history yet to come:

To the unknown, unsung of this radical young generation who will answer Jesus' question, "When I return, will I find faith on the earth?" and whose lives will be his yes.

CONTENTS

FOREWORD

IT WAS A WARM SUMMER Sunday evening and our church building was filled to capacity. Our featured speaker was Nicky Cruz, former gang leader of the Mau Maus who decades before had rumbled right here in downtown Brooklyn. Nicky and I had already been friends for a few years. His dramatic conversion story had become almost legendary through the overwhelming popularity of *The Cross and the Switchblade,* authored by David Wilkerson. The book had circulated around the world and was translated into dozens of languages. It told the story of a young country preacher from western Pennsylvania who felt compelled to come to New York City to spread the message of God's love to troubled young men and women who made up the violent gang culture of that day. David Wilkerson's courage and preaching had reached even Nicky Cruz, seemingly the most hopeless of them all.

In a few minutes, I was to introduce Nicky to share once again his incredible testimony. As my wife's choir was singing, an usher came to the platform and whispered in my ear, "David Wilkerson and his wife just arrived and are sitting in the balcony." I hadn't met David Wilkerson but quickly invited him to join us on the platform. And that was the beginning of my long, valued friendship with the author of *The Cross and the Switchblade* and founder of the Teen Challenge ministry that ministers so effectively to drug abusers around the world.

But David Wilkerson was much more than that. He was a man raised up by God as an effective evangelist both in America and overseas. He authored books that inspired people to be serious about their relationship with Christ. His financial generosity reached around the globe, providing homes for the destitute and feeding programs for the hungry. He later became the founding pastor of Times Square Church. He also was, in some sense, a prophetic voice to his generation, confronting ungodly trends within the church of Christ and warning both pulpit and pew with no thought as to the popularity of his message.

David Wilkerson's outstanding character trait was his passion for God. He longed for closeness to Christ above everything else. His quest was to experience God in deeper ways and not merely understand Christian doctrine. His dependence on the Holy Spirit's empowering and guidance was often breathtaking to behold. When at his best, Brother Dave wanted to be led by God no matter the consequences. Insincere, lukewarm, mechanical Christianity grieved him to the core.

It's ironic that I've been honored with the privilege of writing the foreword to this biography. David Wilkerson spoke countless times at The Brooklyn Tabernacle, and our friendship deepened over the years even though he remained somewhat of a loner his whole life. We traveled together, worked together for the cause of the gospel, and often talked about spiritual matters.

One day we were walking up Flatbush Avenue in Brooklyn toward Prospect Park, where our church had arranged an outdoor street meeting with Brother Dave as the speaker. He opened up to me about a recent misjudgment he had made and some of the spiritual struggles he was undergoing. Suddenly he stopped in his tracks and said, "Jim, just imagine! One day I'll die and someone will probably write a book about my life. They'll paint a picture of some superspiritual giant of the faith who never battled with sin and Satan like everyone else. How ridiculous!" Here was the famous David Wilkerson reminding a young pastor that without the grace of Jesus every moment of the day, he, like everyone else, would quickly fall apart. That was vintage David Wilkerson — unpretentious and candid, humbly expressing his constant need of God's help.

We finally reached the band shell in the park, where people had gathered, drawn by the sound of gospel music. David Wilkerson, then living in Texas, had returned to his element — a street preacher telling folks about the love of Jesus. That afternoon, for some reason, David broke down in tears as he spoke. He seemed to recognize some older, chronic drug abusers in the crowd. "How many more times will you have a chance to come to Jesus?" he asked. "What more can I say to you about Christ and his love? You've heard it all before. You still have time today. Don't say 'tomorrow'; come to him now!"

As he shared the gospel, conviction of sin through the Holy Spirit could be palpably felt. David asked those wanting to receive Christ to step forward closer to the small platform. Dozens moved quietly as the band shell area became an outdoor sanctuary for God. As David asked them to repeat the sinner's prayer, suddenly he thrust the microphone in the face of a Puerto Rican man who was crying like a baby. "Repeat after me," David instructed him, "but say it from your heart!"

What followed was probably the strangest sinner's prayer in the annals of Christianity. David Wilkerson led him along with the others: "God, forgive me of my sin." "I need you, Jesus." "I'm sick of my life." "I put my trust in Jesus." Those were the phrases my friend Dave Wilkerson spoke, but when the desperate man repeated them, amplified throughout the park, he added all kinds of four-letter adjectives to each sentence. With tears of contrition, he seemed so desperate for God to know he was serious, he fell back on the strongest words and language he knew. Suddenly, the park was filled with the sounds of cursing mixed together with a cry for God's deliverance and salvation! And David never pulled the microphone away from him. It sounded wrong, yet somehow it was absolutely right because it was the only language the man knew.

I opened my eyes during that prayer and heard others following along. Dave Wilkerson, with tears rolling down his face, held that microphone in front of a man thrusting his way into the kingdom of God. There probably won't soon be another David Wilkerson among us.

— Jim Cymbala, The Brooklyn Tabernacle

A life marked not by honorarily designated
"miracles" but by what can, and must, accurately
be described in just that term.

Written as fiction, this would not be believable,
yet it is, because it is enacted fact.

— John McCandlish Phillips, reporter, *New York Times*

Introduction

THE MAN WHO BELIEVED

"What do you see?" my father asked.

He had asked me this question several times in my life. At the moment, we stood side by side, sweating, at the center of one of the world's largest slums. The question now — about perceiving something accurately — had always been central for him, no matter where he stood.

Our dress shoes, covered in muck, toed a weedy patch of dirt in Nairobi's steaming heat. A van had dropped us off a half mile away, after having driven us as far as it could. We had walked the rest of the way here, winding along narrow dirt pathways, past row after row of mud huts and lean-tos, our group gazed upon impassively by Kenya's poorest, their tiny, makeshift dwellings jammed into each other for as far as we could see. Some of the huts were made of two-by-fours for corner posts, a piece of canvas or tin for walls. Some were covered by plastic tarp or cardboard. These were permanent homes to multitudes who lived and died in the slum without ever leaving it.

We had come here with a delegation of Kenyan pastors, at my father's request. At one point, our group had to straddle a long latrine that runs between the shacks for block after block. The slum had no sewage system, so people had dug runoff trenches from their homes. The rivulets fed into a river of waste flowing between the rows of huts. We came to a spot where there was no room on either side of the latrine to walk, so we straddled the stream — left foot on one side, right foot on the other. Our waddling might have seemed undignified for a group of men in Sunday suits, particularly for my father, a slight figure in glasses, now in his midseventies and always crisply dressed. But he wasn't fazed; he clearly had something in mind.

Occasionally we had to step over a cable wire that snaked surreptitiously into a shack. Most people in the slum didn't have electricity, so a few brave dwellers had run wires off a main electrical line somewhere on a street nearby. If caught, they faced not just fines but harsh punishments or sizable bribes they could never afford. I admired their ingenuity, not to mention their bravery, in the name of survival. That's life in any slum. My father had been familiar with this kind of desperation all his life, and he had never turned away from it. In fact, Dad was an expert at locating just these kinds of "wires" — lines of human desperation leading him directly to the world's most needy areas. He seemed magnetized by them.

Finally we arrived here at the small clearing. Dad had stepped away from the group of pastors when he motioned for me to stand next to him on the cracked earth spotted with weeds. I glanced at him again for a clue about what he had just asked me. What did I see? A vision of human hell.

The vast Mathare Valley slum is home to 600,000 people. It sits in the shadow of downtown Nairobi — ironically, near the capital's affluent areas. The deeper one ventures into the slum, the poorer it becomes, with its own gradations of poverty. At its very center, encompassing the weedy patch where we now stood, is a city within a city within a city. Each of the slum's neighborhoods has its own schools, churches, and stores, basic human institutions unrecognizable to visitors. At the heart of the Mathare Valley, a half mile back — mired in the worst of its squalor, amid the earth's most deplorable conditions — we had helped to build an elementary school for neighborhood children.

We had met the delegation of pastors at the school, a group that included a Kenyan bishop. Just inside the gated compound, on a dirt and clay patio, our group was greeted by the beaming school staff. "The children made you this plaque," said the principal, stepping forward to present it along with a bouquet of flowers. They were poised to give us a tour of the school, which we supply with daily lunches for the four hundred children who attend. My father was eager to see where the food was prepared and served, the one healthy meal of the day these kids enjoyed. We were led to the kitchen, which was essentially a pit in the ground with a place for a fire, and a huge pot in which large quantities of meat or vegetables could be boiled.

As we rounded a corner into a small courtyard, we were greeted by a chorus of four hundred young voices, all lined up in bright school uniforms our ministry had paid for. "We love you, Jesus!" they shouted in song, one they had written for the occasion. Then came a verse somewhere in the middle: "We thank you, David Wilkerson!"

Dad smiled at this. Yet I could tell his thoughts were elsewhere. I wasn't surprised. As the kids lined up single file to be served lunch, my father turned to consult with the bishop.

Once the kids loaded their plates, they squeezed into a small, walled-in area where they sat on hardened dirt to eat their meal. There were no chairs or tables because the space doubled as their play area. After lunch, one by one a group of them kicked a soccer ball, but soon the area was so crowded the game became a kind of frenzy. I gave in to it, kneeling on the ground among the kids, who within minutes had piled on top of me. When I looked up I saw my father with the bishop and pastors waiting. Dad was antsy, wanting to get moving. He had seen what he needed to see.

Now at the edge of the weed-filled patch of ground where we stood, I was about to learn what that was. "So, what do you see?" my father asked.

Heat rose from the earth in skinny waves. "An empty field, Dad?" I thought of joking. We were at the epicenter of the world's desperation. There was nothing here for the naked eye to take in but bald life-or-death need. Even the bleached ground had been picked clean of any shard of glass that might be sold for scrap. The desolate sight was reinforced by its smell — a mixture of fumes from the oils people burn in their homes for fuel and the urine and feces vacated from their malnourished bodies.

Yet I knew exactly what my father was thinking. There he stood in his suit, despite the oppressive heat, his shoes filthy. He always dressed well to honor those we visited, who themselves put on their best to host us. Now he pointed across the field. "Here's what I see," he said, and he articulated a sharply detailed vision for new school grounds. "The dining hall — here," he said. "The playground, right there." Every gesture pointed to a specific patch of ground. Each signified a specific improvement in exacting detail. I could see it all.

A grin formed as he talked. His juices were flowing; this was my father at his best. The need he had discerned in the cramped quarters of the school had registered in his mind the moment he took it all in, and a vision immediately formed. These children had a classroom building; now they needed a place to play and eat, and these teachers needed help. Before we left the Mathare Valley slum that afternoon, a cell phone call was placed to start the drawing up of plans, which Dad provided off the top of his head.

———

IT WASN'T THE FIRST TIME my father had shown me what he dreamed. In 1973, when I was a teenager and our family lived in Dallas, Dad occasionally took me on his weekend drives eastward where Texas's piney woods begin near Tyler. Those drives were refreshing breaks for him between his preaching trips, long travels that zigzagged across the country between metropolitan arenas and small-town churches, between crowds of ten thousand and merely a few dozen; travels that took him overseas, where he addressed vast throngs in soccer stadiums and small gatherings in hand-built slum churches. At a certain point on our drive, he turned north off Interstate 20 onto a county road and followed its winding miles between groves of post oaks and magnolias. Near a certain bend he turned right onto a short gravel drive and followed a dirt trail that bisected a sprawling property. He aimed the car toward the highest hill we could see and drove along its bumpy incline in grooves made by someone's pickup truck. Finally, at its highest point he parked and stepped out of the car. As we paced forward to the hill's edge, Dad made sure he had my attention, raised an arm, and pointed, saying, "Let me tell you what I see."

On those East Texas trips, he envisioned a leadership school for graduates of Teen Challenge, the drug rehabilitation program he had founded thirteen years earlier. That kind of rehab program had been unheard of when he started it. There were only two centers in the United States that treated addicts — one was part of a psychiatric unit; the other was a wing of a federal prison, institutions that said everything about how the world viewed addicts at the time. Teen Challenge not only removed the stigma of addiction, but it also became renowned for its eighty-six percent cure rate, the world's most successful by far. Its reach had spread to other continents, even communist nations whose drug problems had become societal epidemics. Regime leaders were desperate for the program, fully aware it was fueled by faith in Christ's power to deliver human beings body and soul.

"His preaching in Poland was a near miraculous gospel exploit," wrote McCandlish Phillips, a celebrated reporter for the *New York Times*. He refers to my father's historic 1986 trip, when civil unrest in the communist nation was at a peak. "David's plainness of speech directly from the Scriptures — in halls, auditoriums, and arenas to young people that were bused to these places — was breathtaking in its power. It surely should have been reported."

Phillips himself was renowned in the *Times* newsroom, revered by peers Pete Hamill, Gay Talese, and David Halberstam. For ten years this devout Christian sent memos to his editors before finally being permitted to write a feature on the astounding success of the faith-based drug recovery program that was "becoming a wide-reaching phenomenon." Phillips knew this phenomenon hinged on one thing: the power of God's love to address the world's most intractable problems.

My father's visions weren't just about the transformation of real estate. He envisioned transformed lives. He had embarked on that vision in a way that's hard to imagine today: as a naive, socially awkward, white Pentecostal preacher from a small town venturing alone into the gang zones of New York City in the late 1950s. Yet as my father had come to believe, if God's love could not reach into impossible places to do impossible things, how real was it?

There were thousands of churches in New York City when my father arrived. Many of those churches were afraid to venture into their own neighborhoods for their own people's safety. "We lost forty young people in one summer to gang warfare," says Dick Simmons, director of Men-4Nations today but a pastor in Brooklyn at the time. My dad's efforts on those dangerous streets had a transforming effect on the church as a social force. "His actions were extremely prophetic, cutting edge," says church historian Dr. Vinson Synan. Those actions produced what Billy

Graham called one of the most outstanding conversions of the twentieth century. He speaks of Nicky Cruz, the gang leader whose encounter
with Jesus was emblazoned in the imaginations of generations through
the bestseller *The Cross and the Switchblade*. Nicky had gained notoriety
among New York City crime reporters. His transformation demonstrated
to millions of readers the powerful lessons contained in Dad's enduring
book: God can change anyone. God can use anyone. And God wants you.

His gaze now fixed on the East Texas countryside, my father described
to me in detail what he saw: a graduate program for "recovered" young
men and women who showed promise as leaders in ministry. He wasn't
just thinking of leaders for Teen Challenge centers. He envisioned ministry outreaches of all kinds — urban missions, overseas missions, inner-
city churches — with young leaders drawn from all over the United States
and sent to the world's neediest areas. He pointed to a grove of trees and
said, "That's where we'll build homes for the staff who come to train
them. We'll put the main offices over there. We'll have a gym over there.
The warehouse for the ministry's books will be by the highway, so trucks
can back up to it."

Within three years, what my father described to me during those
weekend drives is exactly what came to pass — and exactly as he had
envisioned it. The properties as he described them stand intact today. Yet
here is what's truly amazing about it: he envisioned it all before he even
owned the land.

This kind of thing happened time after time. More than a decade
later, he intrigued a legendary family of Broadway producers when he
sought to buy their flagship theater in Times Square to house a church.
Standing before them was a Pentecostal minister who for years had been
living in the sticks of rural Texas. Within a year and a half, those same
producers were shaking their heads in disbelief as they signed over the
Mark Hellinger Theater to make it the home of Times Square Church, a
congregation where the humble aromas of homeless people mixed with
the heady colognes of hedge-fund managers, where Tony-winning actors
held hands in prayer with crack addicts. "The Church That Love Is Building" reads the marquee.

"David did things that no one else could do, or even conceive of doing," said McCandlish Phillips. He was friends with my father and knew that Dad possessed the threefold gift of a visionary: He was able to see in his mind's eye what few if anyone else could. He had the pure faith to believe that what he envisioned would come to pass. And he possessed the ability, drive, and trust in God to pull it off. As my uncle Jerry, Dad's younger brother, says, "He could look at something and see what it would be in five years." That included lives.

——•——

DAD AND I HAD COME to the Mathare Valley slum on the heels of a pastors' conference that his ministry, World Challenge, was holding in Nairobi. Dad always allowed time after a conference to visit the local ministries we supported. The conferences themselves are designed to encourage pastors in their difficult work, especially in their service to the poor. The events are always free, because often the pastors are poor themselves. We provide meals for many, some of whom travel great distances to attend. Dad had begun these conferences after years as a pastor himself. He had instructed his staff at Times Square Church, "I know there are pastors crying out from slums around the world, needing encouragement. Go find them." Now, in his last major effort to do hands-on gospel work, he traveled the globe to minister to them personally. In five years' time he went to sixty countries.

On the final day of the conference, we saw a brilliant cultural dance by Kenya's Maasai warriors, whose amazing jumping abilities are renowned. They had performed at the request of the nation's vice president, who shared the platform with us that day in the hotel ballroom. As the Maasai finished their dance, I directed Dad's attention to someone in the crowd whose story I'd just heard. "She's a missionary who runs an orphanage," I told him, gesturing to a woman who jostled a three-year-old. "She rescued that boy out of a garbage can." Little Samuel, I was told, had been left to die as an infant.

Moments later, my father was at the podium. "Before we start, there are some dignitaries here you're going to want to meet," he said. "These are real world-changers, people you will hear about." All eyes turned to the country's vice president and the church bishops. Instead, Dad said,

"I want to introduce you to Samuel." He motioned for the missionary to bring the boy to the platform. Dad took the child into his arms.

"This is Samuel," he said, smiling. "God rescued him from a garbage heap. He's going to be a great man of God in your country."

One by one, the pastors stood and erupted in praise. I glanced at Kenya's vice president. Tears traced down his cheeks. I could read his thoughts: "This is what our country needs to hear. Yes, this is a son of Kenya."

My father had just breached protocol. The proper thing would have been to acknowledge the societal dignitaries, yet no one in the room felt that way, including the vice president. God's reality had broken in. The lens of Christ had cast everything in a different light. It was the same lens through which my dad had first seen Nicky Cruz, with a vision for what his horribly damaged life could become.

What my father had done in that moment wasn't out of the ordinary for him. It was in keeping with how he had always lived. For reasons of his own, he had turned down every invitation from a US president to visit the White House, but he would drive hundreds of miles out of the way during an evangelism tour so he could meet an obscure nun who had written something about Christ that had moved him. Always, he saw the world and those around him through the lens of eternity.

———

MY DAD NOT ONLY SAW what many of us couldn't. He disciplined himself to see what most of us didn't want to see.

He forced himself to go into heroin "shooting galleries," to witness what the world turned a blind eye to: downtrodden young people knowingly killing themselves. He foresaw the same deadly drugs flooding into middle-class suburbs years before secular commentators recognized the shift in society. For the bored generation that succumbed to them, he foresaw their lives five years down the road and was moved to tears again. He founded David Wilkerson Youth Crusades to reach that generation with God's love before despair, addiction, and suicide could, a deadly progression he had already witnessed in urban ghettos.

It's easy to forget the culture of that period, how suspiciously young people were viewed. It was the time of "America, love it or leave it." Any guy with hair touching his ears was seen as rebellious. The same for any girl wearing a miniskirt. Dad pursued them all, the same way he had gone after gang members and drug addicts — not just to rescue them, but because he saw them as God's best evangelists. His faith helped transform the way they saw themselves — as objects of eternal love rather than scorn.

Dad's vision for people also aroused their faith. He preached that supernatural works could be accomplished through imperfect but yielded human beings. Over two decades, that message stirred untold numbers to entrust their lives to Jesus. During the classic era of evangelistic crusades, many Americans accepted Christ as their Savior. At my dad's crusades, they were stirred to more, offering to God not just a believing heart but a life of sacrificial service.

"He was always way out ahead," says Dallas Holm, the renowned musician and songwriter who traveled with my dad full-time for more than ten years. "I don't think he knew how progressive he was. His crusade messages were always about something very relevant to the culture, a specific, unique topic everybody was aware of — drugs, suicide, music, issues of the day. I've heard pastors try to be relevant — you know how that goes — but there was an authority with him. There are people who make themselves relevant because they've read all the information. But Brother Dave lived in the middle of it. So much was going on in California — the biggest services, with all the hippies getting saved — that he moved all of us, his entire ministry, from New York. He said, 'We've got to be out there. That's where God has our ministry.' That's why he was so relevant — he didn't just read about it; he went there."

Over five years, my father had a profound impact on the Jesus Movement as he preached at a series of influential youth rallies held by Ralph Wilkerson (no relation) in southern California. "Melodyland Theatre held thirty-two hundred people, and the services were packed out," notes David Patterson, my dad's first full-time crusade director. "The conviction of God would rest so strongly in those meetings that when Brother Dave invited kids to come forward, they couldn't get up out of their seats. They were riveted. The ushers would have to pick them up and carry them to the altar. It was the most amazing series of meetings I've ever seen. There were hundreds and hundreds of kids getting saved. Every three months, the rally would be moved to the eight-thousand-seat Anaheim Convention Center, and those meetings would be full too. There was nothing like this happening anywhere in America. Some of the early pioneers will tell you that it was the momentum of those meetings that gave birth to a large portion of what became the Jesus Movement."

I'm touched by a relic from that era. My dad had written a book, *Purple Violet Squish*, titled after one stoned kid's conception of God. Inside, the book's owner inscribed her name, "Mrs. Powell," whom I might safely guess was someone's mother, looking for insight. Dad was not only an advocate for young people; he was a faithful translator of their experiences to their concerned parents. He saw the distress that people had over their children's struggles, and he was a compassionate friend to them. He also challenged them, just as he challenged their kids, that God could be trusted in all things. His directness earned the trust of both generations.

That's another overlooked role my dad played: he was an intrepid reporter. Whenever he went to the front lines, he faithfully reported what he had seen. And he didn't embellish; he spoke the truth straight. In 1959, he recruited his youngest brother, Don, to accompany him to a heroin shooting gallery to film teenage addicts. Dad was convinced, "The churches won't believe us unless we show them what's happening." He was right. When they screened *Teenage Drug Addiction*, which showed addicts injecting needles into their blackened arms, people fainted.

———

HE SAW THE CHURCH FAINTING in other ways too — falling into ruin as it descended into a compromise of basic gospel tenets. He boldly called a "fattening" church to account — not judgmentally but because he envisioned the beauty of Christ's bride enacting justice for the poor. He wrote endlessly about that bride, and he led the mission for justice by example.

Long before cable television, he foresaw little black boxes sitting on top of TV sets, piping pornography into homes. He published that prediction in 1973 in his controversial book *The Vision*. Now, when it's estimated that nearly half of all pastors view porn online through little black boxes emitting signals from the internet, it's hard to imagine why he was ever dismissed.

In truth, I was never fully comfortable with my dad's prophetic role; he never was either. I'm very different from my father in many ways — in temperament, gifts, and personality — but the prophetic role my dad played is one I came to respect. He himself never wanted to be a prophet. "No true prophet ever does," says church historian Dr. Stanley Burgess, who encountered my dad in his earliest days of ministry.

When my father saw evil in the world, he never questioned why it existed. Instead, he did something about it. "You can't do everything," he always told us, "but you can do something." He did more than his share. He went to every area of crisis he could — ghettos, prisons, poverty-stricken countries that few evangelists visited — and started works there. "Find the poor," he advised every young minister who sought his counsel. "Help those who can do nothing for you. Then watch God bless you."

He was also a pastor to millions through his writings. He authored more than forty books, each with an urgent message — on suffering, on suicide, on crossless Christianity. His monthly newsletter messages were a lifeline to Christians during some of the church's — and America's — most difficult times. At one time his free mailing list exceeded one million households, with an estimated actual readership well above that number.

But that wasn't the extent of his writing. He had a powerful ministry penning letters to people who wrote to him in agony of soul. He responded by dictating letters — thousands over the years — to prisoners, shut-ins, widows, the mentally ill, anguished parents, and troubled children. He wrote to them as if he knew them and as if he were right there with them in the midst of their pain. I couldn't begin to recount the number of people I've met whom Dad wrote to, personally offering a specific word that changed their lives.

Yet of everything he authored after *The Cross and the Switchblade*, my dad never wrote much about himself. In his last years, my aunt Ruth, a writer herself, did all she could to urge him to reflect on his life. She gifted him with a stack of his preferred lined pads, the kind he used for his favorite writing task — sermons — but he never touched them. My father was comfortable in his own skin, always at ease with who he was, but in some ways he didn't seem alert to his own life.

On the flight home from Nairobi, I was surprised to see him lift a copy of *The Cross and the Switchblade* from his briefcase. He noticed my puzzlement. "I just read this recently," he joked. "Boy, I was a great guy." He hadn't recognized in those pages the young, tee-totaling preacher who founded the world's first successful drug rehabilitation program. Yet history saw my dad very clearly: as a bold, progressive, and fearless spokesman for God. "He was a visionary," says Stanley Burgess, "a man of God's heart who followed the Spirit directly and started a resurgence in social awareness." Vinson Synan adds, "He was one of the most transformational figures in Pentecostal and charismatic history."

Still, Dad had begun asking his trusted friends, "People tell me I'm famous. Do you think I'm famous?" Make no mistake, my father was acutely aware of his reputation, and yet his question was sincere. What he was really communicating was, "I'm unsure how God sees me."

At his most vulnerable times, my father wondered whether he was loved by God at all. He didn't question the Lord's goodness. He didn't struggle over why evil exists. He didn't wonder why people suffer. (And his family suffered as much as any. Through a genetic anomaly, my mother, both sisters, a niece, and now a nephew all have faced serious battles with cancer.) Very simply, my father wondered his whole life whether God loved him. It was a question he kept mostly to himself. Growing up, he had absorbed some of the traumatizing aspects of a theology that leaned toward works and legalism and sometimes fear. Although doctrinally he knew he was free in Christ, something in him still made him feel he had to work hard — that nothing he did was enough, that more was required to fill what was missing in his righteousness in Christ. My uncle Don, who for years worked alongside my dad in ministry, observes, "David had a lot of grace for other people, but he wasn't always able to appropriate it for himself."

Unlike some pastor fathers who battle in this area, my dad never placed that burden on us, his family; he reserved the struggle for himself. Yet in waging that battle alone, my dad withheld an important part of himself from us. It was a part we desperately needed, in retrospect.

That's why, more than three years after his passing, my siblings and I are each still raw in our grief over his loss, still wishing we had a part of him he chose to keep from us. (I don't presume to speak in this book for my siblings. Their contributions here are ones they've chosen to make. Like children of any public figure, we have to work to keep those parts of our father that are due to us alone. Children of civil rights leaders speak of this kind of thing. They understood what their father was doing and why it was important, and that, in effect, they had to share him with the world. But even with that understanding, some say they still feel something crucial had been taken from them, and they wouldn't surrender it again if given the choice.)

The revelation of my father's lifelong struggle was stunning to many. "I preach a lot about the love of God nowadays, and it was David who had the greatest influence on me for that," says Bob Phillips, who copastored with my father at Times Square Church. "It's based on what I learned from him in his years as a pastor, not just from his preaching but from how he believed and lived." Like so many others who worked closely with my dad, Bob never would have guessed this struggle to be my father's deepest.

From the outside, those who understood my dad's early life would say he never stood a fighting chance. Yet, characteristic of my father, a few decades ago he set himself on a journey to correct things within himself. At that time, in the eighties, he was still busy traveling the world as an evangelist. Yet his own soul was dry; he had become weary of preaching the same messages to crusade audiences. Between those events, he began reading a stack of books given to him by a discerning friend, author and preacher Leonard Ravenhill. These were classic works that had endured the centuries, most of them written by Puritans, names many of us have never heard of. As my father dug into those treasures, his heart opened to a new revelation of Christ. Grace awakened in him, coming alive in a way he had never known. The old books stirred him once again to study the Scriptures cover to cover, this time with a new understanding of the gospel. As he explored the full extent of the finished work of Christ, he experienced joy.

Toward the end of his life, my father confided to me that he still struggled to know whether he was loved. He couldn't escape completely the emotional cobwebs, but he was seeing more and more clearly the work that Jesus had done for him. In my last conversation with him, he told me of how deeply he had probed, how he had scoured every page of every writing he could find on the glorious subject of God's covenant grace. And yet I could see in his eyes there was a yearning for more. There were things he still wanted to know about the depth and breadth of Christ's finished work. That's when he urged me to dig deeper in my own search on the subject, not to be satisfied but to go farther. It was as if he were saying, "I got a late start. I want you to have it better. I want my grandchildren to have it better. Don't ignore this truth. If you catch it now, it can save you years. Son — *do you see?*"

A few weeks after my father's funeral, my brother-in-law sent me the last book that Dad had left open on his study table. It was a classic work by Thomas Brooks. Almost every page was underlined and highlighted, with comments filling every open margin. There was my father, nearly eighty years old — after sixty-five years of serving in ministry — still yearning, still reveling in the gospel of Christ, its glories never ceasing to unfold new beauties of assurance.

In this way, my father was like Paul. With every achievement, his estimation of himself had grown smaller. Early on, Paul went from strength to strength in his accomplishments for the gospel. In AD 55 he wrote to the church in Corinth that he was no less than any of the other apostles. Two years later, he wrote something very different to the Ephesians, stating, "I am the least of all saints." Finally, in his last known letter, Paul wrote, "I am the chief of sinners."

That was my father. In the beginning of his ministry, David Wilkerson was a crusading young zealot, making a massive imprint on the world for Christ. Later, as he gazed hard into his own brokenness, he realized, "I am dependent on God for everything," and he offered genuine encouragement to others in their sufferings. By the end of his life, amid his anguished battle to know love, he claimed, "I can do nothing. He did it all. 'It is finished.'"

Here is where God's work in my father began. Let me tell you what I see.

Part One

VISION

David Wilkerson realized at some point, "It's not about my knowledge or expertise. If we all trust God, anything can happen." Of course, it has. What happens in *The Cross and the Switchblade* is not fantasy. It's the story of a real guy who opened a magazine, felt God leading him to a New York courtroom on behalf of teenagers on trial for murder, and ended up ridiculed with his photo in the newspaper. No one could have scripted this except God. It's almost comical. It's as if the Lord wanted to give us an illustrated sermon: "Let's take this diminutive white guy to Harlem. Let's make this self-educated man a prophetic intellect. Let's make this socially awkward guy who doesn't come from means negotiate multimillion-dollar real-estate deals, not with teams of high-powered lawyers but just himself. Let's see how far opposite I can make him of everything you would think is the way to accomplish things." He had nothing going for him in all these things. He just had a drive to act when he felt God told him something. His fearlessness was in proportion to his confidence in God.

—*Dallas Holm*

1
—
TWO SIDES
OF A HILL

Somewhere in a family member's garage, there is reel-to-reel tape that dates back to 1958. It's a recording of my grandfather preaching at his small Assemblies of God church in Turtle Creek, Pennsylvania, a tiny town in the coal-mining hills southeast of Pittsburgh. When I was a teenager, my father played that tape for me. Through the tinny crackles I heard my grandfather preparing to start his sermon. "Before we begin," he interjects, "I'd like to welcome my son Dave and his family, and their newest addition. I'm very proud to announce my grandson, Gary Randall Wilkerson."

My father took joy in playing that tape for me. It was his way of making a generational connection. I never knew my grandfather, Kenneth, because he died before I was two. And when it came to his own family, my dad wasn't a storyteller. He didn't articulate to us his relationships with his parents or siblings, partly because there were no family stories to speak of — none, that is, that didn't center around church or its obligations.

There was another reason my father didn't talk much about his childhood years. He just didn't look backward very often. In most conversations we had, he was always looking forward. Our talks centered more on his views of things and how he might bring about change. "Have you noticed this happening in the world today?" "What do you think about this movement in the church?" "Here's what we're going to do, what we're believing for."

Whenever Dad did speak of my grandfather Kenneth, it was always with reverence and respect. He described his father — a tall, dark-haired, striking man with a persuasive preaching style — as tenderhearted and soft-spoken. But I know my grandfather was also intense and serious. These traits were partly his temperament, reinforced by his training as a US marine. Yet they also extended to a certain legalism — an emphasis on outward behavior to reflect God's holiness — that was part and parcel of the Pentecostal holiness faith that he and my grandmother adhered to. They weren't unique in this. The 1940s — my father's teenage years — were generally a stricter time for a lot of reasons. Those were the war years, and the mood in society wasn't one of frivolity. That generation had also just endured ten agonizing years of the Great Depression. For a while, my grandparents had to rely on a neighbor's kindness to provide their children with food. Yet beyond this were "spiritual" prohibitions against worldly things — not just movies or sporting events but, to people of my grandparents' persuasion, even owning a washing machine.

"There was joy in church," attests my uncle Don, the baby of the family. This was certainly true for his parents. When they looked into the pews, they saw all five of their children in attendance. Church was where the very reserved Kenneth and Ann Wilkerson channeled all their emotional energies, leading two Sunday services — a morning sermon to build the body of Christ and an evening message geared to evangelism. Once the day ended, there was a discernible release in the household. "Dad and Mother were relaxed and loose, and everyone in the family spoke their minds," Uncle Don says. Those free and easy evenings must have been true Sabbaths. My uncle looks back on them fondly as "the Wilkerson jam sessions."

"We would all gather in Dad's study after a Sunday night service," he remembers. "David would be there with his girlfriend. Jerry would be there with his girlfriend. I was just a kid then, but those were some of the happiest times I can remember in our family. Everyone would just talk. Then they would complain because there was a schedule of who should wash the dishes and who should dry. And they would pay each other off. 'I'll give you a quarter if you do mine.' It was a good family time."

Every son desires his father's approval, and it was no secret that my dad, the oldest brother, wanted his father's. He never would have done anything to disappoint his father, much less get crosswise with him. But my dad's outsized ambitions for a life in ministry would inevitably have to collide with his father's — and they did.

Only once did I get a glimpse into any deeper feelings my dad might have had about his father. I recall him once saying, "He was a denomination man." He offered this as a description, not a judgment; Dad never would have disparaged his father. But I know the exact compartment in my father's heart — a palpitating chamber of burning vision and restlessness — that let slip that comment. All of my dad's dreams had to do with serving God, and those dreams ranged as broadly as his imagination allowed.

What I've written up to here is very nearly the extent of what my father told me about his childhood. The one other thing he disclosed was that he loved basketball and that he thought he was pretty good at it. That was it. The past just wasn't his concern. There were reasons for this, which he kept to himself, and others I don't think he was fully aware of. He just knew that everything ahead of him would be a matter of pleasing God. And he trusted that God would make possible things that the church world could not.

——•——

ALBERT STREET, WHERE MY FATHER, David Ray Wilkerson, spent his adolescent years, isn't very long. But it does stretch the length of the plateau that sits atop a steep hill overlooking downtown Turtle Creek. Up on that hill, anchoring the center of Albert Street, was the neighborhood grocery store, a small, narrow building occupying a single corner lot. People weren't allowed to buy a newspaper there on Sundays. But outside was a telephone booth where men made discreet phone calls throughout the day. My uncle Don was just a schoolboy then, but if he happened to be walking by when the phone rang, the store owner would tell him to answer it and to shout out the series of numbers that the caller whispered to him. My uncle had no idea he was relaying illegal bets.

Not far from the grocery store was the Packard garage, where my father and his younger brothers would eye the classy cars as they walked by on their way to the schoolyard basketball court. Their own dad appreciated a good car, but on a pastor's salary Reverend Kenneth Wilkerson could afford only a Hudson. Packards were the Cadillacs of their day.

Down the block from the garage was the neighborhood bar, which my dad and his brothers also would have passed. As preacher's kids, they rarely recognized anyone who came or went through those doors. But they were surprised one afternoon by the sight of their uncle Frank, their mother's brother from Cleveland, emerging from the bar in his navy uniform on his way to visit them.

Up and down the neighborhood streets of Turtle Creek, soot of all kinds gathered on window shades, floating in from the various industries: the Westinghouse factory that employed so many townspeople; the electric plant down at the creek bottom next to the railroad tracks; the coal mines in nearby Forest Hills, a town just down the road.

Like a lot of working-class homes on Albert Street, my grandparents' three-story wood house, humble but spacious, sat on a narrow lot. Its enclosed front porch jutted almost to the street. The driveway led to a backyard garage where my dad and his brothers had set up a hoop so they could spend hours shooting baskets. When the weather was bad, they unleashed their energies playing ping-pong in the basement. And in summers they enjoyed the shade of the back alley, where neighborhood kids gathered to play baseball. One inventive mother improved their games by producing a baseball-sized sphere from yarn, woven tightly so it wouldn't unravel when battered, yet staying soft enough not to break a windowpane. She should have patented it.

In that hilltop neighborhood in Turtle Creek were two spots that occupied my father's imagination for most of his teenage years. They were located on opposite sides of the hill — and opposite ends of my dad's dream life.

◆

AT ONE END OF THE hill, perched on a slope overlooking downtown Turtle Creek, is the Assembly of God church my grandfather pastored. It's a modest, simple brick church he had led his small congregation to build, and they all were proud of it. It replaced the cinderblock structure where they used to meet, directly below at the bottom of the hill, beneath a clattery raised railroad track that ran parallel to a flowing Turtle Creek. In those two church buildings, a central part of my dad's imagination was fed and formed. Despite the restrictions of his family's brand of faith — or maybe because of those restrictions — church was the one safe place he could let his imagination run free.

Dad's preacher father may have been soft-spoken in person, but in the pulpit Brother Kenneth Wilkerson didn't flinch from preaching on God's judgment. In my dad's young mind, the flames his father described morphed into fireballs — exploding World War II fighter planes, Japanese Zeroes and German Messerschmitts he imagined crashing into Turtle Creek's hillsides. Yet it was the sermons on Christ's second coming — when a trumpet would sound, lifting the faithful into the air and leaving the world to face destruction — that left the deepest impression on him. The end of all things wasn't hard for my dad to imagine: two of Japan's major cities had been decimated in the twinkling of an eye by atomic bombs. With a single newspaper photo, everything that Christians had believed for two millennia about the earth's sudden destruction became plausible. And though his thoughts of end times would be tempered by his maturing years in ministry, my dad could never dismiss those images of mushroom clouds as imminent possibilities.

At the opposite end of the hill — just three blocks from the Wilkerson house — Albert Street dead-ended at a beautifully impressive overlook. Outstretched below was Turtle Creek High's football stadium, cradled in a natural amphitheater of leafy hills. Football was big in Turtle Creek, so big that if the high school team beat their archrival, Scott Township, all the schools in town got a half day off.

Every other Friday afternoon, my father and his brothers walked the three blocks to sit on the hillside and gaze below at the stadium, a mesmerizing world of daring and stardom. There on that field played Leon Hart, the great end who became a hero at Notre Dame, winning the Heisman Trophy and later starring for the Detroit Lions. But the stadium below was more than that; it was also a world of exhilaration and freedom. My father and his brothers watched as their classmates filed into the massive concrete grandstands on the facing side. Some clasped hands with their dates, others shouted rowdily with friends, all encouraged to go wild with school spirit. These were the kids who ran free in gym class, a class forbidden to the Wilkerson boys, who were pulled from it at their parents' request.

"David-Jerry-Donald. Time for prayer!"

Mom Wilkerson's shout reached them easily on their hillside perch. Her voice could be heard to either end of Albert Street, and it tolled with authority. I wouldn't be surprised if startled fathers along the block dropped their newspapers and momentarily considered their souls. Mom Wilkerson had the physique of a bird and was quiet and reserved, but when she spoke, it counted. It didn't matter how involved in a game her boys might be when she called them. My dad or uncle Jerry could be up to bat in the ninth inning of the Albert Alley World Series, but they knew not to balk at her summons. If they mumbled something on arrival, they could expect their mother's singular response: "You know where you belong."

To youngest brother Donald, those words contained a mild reassurance. To middle brother Jerry, they added one more brick to a wall slowly being erected between his parents and himself.

"Family altar" in Brother and Sister Wilkerson's household was not meant for spiritual discussion. It was a solemn time for all five Wilkerson kids to gather in their father's study on the second floor of the house and hear their parents' prayers. Other than meals and church, it was the only activity that gathered everyone as a family. And each of the five children came to it with his or her own level of interest or toleration.

Juanita — or Nan, as her younger siblings called her — had chafed at her parents' restrictions. The oldest, she resented being sheltered and overprotected. At seventeen she was still threatened with spankings. She wasn't allowed to style her hair. She had been made to wear unstylish long stockings while her classmates wore ankle socks. She was forbidden to date until she graduated high school. Now she had begun lashing back at her parents without remorse. Her heroes were Hollywood icons, not Bible figures or missionaries, and she resisted every restriction placed on her.

In truth, my grandmother was desperate to bridle Juanita because she reminded her of her own younger self. Mom Wilkerson looked back on her youthful years as wild ones, which may have been somewhat of revisionist history. She was probably as close to normal as any first-generation child in an immigrant family could be, which of course carried its own burdens. In the 1920s my grandmother had been an independent young working woman — a "modern girl," with a job as a secretary, dressing in current styles and spending her evenings in dance halls perfecting the Charleston. If that kind of nightly release carried any guilt, it wasn't because she had a serious faith commitment — she didn't at the time — but more likely because she had hardworking immigrant parents who didn't indulge themselves. For a working girl from an austere home in which English wasn't spoken, the dance floor was a place to cut loose and be free, which happened to be where she met my grandfather. Kenneth Wilkerson was a marine recruiter who at the time was sidestepping his own Pentecostal restrictions and was still a few years away from returning to his roots to become a minister. It took him some time to give up his drinking habit, however, his chosen means of drowning the pain of his own growing-up years.

My grandparents didn't want their oldest child repeating their "mistakes." Aunt Juanita wasn't aware that in a few weeks she would be sent away to Cleveland, to stay with an uncle and his family. After a few months there, Juanita would seem to have changed; she would write her parents that she was interested in going to Bible school to become a missionary. That was the ultimate vocation for any Pentecostal girl, in a hierarchy that held missionaries at the top, followed by evangelists and then pastors. Ultimately, though, Juanita wouldn't recover from the binding legalism she tied inextricably to her parents' faith. After graduating she would marry a Catholic man, which would be a slap in the face to her father. In turn, her father would never talk to her again. In both my grandparents' eyes, their daughter had backslidden, a conclusion that may have been their way of steeling themselves against heartbreak.

In years to follow, Juanita effectively disappeared from her family — calling herself Joan, moving to Arizona, raising two sons, and divorcing. She pursued eastern religions, even traveling to the Far East to study, as many searching souls did in the sixties. She became a cautionary tale to us through our grandmother. "You don't want to end up like Juanita," Grandma would tell us. "She had a call to Africa, but she ran from the Lord." That caution registered with us grandkids the few times we were around our aunt. Juanita's humor was brazenly sarcastic and at times caustic, and she seemed to try to shock her adult siblings with tales of her lifestyle. In retrospect, perhaps she was instead trying to impress them — and maybe, deep down, wanting to endear herself to them again.

When we were growing up, Aunt Juanita was a source of confusion to some of the Wilkerson granddaughters. Some saw her as a glamorous figure — beautiful and smart, worldly and well-traveled, interesting and free. And she was striking, with large, dark-brown eyes, high, pronounced cheekbones, a pointy chin, and olive skin. She had entered the education field and ended up doing stellar work among children with learning disabilities. But ultimately my grandmother's view of Juanita held sway with us. Between the two of them, Grandma was the one who had authority to speak for God. We saw her pray for her daughter with every good intention.

Yet the traits we saw in our aunt Juanita — intelligence, spirit, vision — were the very ones Grandma esteemed, but for God's use, not worldly pursuits. The only Christian doctrine our grandmother knew very narrowly defined what it meant to serve God.

———

AT FIFTEEN, MY FATHER MIGHT have fallen in line with his parents' view of Aunt Juanita. I picture him sitting across from her in the study as their parents prayed. If during those times he thought of his sister as lost, he couldn't be blamed. Certain Pentecostal churches didn't preach grace for sins back then; if you sinned, you had to get saved all over again. In that environment, I wonder what my father's thinking was regarding his sister. Later in life he came to believe she had borne an unfair share of their parents' legalism. But at the time, his sister's example might have been something he learned from, as any second child would.

My dad wouldn't have identified with Juanita's disrespectfulness. But to find his own way, he would have to do some rebelling of his own. The rules he broke didn't have to do with God's law; he rebelled instead by circumventing his parents' legalism. He didn't tell them, for instance, about sneaking a TV set into the attic bedroom he shared with his brother Jerry and watching *The Milton Berle Show*. Or taking his two brothers on the trolley to Pittsburgh (which was allowed) to enjoy the amusement park (which was not) or to Forbes Field to watch the great Pirates slugger Ralph Kiner (also forbidden). He brought home board games of their favorite sports, but he had to keep an extra pair of dice handy because when their mother found them she threw them away.

A brasher act of my dad's was auditioning for the lead role in the high school play, *The Scarecrow*, and landing it. Juanita was wounded when she found out about it; she'd been strictly forbidden to take part in any school activity. But her siblings swore her to secrecy for their brother's sake. Their undersized, socially awkward sibling had conquered something in an outside world they had not been allowed to enter, and they were proud of him. Somehow the siblings were even able to slip away to see the production without their parents knowing, and they were thrilled at the boisterous applause my dad received at the curtain call.

I'm trying to imagine what inner part of my father would have come into the open during that performance. According to descriptions of the play, the role demanded some emotional range. My father was no extrovert — quite the opposite, in fact — which would have made his performance all the more mesmerizing to his siblings. For a moment, they wondered whether he might go into acting; his onstage presence had seemed that natural.

It shouldn't be surprising that any preacher's kid might project a sort of "theater" onto a church service — the spotlight of the raised platform, the dramatic telling of a biblical story, the endpoint of redemption. But I don't think it was unconscious training that summoned my father's powers for the role he played. I think there was something else going on when he took his bow — an inner drive for affirmation.

•————•

IT WAS THIS SIDE OF my father's personality — what the family called "theatrical" — that upset his parents. It was assumed from early on my dad would be a preacher, something he desired and was gifted for. Yet I think he knew deep down that conventional church life couldn't contain all that he envisioned doing for God. It certainly couldn't contain the great emotions churning inside him. Years later he would write of his boyhood dreams, "I composed sermons in my mind, sermons that made people laugh or cry. When my dad found out about these imaginings, he chided me: 'David, why do you get so carried away?'"

His parents were simply distrustful of emotions. (It was a running joke in our family that if you wanted a hug from Grandma, you had to make the first move.) Yet it's clear to me that getting "carried away" was my father's only way to handle fears produced by certain Pentecostal-holiness beliefs. My father was prone to all of them. He told me that while growing up, he feared missing the rapture, the sudden event signaling the end of all things. In his mind, the sound of the "last trump" was both fascinating and terrifying. What if he wasn't ready? What if he was at Forbes Field when it happened? Would he be left behind for eternity?

He had a powerful imagination already, but the church's emphasis on the rapture did some damage to a lot of earnest believers. It placed great pressure on them to witness for Christ, getting as many souls as possible into heaven because the clock was always ticking down on Jesus' return. Any idea of a "social gospel" — helping others through charitable works — was barely visible down the list of priorities. The other mental burden was having to avoid committing any sin at all. If you were "fallen" — or even distracted — at the moment Christ returned, you were lost forever. It was a doctrine that forced a believer to organize his or her every thought around spiritual matters. My father eased his mind from that pressure through the years, but he never escaped it entirely. As much as he grew in his knowledge of God's grace, he never stopped wondering whether his life was pleasing to God and, more especially, whether he was deserving of God's love.

——

MY QUIET UNCLE JERRY WOULD have come to the family altar with pain as deep as his older sister's. What his parents saw as their athletic, blond-haired son's "rebellion" was never about belief in God. Jerry just didn't compute their legalism, and it wasn't in him to fake it. He couldn't adopt behaviors to accommodate religious rules that he didn't grasp. At thirteen, he had become a watchful, observant boy of few words. It was his only strategy to withstand what he couldn't comprehend.

In adolescence, Uncle Jerry's resistance to legalistic rules was interpreted by his parents as stubbornness. When he was punished for something, he didn't cry, the way my father did. He dug in. "Son," my grandfather would say, brandishing a leather belt, "I'm going to knock that stubbornness out of you." My grandmother intervened to protect her middle son, seeming to understand something of what went on in him. By that age, Jerry had learned how to ride the trolley on his own. Some Sundays after church, he would hop on it by himself and ride all the way to his Czech grandparents' house in Canonsburg, more than twenty miles away. Despite the language barrier, my uncle was content just to be with them. When he returned home later in the afternoon, after a nearly fifty-mile round trip, sometimes his parents weren't even aware he had been gone.

Soon after high school graduation, Uncle Jerry left home and took up drinking. He also entered military service. Perhaps not coincidentally, those were two things his father, Kenneth Wilkerson, had done at the same age — in reaction to his own preacher father.

Thankfully, these wouldn't be the defining actions of my uncle's life. Despite several rocky years early in his adulthood, he forged his own idea of family, and years later he reconnected with his family of origin in a meaningful way.

⊢——⊣

EVEN AT AGE TEN, my aunt Ruth brought to the family altar a spiritual inclination as clear as my father's. Modest and reserved, she was bright and studious and she loved the Bible. Ruth looked up to her older sister, as any little girl would, longing for Juanita's attention, despite the difference in years and temperament. But at her tender age, Ruth couldn't comprehend Juanita's arguments with their parents. She recoiled when her sister talked back to their mother. Ruth loved church life, her parents, and her siblings. And gradually, she wanted less to do with the sister who seemed antagonistic toward it all.

As years passed in the household, my grandparents' legalism waned a bit. Ruth and her younger brother, Donald, were allowed to do some of the things their older siblings couldn't. Ruth even dated a young man who lived next door. But the priority at home was still — as my uncle Don recounts — "God first, church second, and family third." When Ruth received a four-year scholarship to the University of Pittsburgh, her parents asked her to turn it down. They weren't biased against education. They were simply poised to take the reins of a larger church in Scranton, double the size of the congregation in Turtle Creek. Church was like a family business to my grandparents, and they needed their daughter's help.

Torn but loyal, Aunt Ruth obliged. In time she found her own wings in a life she loved, serving in ministry. She married a pastor and blossomed as a writer. The view she formed of her family's spiritual heritage honored her parents, but by then it was completely her own.

In homes like theirs — where every child is conscious that God, rather than family, is the focus — each young mind is convinced that he or she suffers alone. Years later, after their parents had died, my two aunts grew closer. Whenever they got together, they reminisced mostly on safe topics, recalling the jokes they played on each other. But eventually Ruth revealed to Juanita how lonely she had been all those years — and that she could have used a big sister's help. Juanita seemed shocked. Being labeled the black sheep of the family had made her feel alienated from them all. Both sisters realized it hadn't needed to be that way.

———

LIKE HIS OLDER SISTER, RUTH, curly-haired Donald had no reason to resist the family altar, other than the boredom that would torment any seven-year-old. With his father's dark hair and rangy build and his sister Ruth's shy reserve, Donald got the affection — minimal though it was — that comes with being the last child. In years to come he enjoyed a few concessions that had been withheld from his siblings. One was getting to play Little League baseball.

Uncle Don pitched for a team sponsored by the Lions Club. By that time, his father's church had grown to include civic leaders — merchants, doctors, and businessmen — which may explain the easing up on prohibitions. My grandfather had also become part of the town's ministerium, a group of pastors that included mainline denominations. He even had a radio broadcast. All these respectable activities may have spelled compromise to stricter Pentecostals, but my grandfather had his own, deeply personal reasons for pursuing them, reasons that superseded doctrine.

Still, the emotional tenor of the Wilkerson household remained subdued. One day, my uncle Don pitched a three-hitter for the Lions, and his coach rewarded him with a quart of ice cream. Bouncing up the hill with a skip in his step, he couldn't wait to share the news about his achievement, but as he rounded the corner to Albert Street, he found his pace slowing. As he approached home, a cloud came over him. Pacing up the driveway, he peeked around the corner of the house to see his father sitting in the back yard. "Dad," he began — and stammered out his accomplishment. Then, Uncle Don recalls, he was met with nothing. "Not discouragement," he says, "but no encouragement either. It just wasn't going to happen." In any other house along Albert Street, he thought, maybe there would have been a celebration.

Young Donald, however, was allowed to go to Forbes Field for Pirates games. He remembers being with Jerry amid a sea of African Americans — the first he had ever seen en masse — who had come to witness Jackie Robinson perform with the visiting Dodgers. He and Jerry would have ridden the trolley to get there, but never with their father.

It wasn't just rare Little League feats that my grandparents gazed past. They didn't give hugs. They didn't celebrate birthdays, their own or their children's. And they never told their children, "I love you." Strange as it sounds, they weren't all that different from other parents of the era, particularly those from stricter holiness churches. To stand out in any way was prideful.

In my grandparents' case, I'm convinced it was a matter of emotional frozenness. Because of their own difficult backgrounds, they had never learned something essential about the human experience. They simply didn't know to give that essential thing — affectionate love — much less how to give it.

———

"Boy, what they went through," Uncle Don says of his parents' lives. "We heard them talk about the hard times. It always broke my heart to know how it affected them." Try as they might to conceal their burdens, my grandparents bore them nonetheless to the family altar.

My grandmother Ann had her share. Like all people with foreign accents, her family had been suspect in a culture that resented the great flood of immigrants in the early twentieth century. The Marton children kept their heads low. This wasn't hard for Ann, who was naturally reserved and quietly discerning. Keeping her guard up was a good trait for protecting herself, but not great for making friends. "She wanted to live and think the American way," my aunt Ruth wrote. But even my grandmother's faith experience, which came later, "did not change her longstanding habit of keeping her thoughts and problems to herself."

My dad admired his mother deeply, and I think he saw her guardedness as a spiritual strength. He was made of the same basic stuff — no nonsense, forthright and direct, a loner by nature — and that was the way he led his ministries for years. In the early days of Teen Challenge, he never revealed the pressures he felt, and there were plenty to be borne in a pioneering work like that one. When my uncle Don joined the ministry, he sometimes opened up to a staff member about a distressing concern. My dad dressed him down for it. "Don't lay your burdens on them," he warned. He worried about the effect on the staff if they saw their spiritual leaders struggling.

That advice was easier for my father to live by than for others. He went to God alone — with everything. "Part of it was his theology," says Uncle Don, "and part of it was just his personality. His approach to life was, 'It's me and God.' I really think that was enough for him, in some ways."

It was an unusual makeup to have, yet I think my father made up his mind early on that it would always be that way for him. Thankfully, throughout their marriage he and my mother always had another couple or two with whom they could relax and be themselves. My dad loved to laugh and have lighter moments, and he shared some of his worries with those cherished friends. But he rarely opened up to anyone about the deepest concerns of his heart. Try as he might — and he tried hard — he could not unlearn the guarded ways he absorbed from the mother he admired.

Sadly, for my grandmother, the guardedness translated into panic attacks. She was never confident in her abilities as a minister's wife or to run a household. She did all of it well — when she preached in her husband's absence, it was with an acknowledged authority — but deep down she was an independent soul, never quite suited to any of the roles she had taken on. And she couldn't help questioning her performance at them.

NOT SURPRISINGLY, MY GRANDMOTHER MARRIED a man with emotional walls nearly as high as her own. The son of traveling evangelists, my granddad Kenneth had twice been sent to boarding school by his parents as a boy. That wasn't unusual around the turn of the century, but all indications are that my grandfather never got over the rejection he felt from it. He was a teenager when his mother died. When his father remarried a much younger woman — a girl just a few years older than sixteen-year-old Kenneth — it was more than his neglected young soul could take.

He signed on with the marines, and military life brought order and guidance to the inner chaos that ruled my grandfather's emotional life. "Adhering to rigid rules gave him a sense of accomplishment and security," Aunt Ruth writes. "Years later, Dad would tell us that he could read a man's character by the way he respected the laws of God and government and by the neatness of his clothes and the shine of his shoes."

That's why punctuality — US marine style — was the first order of business at the Wilkerson family altar. Nobody made my grandfather wait. That kind of consistency and reliability can provide children with a sense of security. But any security the five Wilkerson kids felt was offset by their father's bleeding ulcers. For ten years they threatened my granddad's life. The family could never anticipate when he would suddenly double over from a potentially deadly attack, and the specter of death loomed continually over the household. "I bawled my eyes out as a boy, wondering if my dad was going to the hospital again and not coming back," Uncle Don says. I know my dad absorbed those traumas in his own way.

My grandparents were leading the family as best they knew how. But as I picture them gathered in the second-floor study for family altar, I wish with all my heart they could have just told stories to each other — stories about their day, their thoughts, their history, stories that could have helped them through it all.

They could have started with the amusing way my grandparents had become a couple. Ann Marton's walls came down momentarily in 1928 the night she and Kenneth Wilkerson first danced the Charleston together. The next day, when Ann clocked out of her job, she found Kenneth waiting on the sidewalk outside her office building, dressed in his US marine best. "I want to marry you," he declared. "But I'm engaged," she said. "Break it off," he told her. It took him three months to convince her, but she did it.

They also might have told their kids about the odd thing that happened when Kenneth was a marine and still drinking. He had hidden his church background from his fellow troops, but after too many drinks, he started preaching — right in the middle of a bar. A couple of rounds turned the soft-spoken sergeant into a tent-revival evangelist, his fiery sermons turning heads throughout the bar. For most marines, cutting loose meant brawling. For my granddad, release meant speaking his deepest heart and mind, and what came pouring out was gospel fire.

Those aren't the stories that got told at the Wilkerson family altar. Instead, the kids listened as their father and mother cried out to God for their own souls, for their children's souls, and for the church congregation that God had entrusted to them. "We lacked a close bond with our siblings because of the nature of our household," Aunt Ruth writes in her book *The Wilkerson Legacy*. She writes respectfully yet perceptively of her family, observing that "too many ordinary pleasures were taboo; there were few family fun times. I don't recall either Mother or Dad sitting down with us for a game of checkers. And card games were definitely forbidden. We ate together, listened while our parents prayed at family altar time, sat separately in the church services, and attended church camp without ever meeting up with each other. This emotional disconnect, although unintended, left a void in us, and eventually affected each one of us deeply."

That effect would show up in each of their lives and marriages. Aunt Ruth says, "I did not know how to converse with people who could not talk about 'the things of the Lord' ... Don speaks of having had difficulty socializing with people outside our church community. It became a hurdle we all had to overcome."

After my grandfather's death in 1960, his adult children didn't stay in touch with each other very much. Nearly fifteen years passed before all five got together again.

⊢━━━┤

YET AS MY AUNT RUTH makes clear in her book, family is also where my father and his siblings found faith — true, spiritual, grounded faith, the kind a person can live by.

My grandmother didn't compromise when it came to the gospel, to speaking truth, and to relying on God through trusting prayer. She had a great burden for the lost, and she evangelized with passion. These unshakable traits made her a fixture in my father's early days of ministry in New York City. When my grandfather Kenneth died prematurely, at age fifty-three, Dad made a place for my grandmother at Teen Challenge. She preached there as she always had, in her direct, authoritative style. And she gained the same respect from tough New Yorkers that she'd earned from small-town Pennsylvanians.

From my grandfather, my dad heard the exhortation again and again, "God always makes a way for a praying man." My grandfather lived by that truth, convincingly enough that my Dad adopted it as his own way of life.

Somehow, at the intersection of my grandparents' towering faith and their sad void of affection, my dad's faith formed. For better or for worse, he had learned to see the world without illusion. And he had learned not to expect its affection. He had these two things in common with the downtrodden people he ministered to throughout his life. It helped him preach convincingly to them of their one hope — God's unconditional love — because it was something he had to know for himself.

———

IT'S SAID THAT ONE QUALITY of leaders is their ability to compartmentalize. This doesn't mean they deny one thing to be able to accept another. It means they're momentarily able to set aside one troubling set of issues to tackle another. My father had that ability.

It's what helped him know that he could love his sister Juanita, sitting bitterly across from him during family altar, without seeing her solely as an object of prayer. It's what helped him later, when his marriage was in serious turmoil, to preach of God's trustworthiness to crowds of ten thousands. When he delivered those messages, he knew he was preaching to himself first and foremost. That ability also gave him peace when one of us kids was deep in trouble. My dad never denied the problems life sent his way. He might have mishandled them at times, but he didn't turn away from them. As broken as he was by life's struggles, he kept moving forward through them. He had learned that at home.

God first, church second, family third. "David reordered those priorities in his own family," Uncle Don says. "We all did — but David probably more so than the rest of us." My father had learned the one essential thing about the human experience — and the spiritual experience — that my grandparents had missed: that love is at the center. It became the focus of every street rally, every outreach, every David Wilkerson Youth Crusade event: the piercing, enveloping, powerful love of God.

Yet that focus didn't make it any easier for my dad to show affection that he himself had never received. He tried to be affectionate with us, but those times could be awkward. So he usually demonstrated it with gifts rather than hugs. Growing up, we were never aware of the inner barriers he struggled through to reach out to us. And we had no trouble laughing when he fumbled his way through an emotional moment. Even those attempts must have been major victories for him.

My uncle Don once told someone, "In all the years I've known Gary, I've never seen him struggle with his security in Christ." He's right about that. I never have, in any serious sense. What made the difference for me?

Deep down I knew that, despite his many absences in my growing-up years, my father loved me.

It's ironic — and saddening — that although my father knew God's steadfast promises better than I ever will, he could never be sure he was measuring up. My father and I occasionally had conflicts, for a variety of reasons, but I never doubted his love. To me, that's a tribute to how hard he battled to show to me the very thing he lacked. It was the conflict of his life.

Dad admitted to me that he always wanted to please his father. Any child does, and that desire is stoked when affection is withheld and love is in doubt. I'm sure that's what was behind my dad's Sunday night telephone calls to his father. After my dad struck out on his own in fledgling ministry, he took time each week to report back home on what God was doing. I see now that he did it for his own sake as much as his parents'.

———

WHAT I CAN PROUDLY AND confidently say about my family — my grandparents, my father, and the heritage they left us — is that they loved God. No one who knew them doubted this. Their hearts were set on Jesus and their gazes were aimed forward, all based on one thing: the faithfulness of the one in whom they believed.

So why would I frame my father's early life in the interpersonal terms that I have here? You don't have to subscribe to psychology to understand why. You don't even have to subscribe to biblical counseling. Stories like ours play out throughout the Bible — of favored sons, of prodigals, of overlooked and alienated children. Thankfully, Jesus changes our understanding of who prodigals are and what it really means to stray from God. Prodigals are not always the runaways but sometimes are those who stay on the family path. My father and my aunts and uncles all had a little of both in them. So did their parents — and so do the rest of us. The only people who get disparaged in Scripture are those who don't face the truth about themselves and who end up inflicting damage on others because of it. As one perceptive theologian has said, "If we don't deal with the sin that has been done to us, we're destined to sin against others in the same way." That's not a psychological statement; it's a statement of how grace works — and of its absence.

My grandparents didn't have a vocabulary for the traumas they suffered, much less what they unknowingly passed on. But even my father, who resisted psychology and counselors for much of his life — until, notably, he became a pastor — was aware that these dynamics played out in his life. God's Spirit was faithful throughout the years to compel my dad to face down his inner conflicts, and Dad was faithful to respond, eventually, as that light came to him. Like his own praying parents, my father listened faithfully whenever he thought God was speaking. He was like a lot of men of his era: he neglected some important things — both with our mother and with us — out of emotional convenience. But he kept listening to God, and he didn't turn away from what he heard. And he came to us in tenderness whenever he thought he had failed.

My dad never would have written of psychological matters to his newsletter audience; that wasn't their interest. But he often revealed deeply felt convictions in the personal notes he wrote to individuals. As those recipients attest, his words were usually pungent and on the money. He once wrote something very telling in a note of condolence to a staff member whose dad had just died. The note consisted of just two sentences. The first read, "I'm sorry to hear of your father." The second was equally simple and true to his experience: "You'll never get over it."

2
—
RESPONSIBILITY

"Gwen. Eve. I need a song tonight."

It was the sort of request my grandfather would make if you happened to be sitting in his living room on a Sunday afternoon. And if you happened to be "dating" his older sons, Dave and Jerry.

I put "dating" in quotes because the teenage girl who would become my mom — Gwen Carosso — wasn't permitted to date. Not even a nice Christian boy like Davie Wilkerson. Her strict Italian father wouldn't allow it. But she *was* allowed to take part in the youth group at Turtle Creek Assembly of God. And she was permitted to be driven home afterward by the pastor's son Davie. He was given driving privileges with the family car because he contributed to the household income as a clerk at Harkins Market.

The other teenage girl sitting in my grandfather's living room — Eve Wood — became my aunt. She was dating my uncle Jerry, who also worked at Harkins Market. Sunday was a big day for all four teenagers, because they got to double-"date" after the evening service.

Before that could happen, though, there was a matter of putting together a song for Brother Kenneth Wilkerson. This wasn't just a request; it came from the pastor, a figure of no small authority in Assemblies of God circles. I picture my mom gulping a little, maybe limbering her fingers for the piano. Aunt Eve might have cleared her throat nervously, to pipe out a song to my mother's accompaniment. Despite any butterflies, both young women knew it was a chance to show their stuff.

Dad and Jerry probably chuckled at the sight after their father had left the room. Secretly, my dad would have been pleased that "his girl" was suited to church life. At sixteen, he was already filling pulpits in the area, preaching to small congregations whose pastors were absent. Those jobs added to his income, but he did it because he loved it. All his growing-up years he had dreamed of preaching God's Word. Now he eagerly followed his father's advice on developing sermons, which was to write an outline and practice it. For my dad, this meant full-sentence outlines. He wrote out his sermons and read them word for word, a practice he never veered from through six and a half decades of preaching. His evangelistic crusades were known for ushering in the palpable presence of God, but no one noticed that the convicting sermons he delivered were basically read from his script.

Even as a teenager, my dad branched out from the confines of pulpit ministry. On his own, he had learned ventriloquism. That may sound funny and maybe even a little weird today, but in the fifties ventriloquists were a staple of TV variety shows. Of course, my dad channeled his new skill into ministry. "Child evangelism" was a common field within the Assemblies of God for young ministers to pursue, and that's how Dad used his dummy, "Red." His parents kept their reservations to themselves, but on the sly my grandmother was heard to mutter, "Which one's the dummy?"

It was this industrious Davie Wilkerson that my mother was taken with the first time she saw him. She was gazing out the window of her grandparents' house when the new pastor, Brother Kenneth Wilkerson, brought his family to Sunday lunch. Mom described her impression as she watched my dad amble up the walk amid his siblings: "Too skinny. His sandy hair was too unruly. There was nothing about his physical appearance that I found especially attractive. Except for his startlingly blue eyes. Nevertheless, after seeing him from Grandma's window, I never really looked at another boy."

It didn't hurt that Davie Wilkerson was the youth group leader at Turtle Creek Assembly. My mother had grown up in a somewhat volatile home. Her dad didn't go to church, so her kindly, submissive Welsh mother took her to services. I think my mother might have idealized my dad's family. She was impressed, for instance, that both of my dad's parents were ministers. But my mom's own father was never keen on my dad. The man who became my Grandpa Carosso was a foreman at the local Westinghouse factory, and he didn't think any minister, no matter how hardworking, could ever be a good provider. Truthfully, I think he was just down on my dad. "This guy never has time for you," he would tell my mom.

Meanwhile, to my dad, my mother must have been a godsend. None of the girls he had crushes on in high school would have been interested in the kind of life he dreamed of. Then along came Gwen Carosso — beautiful and shy, with lively humor — and she loved God. None of the teenagers in the church youth group ever dared to pair off, but everyone knew who were couples, and Davie and Gwen were the most obvious.

Traditionally, the Sunday evening service at any Assembly of God church was evangelistic. It was the service you brought friends to if you wanted them to hear the gospel. But for my dad and Jerry, Sunday evenings meant one thing — date night. It commenced with the youth meetings, which I'm sure were designed to be serious, but under my dad's leadership they were punctuated by informal comedy routines. These were unplanned bits that he and Jerry naturally fell into, unfolding as the evening went on, everyone laughing as the brothers played off each other. Clearly they had picked up a few bits from watching Milton Berle.

An hour or two later, four teenagers scurried out of the church to squeeze into a green Hudson in the parking lot. Their first stop was for ice cream, and afterward they drove across town to Elder Beck's church, an African American holiness congregation. Aunt Eve remembers the distinctive beauty of those services, the people "singing the old, old songs" by memory, without hymnals. It made for a late night on Sundays, but it was safe enough entertainment for Assembly of God kids.

The last leg was the drop-offs, with the boys' strict 11:00 p.m. curfew in mind. The first stop was Eve's house. Jerry would slip out of the car with Eve, and then my dad drove my mom to Forest Hills, two towns away. The distance was no bother since it allowed them time alone together. Once they said good night, my dad sped the green Hudson back to Eve's house, idled at the bottom of the hill, and honked. He would watch his burly brother amble down the slope and jump into the car, and Dad would gas it home. They would pull in by 10:45 — which was already 11:00 by marine time.

———

DATE NIGHT WASN'T THE ONLY time the two brothers had to hustle home. Little Aunt Ruth remembers Dad and Jerry bursting through the front door after school, shucking their books aside and wolfing down a meal their mother had set out for them. They had only a few minutes before the trolley came by, taking them to their jobs at Harkins Market in the next town. After that, they were gone until late evening.

For years my dad and his brother had done most things together. Dad had tried to teach Jerry basketball, his own favorite sport, but Jerry says he could never master the dribble. For his part, Jerry developed ace pitching skills, spending hours in the yard bouncing a ball against the wall. The brothers also competed for long stretches at ping-pong in the basement. It surprised no one that when they found an after-school job, they could do it together. Mrs. Harkins, a devout evangelist, knew the pastor's family could use the income and had offered work to the boys.

Despite being constantly together, the brothers had begun drifting apart in their adolescent years, as many siblings do. The way my dad described it years later, he immersed himself in the things of God, while Jerry immersed himself in sports. As adults, both brothers used the same phrase to describe their separate paths: "We were just on different planets."

That distance grew more pronounced, in Dad's mind, as he noticed girls giving his athletic younger brother the eye — but not him. When my mother said he was skinny, she wasn't kidding. My dad's arms were so remarkably thin he wore long-sleeved shirts to hide them, even in the stifling summer heat. At the time, Charles Atlas's "he man" ads were plastered everywhere, in drugstores, in magazines, and on the back covers of comic books. It was one more message from the world that my dad didn't belong.

———

THERE WAS ONLY ONE KIND of vacation my dad's family ever took. They spent a week each summer at Living Waters Camp in Cherry Tree, Pennsylvania, the regional worship gathering held each year by the Assemblies of God. These were gatherings in the classic "camp meeting" mold, drawing people from several states away.

The campground sat in a clearing amid a wooded grove dotted by a dozen or so cabins. Most people brought tents to set up as living quarters for the week. While adults made camp, the kids met at a tree swing in the midst of the clearing. From there they could run down to the creek to draw water for their families, or splash their way across and then down a long slope to a grassy field. Once there, all they needed was a bat and a ball because the field made a perfect diamond.

Anchoring the campground was the Tabernacle — a two-hundred-foot-long wood structure hand-built by the men who came to Living Waters each year. On the first day of camp, a caravan of semitrucks rumbled in carrying massive mounds of hay. It was dumped and spread throughout the sanctuary, which was three pew-rows wide and twenty or so deep.

The speakers who converged on Living Waters were heroes of the faith — some missionaries, some evangelists, some pastors, and some powerfully Spirit-gifted laypeople. Their names meant something special in Assemblies of God circles — C. M. Ward, Dan Betzer, Paul Wysocki, the great gospel songwriter Ira Stanphill, and Esther Cox, the gifted teacher who led children's Bible school. These were the human vessels through whom, year after year, God changed lives forever.

My dad was one of those transformed. He had been saved at age nine, which had been cause for excitement in the family. But two years later, things had changed. On the cusp of adolescence, my father was preoccupied with his appearance. That summer he chose to wear a corduroy coat all week long under the summer sun to hide his arms. He even kept it on during baseball games at the grassy field.

My father's need was like any other kid's at that age. To him, though, that need was something the world couldn't satisfy, nor could his parents. On the last night of that year's camp, in a message aimed at young people, the speaker said something that went straight to my dad's heart. Aunt Ruth writes:

The preacher's sermon caught David's attention: "I don't care what you look like — your outward appearance doesn't matter to God. It is what is inside that matters. God is looking for young men and women who will love Him with all their heart and mind and faithfully serve His Kingdom on earth....

"God is calling some young person tonight. He wants to use you to reach thousands of souls for Christ's sake. All he asks of you is that you come and present your body as a living sacrifice for Him. You are never too young to make this consecration to God." ...

Never before had the words of a sermon struck him as those did. He loved God and he knew God loved him; but to think that God could use him, that God actually wanted him — skinny and all — was an awesome revelation to David.

He could barely wait until the altar service. At the invitation to go forward, he jumped up, ran down the aisle, and flung himself down on the straw. With arms raised up toward the heavens, he cried out: "Jesus, use me. Put your hand on my life." A nearby minister placed his hand on David's head and prayed: "Lord, use this young boy for your service. Let him never lose this zeal and desire to serve you that he feels so strongly this night."

David got up, his face beaming. He had received "the call." ...

Dad referred to this experience continually throughout his life. Yet two very different realities marked his calling that night — one expected, the other not. The first was the affirmation his father gave him. When the family got home, his father presented him with a copy of *Foxe's Book of Martyrs*. Then he offered counsel that I would hear my dad repeat throughout his life: "God always makes a way for a praying man. You may never be able to get a college degree, you may never get rich, but God always has and always will make a way for a praying man."

The second thing my dad experienced after his earth-moving experience was surprising: *nothing*. The whole world looked different to my father after that experience with God, yet the world itself hadn't changed. As he put it, "I assumed that the world was going to be different after that.... But as a matter of fact my world didn't change much. Mother remained her collected self. Dad's duodenal ulcers continued to give him both fear and pain and left him keyed up emotionally.... I couldn't understand this, for to me the things of God were becoming more important every day."

I know Dad wrote those words gently, because they involved his family. When I read them now, I picture a boy who needed some follow-up after a crucial moment in his life, some kind of guidance, direction, or reassurance, even if he couldn't name what it was. From what he wrote here, it was clear to my dad he wasn't going to find that at home. At this pivotal moment, he turned to God alone to fulfill his need, a practice he would follow the rest of his life.

———

AT HOME, DAD LEARNED THE practices of a consecrated life from his parents. His father's study on the second floor was a sacred space where Brother Kenneth paced back and forth practicing his sermons, his intonations a familiar sound to his children. He also spent hours there studying the Bible, which to my grandfather contained everything a person needed to know about life — truth, wisdom, history, human nature, and most important, the character of God. The Scriptures translated every earthly experience in light of truth that was timeless, permanent, and revelatory.

My dad adopted these same convictions and practices. As a pastor he made his study the one place where he could be completely himself — open before God about his sins, vulnerable about his needs, anguished over a broken world, and able to refresh himself with hope.

My dad also learned another important spiritual practice from his parents that he continued throughout his life — compassion for the poor and troubled. With parents in ministry, my dad and his siblings were constantly surrounded by needy, broken people. Uncle Don recalls a core lesson he learned the night a schoolmate unexpectedly came to church: "My friend Larry showed up and said, 'You didn't tell me you were a holy roller.' I was so embarrassed because I didn't want anybody to know." Don went to his father about it, asking, "Dad, why do all the strange people have to come to our church?" His father answered with his own pointed question: "Where else will they feel comfortable?"

My grandfather always had a moment to spare and a gentle word for people with "broken wings." Uncle Don remembers a Mr. Powell, a gruff man who brought his wife to church but could never bring himself to enter the doors. After every service, Mr. Powell stood outside the church waiting for my grandfather to emerge. The few minutes he spent with Brother Wilkerson were the only times anyone ever saw Mr. Powell smile.

My grandparents' godly compassion extended to the poor in their midst. My grandmother seemed to specialize in giving, passing out food to homeless people who came to the back door, until so many showed up she didn't have enough for them all.

———

IF MY DAD WAS GUILTY of anything by temperament, it was impatience. At fourteen he had already written more sermons than he kept track of. He was ready to be in the pulpit, or so he thought. "I remember the night David kept after Dad," Uncle Don recalls. "He kept asking him, 'When can I preach?'" Finally, their father scheduled my dad for a Sunday evening service.

"David got up," Uncle Don says, "and he froze." My dad gripped the pulpit as if hanging over a cliff. It must have been the enormity of the moment, the responsibility of a role that to this point had been all dreams and play. Was he ready?

"Our dad had to come up, lay hands on him, and pray over him," Uncle Don says, "and then David was fine. For fifteen or twenty minutes he preached the house afire."

At church, my dad and his siblings were exposed to God's work throughout the world by the overseas missionaries who passed through. "It was Holy Ghost *National Geographic* at least once a month," Uncle Don says. One of those missionaries was fairly well known, Charles Greenaway, whose ministry was having a great impact in Africa.

Yet something just as exciting, yet controversial, was taking place closer to home, a few miles away in Pittsburgh. Kathryn Kuhlman, a

Pentecostal healing evangelist, had gained notoriety for her services at Pittsburgh's Carnegie Hall. A flamboyant figure — she was divorced, a strict taboo then, and claimed to "dress for Jesus" in her flowing chiffon gowns — Kathryn Kuhlman was held in suspicion by a lot of Christians. Church leaders scrutinized her, but evidently the results of her ministry could not be denied.

My grandparents remained skeptical until a respected evangelist couple came for Sunday lunch. The couple had attended one of Kathryn's services out of curiosity, and at one point Kathryn pointed to the wife in the balcony, summoning her to the stage to receive healing prayer. Kathryn had no way of knowing that this woman suffered from a chronic ailment. When Kathryn prayed over her, the woman was healed instantaneously. "What she's doing really is of God," the couple testified to my grandparents.

Faith healing would not have been unfamiliar to my grandparents. It was the core testimony of a central figure in the family — Kenneth's father, the well-known traveling evangelist J. A. Wilkerson.

If there was one concern Davie Wilkerson's parents had about him, it was that he was too much like the old man. J.A. was an effective evangelist, with a special gift for connecting with men who resisted the gospel. He had even preached at Living Waters Camp with other notables of the day. But the Assemblies of God was constantly on pins and needles because of J.A.'s flamboyant style. Every so often they got wind of something he'd done to upset local pastors, an act of grandeur committed during one of his crusades. The truth is he was an unapologetic showman, and that cut against the grain of a still-young denomination struggling to establish credibility.

J.A. had a stiff leg that he swung over altar railings to prove God had healed him from a fatal disease. He had been on his deathbed with tuberculosis, written off by his doctor, when he miraculously recovered, all of which he attributed to God's merciful power. With that kind of testimony J.A. didn't need gimmicks in his ministry, but he used them; spectacle was simply in his nature. Prior to a service he would set exploding powder on the stage floor behind the pulpit, and at the climax of a sermon on hell, he would step backward onto the powder, sending up smoke and sparks.

"Grandpa was very flamboyant," Uncle Don says, "and David was in that vein." To my dad's parents, this trait was something to be feared — and "prayed out" of their son. Yet what my dad saw in his grandpa's life and ministry was the reality of God. It didn't matter how J.A. drew men to him; when it happened, it was under the genuine drawing of the Holy Spirit. A grandfather like that was someone to be emulated, because he represented a gospel of action and, in turn, a living God.

———

THERE'S AN OLD JOKE ABOUT why the bond is so strong between grandparents and grandkids. Answer: They have a common enemy. I wonder about the war my father felt in his soul between loyalty to his father and adulation of his grandfather. It had to be tense for him, because there was always an undercurrent of tension between Kenneth and J.A.

Kenneth might not have shared the same high opinion of J.A. that my dad had. It was J.A. who had sent Kenneth to boarding school as a young boy so that he and his wife could travel freely as evangelists, leaving the son to find his own way. Years later, it must have been a kind of compensation to Kenneth to be involved in so many respectable activities — the local ministerium, the radio broadcast, church services that attracted civic leaders. Those things told Kenneth he belonged, something he hadn't felt as a boy.

Maybe they were also a kind of vindication. His father, J.A., had been held in high esteem as an evangelist, despite all the flamboyance. Now that Kenneth's work was flourishing, maybe the old man's theatrics seemed less of a threat. Once, when J.A. came to preach at Kenneth's church, he purposely put on a sort of spectacle, opening the windows of the church and leading the congregation in a march through the sanctuary, urging them to shout praises loudly enough for the whole neighborhood to hear. He did this because he had sensed his son's congregation was "acting uptown."

Watching all this, my dad had to feel the tension. He was loyal to his father, but he resented the message he got from him from time to time: "If you make a fool of yourself, it can reflect badly on my reputation and on the denomination." My dad never liked hearing that. At the same time, he saw that as a pastor his father had to swallow a lot of unjust criticism. "To read our father's diary of how vicious certain people were in those days — wow," Uncle Don says. "All the petty gossip, the minor decisions that got blown up."

Yet if there's one tension from my dad's childhood that trumped all others, it was the trauma of his father's ulcers. Kenneth was in continual pain for ten years, on a death watch all that time. I can't fathom what that might do to children in their most tender years; or to my grandmother, who had to preach in her husband's stead, triggering her own anxieties; or to my aunt Ruth, who had to forego college to help her parents out. As if those crises weren't enough, there were the near-death incidents themselves, full of agonized screams, bloody bed sheets, and bloody floors.

There was a lot of responsibility to go around in the family. My dad took on his share, working at Harkins Market and preaching around town, and he didn't seem to mind. With the extra money, he was beginning to dress snappily. I have pictures of him in a sports coat, broad collar jacket, and baggy slacks. His hair is casually pomped, neat but with a few locks strategically loosened, enough to look relaxed and happy to be himself.

Maybe the day came when he wanted to spend more time with his girlfriend. Maybe he wanted to preach more and work less at the store. Maybe he was just tired of all the tension and working all the jobs. Whatever the reason, he surprised the family on a rare evening when he and Jerry were at home for dinner. Their pastor father had just said the blessing and everyone had dug into the meal when my dad nervously made an announcement.

"I'm thinking about quitting Harkins Market," he said.

At the far end of the table, his father stopped eating. He stared down at his plate. Finally, he said, "David, we won't make it."

My uncle Don, in grade school, remembers the moment with crystal clarity. "A look crossed David's face," he says, wincing. "*We won't make it*. Think about that. David took on the responsibility."

Uncle Don shakes his head at the memory. "David and Jerry never had teenage years," he explains. "They had to work to help support the family. That became David's lot in life. When David went into ministry and then Dad died, he became head of the house. Now he was responsible for my mother and for me. Responsibility was thrust upon David at a very early age. I think a lot of his financial fears were driven by that."

Dad didn't quit his job at Harkins. He never quit anything that mattered to him. He did quit Bible school after one year, but I'm pretty sure that was to come home and marry my mother. A few years later, he refused to quit reaching out to gang members, even when he was slapped and spit on, even when pails of sand were aimed at his head from ten-story buildings. He didn't quit during the years when his marriage seemed beyond repair. He never gave up — not when it would have been easy to, nor when it would have been hard to. But he also didn't surrender responsibility at times when he should have — not even in his seventies, when he was attending to my mom's many health issues, reducing him to skin and bones. In his mind, the responsibility would always be his — and for a son desperate to please his father, that wasn't something easily let go.

3
—
A WAY FOR
A PRAYING MAN

IN 1957, SOMETHING UNUSUAL BEGAN to happen to a young man named Dick Simmons. A recent seminary graduate, he had accepted the pastorate of Brooklyn Presbyterian Church, not far from the Fort Greene Housing Projects in Brooklyn's Navy Yard. The church was a beautiful old structure with a storied history that dated back to renowned nineteenth-century revivals. Its proud congregation had numbered more than fourteen hundred people until recent years, when gangs had overrun the neighborhood. The congregation had dwindled to less than a hundred, some of whom needed a police escort on Sunday mornings. This was Mau Mau turf, home to the most feared gang in New York.

On most days, Reverend Dick Simmons had the church to himself. One morning as he made his way up the sidewalk, he saw a police vehicle parked in front, with two young men being loaded onto stretchers. Dick saw blood coursing from their midsections. He later learned that one of the teenagers had been on his way to see him, desperate to talk to a preacher. But the boy had been intercepted on the steps of the church manse by the other young man, a rival gang member.

The sight of the two bleeding, semiconscious boys sent Dick to his knees. He spent the entire morning in the living room of the manse praying, "God, how long? When will you send revival to change this?"

"It provoked me to begin getting up very early in the morning and going to the church to pray," Dick says. "The Spirit of God came on me, and I found myself praying all day long — eight, ten, even sixteen hours. The fire of the Lord would fall on me, and I couldn't stop. My whole body was engaged, until I was perspiring. I would get up to pour myself a cup of tea and the Spirit would pull me back into prayer."

Dick wasn't surprised by the experience. Five years earlier, he had been baptized in the Holy Spirit as an undergraduate at the University of Washington during a revival on campus. What was happening now reminded him of that deep and holy experience. He would learn the serious, vital nature of prayer at New York Seminary, where he joined an intercessory group including a young Pat Robertson and Eugene Peterson. "We were desperate to see revival," Dick says.

At one point, Dick and his wife had served as house parents at an orphanage for Korean children in Fort Lee, New Jersey. Fort Lee sits atop the Palisades cliffs, near the George Washington Bridge, directly across the Hudson River from Manhattan. The setting gave Dick a panoramic view of New York City that broke his heart.

"The orphanage had a playground area, and behind that was a forest," he says. "Just beyond that was a promontory point, and I would go out there and pray." There, in that idyllic setting, Dick found himself in the grip of long, intense prayers in the Spirit. He was moved in ways that were beyond himself to pray, but for what? "My primary prayer," he says, "was that God would thrust worthy laborers into the harvest field across the river."

———

EIGHT HOURS WEST OF THE Hudson River, in a small hill town in western Pennsylvania, my dad was disconsolate. It was Sunday night, time to call his father to check in. He would tell his father about the growth of his two daughters, my older sisters — Debi, the little sandy-blonde toddler, and infant Bonnie, who had our mother's dark eyes and dark ringlets of hair. Dad would report what the Lord was doing in his small church in Philipsburg — what he had preached about, how many people had come to the altar, and other things that would have interested his father.

But more and more, my dad found these calls hard to make because of a growing restlessness. First, there was the mundane reality of church life. On one hand, Dad loved the people he pastored in this small town. Some were farmers, hardworking people, many of whom paid his salary in the vegetables they raised. Others worked in a nearby factory that made men's clothes. All were humble people who supported him, and for that he was grateful. But every church service followed a certain predictable course. Sister so-and-so played the organ and the congregation sang gospel songs. Someone stood and delivered a message in tongues, followed by another who provided the interpretation. Dad then preached. Afterward, he offered a brief altar call, and people came forward crying for the Holy Spirit to come down. Then everyone went home.

The tiny congregation of Gospel Tabernacle had doubled since Dad's arrival, from around fifty people to more than a hundred. That growth may have been the reason the congregation supported Dad in his decision to erect a new church building. The church moved from its downtown location to a larger structure on a road leading out of town. The new building was bordered on one side by a vast grassy lot that had been a baseball field where Lou Gehrig made his way up to the majors. Now it was a yard where the congregation held lemonade socials. Behind the church building stood a grove of trees where my dad spent his afternoons praying. Beyond those woods was a bluff overlooking town, where Dad sometimes parked his car for special, extended times of prayer.

In some ways, Philipsburg was an ideal place for a young family man to settle down. But as my dad confided to me years later, it wasn't the life he had envisioned in service to God. After four years, he pondered what his ministry had become. "Is this all?" he wondered. "Is this everything that the work of God is supposed to be?"

Dad had been happy to take the job. Before that, he had been on the road for three years as an evangelist, sometimes holding children's crusades with his dummy, Red. Now with a growing family, he had less of a taste for the constant travel.

His decision to pastor had come as a relief to his parents, who by this time had moved to Scranton. But to their chagrin, Dad hadn't given up ventriloquism. Evidently he was very good at it. "There was a big church in Atlanta, and the well-known missionary Charles Greenaway made a call there to open a door for him," Uncle Don says. After that, Dad's ministry as a child evangelist took off. He traveled heavily through the South, in Mississippi, Alabama, and Georgia, with great success. At one point he was even asked to host a secular TV program for children. According to Dave Batty, a director at Teen Challenge, "My understanding is that Fred Rogers filled that slot. Had David said yes to that, there might not have been a Mister Rogers; there might have been a Mister Dave."

"He always thought outside of the box," says Uncle Don. "He wrote up a pamphlet about Red and published it. The cover was a photo of Red sitting in a cupboard. Then he would set Red in a little chair, tie it to the top of his car, and drive around town inviting kids to the crusade."

Now that Dad was a pastor, my grandmother was convinced she had prayed him out of a showman's field. But she hadn't yet prayed the showman out of him.

———

THAT FIRST YEAR HE PASTORED in Philipsburg, Dad invited Uncle Don — then sixteen — to spend the summer with his family. It would be a kind of ministry apprenticeship, as Uncle Don saw up close my dad's gifts for ministry in nascent form.

"It was the beginning of his developing a voice," Uncle Don notes. "He was transitioning from being a child evangelist to being more evangelistic. It wasn't prophetic yet. But I do remember that men would get saved under his ministry, and that was like our grandfather J.A. For some reason our granddad was able to reach men, maybe because of his style, which fit the era. David was able to do that."

Dad's most significant impact at Gospel Tabernacle may have been on the young people. Uncle Don recalls those meetings as "some of the greatest youth prayer times. There were tremendous, awesome times of worship. I remember two full rows of young people, all of us crying out to God. Someone's unsaved father happened to be sitting in the back during a service, and David went to talk to him. The man was somewhat reluctant, but David pulled him to the altar — literally pulled him — and he got saved."

During the afternoons, Uncle Don saw his older brother walking through the field behind the church, heading to the woods to pray. "I was a teenager, and I didn't think of the significance of it then," Uncle Don says. But his brother's devotion to prayer made enough of an impression that Don came back the following summer. "I preached my first sermon there," he says. "It solidified my own calling to ministry. David allowed me to do what our dad had allowed him to do when he was my age, and a bonding took place. David was already becoming a father figure to me."

Uncle Don's reports from Philipsburg to his parents in Scranton might have been glowing, but they could have been disconcerting had they included news about the showman who was emerging. Dad had taken on side projects to bring in extra income, including the sale of used cars in the vacant lot next to the church. "He always had four or five cars in the lot," Uncle Don says. "One Sunday night he told me, 'Don, go move all the cars and park them in front of the church.' I asked why, and he said, 'Because I want people to think there's already a crowd gathering.'"

During one service, Dad drove a tiny three-wheel car up the center aisle. It might have been the Fiat he bought in Pittsburgh to sell on the lot. "It had a door that would open from the front," says Uncle Don. "He drove it through all the towns, everywhere he went, to draw people's attention. David was always bordering on the sensational."

Dad then bought an even more unusual car for use in his ministry — a Messerschmitt KR200, also a three-wheeler. Slightly smaller than a MINI Cooper today, it was equipped with a glass-bubble dome top. Painted on each door was the title of Dad's TV program — yes, a television show — "The Hour of Deliverance." Just below the door handles appeared his name in slightly smaller script: "Brother 'Davie' Wilkerson." "That car was how he advertised his show around town," Uncle Don says.

My grandparents must have despaired over the Bible verse Dad used in his newspaper ads: "'The prince of this world cometh, and hath nothing in me' (John 14:30)."

———

GIVEN THAT HE BORE J.A.'s genes, it's no surprise my father wanted a TV show. It was a fifteen-minute program, taped midweek in the Philipsburg church's sanctuary, and consisted of the choir singing a gospel song, followed by my dad preaching a brief sermon straight into the camera. Judging from a publicity photo, it was an impressive setup. Studio lights were hung from the ceiling of the sanctuary, and the sizable choir stood three rows deep on a raised platform. Next to them stood my father and mother, beaming in their Sunday best, with Dad in a trendy sports jacket.

The show was broadcast from a station in Altoona and aired on several channels in Pennsylvania and parts of eastern Ohio. My uncle Jerry and aunt Eve remember seeing it and thinking it was "cute." "Dave appeared kinda stiff," Eve says. "But then, his dad was sort of stiff when he preached. He didn't use a lot of movement, just a lot of voice."

"That was just the era," Jerry says. "TV was still in its infancy then, and people didn't know how to look or act. If you showed it today, it would compete for *America's Funniest Home Videos.*"

David Patterson saw those shows years later, when he was director of my father's crusade ministry. A tall, quietly astute Canadian, David notes, "The shows had been transferred from the old kinescope technology, and Brother Dave let us show them at a staff banquet once. I'm telling you, he was just as anointed on those programs as he was later in life."

I have no idea how Dad financed all the ventures of his early ministry. He may have jumpstarted them with car sales, or perhaps the TV show generated income. "He had worked out a circuit of where his program was being shown," says David Patterson. "He went on the road every week for several nights, preaching in towns where it aired. I think he liked the circuit kind of thing — one night here, one night there. He appreciated the energy that came out of it."

"David was the first to buy our parents a TV, so they could watch him," says Uncle Don. "He wanted to please Dad, which I didn't see then; I see it only in retrospect. It was a little portable TV, and Dad would wheel it out of the closet to watch the program on Sunday afternoons. Then he would wheel it back into the closet, because he didn't want anyone to know he owned a TV."

My father developed enough of a reputation in the region that he was asked to assist with a church plant in a nearby town. He used the connection to his advantage. "David's Sunday night services were evangelistic," Uncle Don says. "He would bring the other pastor to Philipsburg, and the congregation would come too. Then other people would come because they'd seen the TV program, so the place would be packed. David would stay in the back room until it was time to preach. The other pastor would lead the service and then finally announce, 'I now present to you evangelist Davie Wilkerson.' David would come through the door and bound onto the platform wearing a white suit — the great man of God!"

Uncle Don and Aunt Ruth recall this stage in my dad's life as "the days of his flesh." "They were the days of 'Davie' Wilkerson as opposed to David Wilkerson," Uncle Don says. "In the pulpit he was trying to be a rock star."

My uncle Jerry saw the same thing. "Being a pastor was too restrictive for him," he says. "I think he wanted to reach more people. I'm sure that was in his mind when he went to New York the first time."

Reaching more people wasn't the only thing on Dad's mind then. In later years, he disclosed to me that when he first went to New York — after being stirred by the images of the boys on trial in *Life* magazine — he was convinced he would return to Philipsburg to keep pastoring. He had viewed that initial trip to the city as a onetime act of obedience to a powerful prompting from God. But something happened in the meantime that ultimately redirected his course: my dad had begun to empty himself through prayer.

——————

"THAT'S WHERE IT HAPPENED, IN Philipsburg," Uncle Don says. "That's when he went from being 'Davie' Wilkerson to being David Wilkerson. It was when he discovered his prayer life."

Of course, my dad already had a prayer life. Uncle Don had witnessed that daily when he saw my father trek into the woods to commune with God. Yet this same prayerful pastor still had all kinds of side projects bubbling in his mind. He had decided to partner with a local doctor to start a larger car lot and call it "REV-DOC AUTO." It didn't get off the ground.

Yet something profound was indeed happening in my dad's prayer life. He no longer prayed only in the afternoons; he now prayed late at night, when his family was asleep. He had stopped watching late-night movies out of conviction, to avail himself to God, and that's when the change began to happen. My father wasn't any holier because he prayed more — he was still a restless, ambitious man — yet it was *that* man who was found by God in prayer. I believe it is one thing to ask, "What was David Wilkerson's understanding of God that gave him such boldness in his work?" It's quite another to ask, "What was God's understanding of David Wilkerson — the drive, the temperament, the determination, as well as the weakness, the blind spots, the temptations — that he would choose *him* to accomplish his divine purposes in the world?"

Dad's transformation began just in time. The president of the Assemblies of God at the time was Thomas Zimmerman, a well-respected leader who by all accounts had done a lot for the denomination. Among other things, he had brought more respectability by persuading the Assemblies to join associations with evangelical groups. He later served as president of the National Association of Evangelicals.

But Reverend Zimmerman also knew of my great-grandfather, J. A. Wilkerson. In his view, my dad had begun to develop the same kind of flamboyant reputation, and he had concerns about how things would turn out. Reportedly, he asked someone, "So this young David Wilkerson — would you say he's a lot like J.A.?"

"People don't know that back then Brother Dave traveled as a healing evangelist," says David Patterson. "He didn't talk much about it. I don't know whether he was embarrassed about that part of his past, but he never brought it up."

Two things come to mind for me on this subject. One is that as a boy my dad must have desperately wanted his suffering father to be healed. The other is that Dad very genuinely might have possessed the gift of healing, as listed by the apostle Paul among the spiritual gifts in 1 Corinthians 12. In any case, my dad added to his expanding ministry by holding Sunday afternoon healing services at Gospel Tabernacle. During those services, by my father's own accounts, the gifts of the Spirit flowed through him freely. He would be given a "word of knowledge" about people in the pews, so that as he walked down the aisles, he told them things about their lives he couldn't have known otherwise.

It sounds spooky, yet Dad used those same gifts years later to touch countless lives in crusades and street meetings over the next half century. He looked into the eyes and hearts of drug addicts, homeless people, even the demon possessed, and spoke directly to their hearts with a specific word from God. Those words were never vague or general; they were always detailed about the person's life. And they were no spectacle: they brought kingdom results, ministering salvation and healing to broken people.

In small-town Philipsburg in the mid-1950s, however, those gifts caused a sensation, attracting busloads of people from churches in other towns. Then, suddenly, one Sunday afternoon it all stopped. Dad describes what happened in one of his old sermon tapes. Before the service, he and my mom had an argument, and Dad stormed out of the house, driving to church on his own.

He said he was in a bad frame of mind — in a self-righteous rage, really — as he began the service. Yet as he ministered, the gifts of the Spirit still operated through him freely. He had words of knowledge about people and prophesied over them. Then, in the midst of it all, he heard a voice within him asking, "Who told you to say that?" It frightened him.

On the way home my father discerned the Holy Spirit speaking to him, saying, "David, you're not going to be flowing in these gifts now — the word of knowledge, the word of wisdom, the gift of prophecy." After that, Dad didn't even try to minister in the usual way. He stopped telling people about their lives, and not surprisingly the crowds stopped coming, and the meetings dried up. Years passed before these gifts reappeared in his ministry.

But my dad never stopped praying for God to perform physical healings, whether in his suffering audiences or in himself or in his family, who needed it desperately. But his broader conviction about healing, which developed over time, is expressed in a sermon he preached in the 1990s titled "Resurrection Now":

> Some faithful believers are enduring a physical tribulation they may never be freed from in this life. God sends his comforting Holy Spirit to these suffering saints, renewing their spirits so they may endure to the end. The Holy Spirit abides in them, raising

them up from their anguish day after day, building in them a total dependence on the mercy and love of the Father. Day by day these saints' spirits grow while their bodies endure.

Perhaps you are enduring pain that has never been clearly diagnosed. You've seen one specialist after another, and no one has been able to answer your inner cry. Now the pain has become unbearable, and you are convinced you'll never get a diagnosis. Despair sets in as you wonder, "Will I ever be free again?" Like Paul, you have given yourself the sentence of death.

Or perhaps you have received your diagnosis and it is bad news: Your illness is incurable. How does God's resurrection power answer you? How do you pray? Dear saint, I believe in miracles more than ever. Yes, we are to seek the Lord for physical healing. Yet the Spirit of comfort and hope must also be raised up in us.

Here is my prayer: "Holy Spirit, quicken this suffering man's spirit. Bring this anguished woman your peace which passes all human understanding. Let your enduring servants see you standing by them so that their spirits are lifted by the flow of your love. Comforter, sweep over them this very hour with your holy rest. Take away their grief, their fear, their spirit of mourning. And replace it all with your spirit of peace."

•———•

MY FATHER DIDN'T FIND WHAT he was looking for in a healing ministry or a TV program or ventriloquism or a used car lot filled with exotic vehicles. Deep down, he knew these ventures were not where he would find satisfaction in Jesus. After four years of pastoring and other pursuits, he had become disconsolate.

Late in his life, my dad spelled out for me what bothered him most about those years in Philipsburg. When all was said and done, he realized, not much happened apart from his own zeal. The church had no evangelistic outreach. It had no ministry of mercy. Few people came to Christ through its ministry. Dad concluded, "We're Christians who seek Pentecost only for ourselves. Can that really be Pentecost?"

My father wasn't just heartbroken; I believe he was angry. He told me he prayed, "Lord, if this is Pentecost, I don't want it. If it's about having a 'bless me' club week after week, I'll have nothing to do with it."

What he was experiencing was a holy discontent, and it stayed with him his whole life. It began the moment that voice rose up in his heart and said, "You can be a famous minister by your own hand, and be happy with that. Or you can see that working in your own strength leaves you empty when it comes to serving me."

That's when my dad came to the end of himself. He began to empty his soul before God, and he started to listen. As he replaced all his pursuits with spiritual conviction, his discontent grew. During those late-night prayer sessions, he began to experience the very emotions of God. He wrote about this in the margin notes of his Bible: "God grieves. He repents. He rejoices" (in reference to Gen. 6:6). A few years later my dad lost that Bible, but it was returned by someone who had glanced at the margin notes. The person commented to Dad, "You know what these margin notes say to me? They're a picture of a soul both in ecstasy and in torment." I can think of no more accurate picture of my father.

There were certain traits in my dad he would never depart from, things that were part and parcel of his being, yet even those would be transformed. His flamboyance would become innovation. His natural restlessness would become a holy hunger. His self-judgment would become a spiritual discontent. And late one February night, when he took a break from praying to glance at a magazine article, he would absorb the story with eyes of the Spirit and not his own, and it would change everything.

My dad followed his discontent when he accepted a missionary's invitation to come to Argentina. When he arrived, he had to take a train into the country's interior to reach the mission station. As Dad stepped off the train, an image on the platform took him by surprise. Hanging on the station wall was a picture of Elvis Presley.

The missionary was working with a group of young people, and he had urged Dad to come prepared with a message to preach to them. But as my father interacted with the kids, he realized he couldn't relate to them. They wanted to know all about teenage life in the US, the rock-and-roll revolution, the teenage gangs in New York. Dad knew nothing of what they were talking about.

"I think David was looking for his next challenge," says Uncle Don, whom Dad told of the experience. "Those youth in Argentina were more interested in what was going on in America than he knew about. Remember, all our lives we'd grown up thinking of foreign missionaries as superstars. It was then David realized there was a mission field in America. The church back then didn't see America as a mission field, and they certainly didn't see the youth culture as a mission field, especially troubled youth. To me, there's a connection between that trip to Argentina and David's call to New York City. Sometimes you have to go halfway around the world to realize you're not called there, that God has called you home."

———

THE MICHAEL FARMER TRIAL IN Manhattan was the O. J. Simpson case of its time. Seven young boys of four ethnicities were on trial for taking the life of a defenseless white boy disabled by polio. Broadcaster Edward R. Murrow covered it, and the judge who presided over it wrote a book about it.

There is no rational reason why Dad wouldn't react with the same fury and disgust as the rest of the nation to a pen drawing of the accused in *Life* magazine. By Dad's own admission, the expression on one boy's face was ugly, filled with "bewilderment and hatred and despair." But it was that one face — the worst of the seven — that brought tears streaming down his face.

I have to wonder what went through his mind when, late that February night, he took a break from praying to glance at the magazine article and absorbed what he saw with the eyes of the Spirit. Why tears? What about grief for Michael Farmer? What about the loss to his family? What about God's justice? I know my father, and I know those very thoughts went through his mind. So why did he pursue the murderers? Why did he follow the voice inside that urged him, "Go to New York and help *those* boys?"

It was anguish — holy anguish over what the world had become.

Anguish over the senseless murder of a defenseless boy. Anguish over the seething hurt and deprivation that had boiled over in the boys who committed it. And, finally, anguish over their fate, the waste of every life involved. To God, they were all precious, and that night in the small study of his Philipsburg parsonage, looking at that image in *Life*, Dad felt wave after wave of God's anguish.

To my dad, New York City was the culmination of all the sin, injustice, pain, and hurt of the world centered in one place. As he wrote in the opening page of *The Cross and the Switchblade*, "I'd never been to New York City, and I never wanted to go, except perhaps to see the Statue of Liberty." That view of the city as a brutal and broken place never left him. It's what pulled him back thirty years later, to start a church in its very heart, when Times Square was at its lowest, plagued by the trafficking of crack cocaine.

It was tears that first caused Dad to go — inexplicable tears. Little did he know that at the same time in an Upper Manhattan magazine office, a journalist named John Sherrill had begun crying inexplicable tears too. So had Dick Simmons, his body wracked by God's own emotions over the mission field across the Hudson River.

One especially dark night on the promontory point, Dick was praying near the edge of the woods. "I was down on my face crying to the Lord when suddenly a light appeared in the trees," he says. "A policeman came stumbling out with a big flashlight. He pointed it at me and said, 'What are you doing out here?' I said, 'I'm praying that the Lord will send laborers into the slums over there. That he'll reach the gangs, the teenagers, and the drug addicts.' 'Oh,' he said, 'there's nothing wrong with that.'"

If Dick and that policeman had turned their heads north at that moment, they might have seen a lone motorcycle rider crossing the George Washington Bridge a quarter mile away, heading into Harlem. As Dick says today, "That was when the Spirit of God fell on Dave Wilkerson in Philipsburg."

Part Two

REVIVAL

That is actually the heart of David's story — the power of the Holy Spirit to move into the world *right now* and change things.

—*John Sherrill*

4
—

"YOU MUST BE ON OUR SIDE"

The broken windows, the missing light bulbs, the plaster cracking from the walls, the pilfered hardware, the cold, drafty corridors, the doors on sagging hinges, the acrid smell of sweat and garbage, the ragged children, the plaintive women, the playgrounds that are seas of muddy clay, the bruised and battered trees, the ragged clumps of grass, the planned absence of art, beauty or taste, the gigantic masses of brick, of concrete, of asphalt, the inhuman genius with which our know-how has been perverted to create human cesspools worse than those of yesterday....

If these words seem strong, visit these massive barracks for the destitute yourself.... It is described as the world's largest housing project. It is better described as a twenty-million-dollar slum. Fort Greene and projects like it are forcing centers of juvenile delinquency. They spawn teenage gangs. They incubate crime. They are fiendishly contrived institutions for the debasing of family and community life to the lowest common mean. They are worse than anything George Orwell ever conceived.

— HARRISON SALISBURY, *THE SHOOK-UP GENERATION*

—•—

LIKE WILLIAMSBURG, RED HOOK, AND other gentrified sections of Brooklyn, Fort Greene today is a trendy place to live. It draws creative, innovative types to its renovated brownstones and century-old apartment buildings or, for those in slightly higher income brackets, to glassy new high-rises. It's one of the areas where visiting hipsters go when they want to see the "real" New York City beyond touristy Manhattan. One travel guide calls Fort Greene "a truly racially and economically diverse neighborhood with what the *New York Times* referred to as a 'prevailing sense of racial amity that intrigues sociologists and attracts middle-class residents from other parts of the city.'"

It's safe to say that nobody living in Fort Greene today would remember the old Fort Greene. That's because anyone living there in the 1950s moved out when they could. Mike Zello's family did. They had to once their neighbors on Carlton Avenue started being killed.

Harrison Salisbury was a renowned reporter for the *New York Times* when he vented his outrage over those projects, located just across the street from the Zellos' home. What he described is exactly what any poor, displaced, or immigrant family had to endure as residents. Thirty-five buildings housed fifty-two thousand people in a few square blocks. What Salisbury forgot to mention is that most people in those buildings took the stairs because the elevators were used as toilets. The Fort Greene Projects had its own hospital, police station, and library, but those institutions were under siege by a desperate, forgotten people. The living conditions, according to *Newsweek*, were "one of the starkest examples of the failures of public housing.... At one time a grand American housing experiment ... [it,] like many others across the country, turned out to be grossly inhumane."

Each of these descriptions puts it mildly. As Salisbury points out, no one should have been surprised that the Fort Greene Projects produced gangs. These were the Bloods and Crips of their day, turf-driven groups with the power to take out a life, which they did with such frequency that government powers virtually threw up their hands. Like other areas of the city, Fort Greene was divided into blocks of ethnicities — Italians on Carlton Avenue, African Americans along Myrtle Avenue. But in the projects, all those ethnicities were flung together in buildings rising from five to sixteen stories. It was a cocktail of continual violence.

———

MIKE ZELLO WAS A TEENAGER in the mid-1950s when fights broke out on his street between his fellow Italians and African Americans and Hispanics. "It was usually over a girl," Mike remembers. "Just teenage stuff, but it was serious." Kids in the projects didn't have anything to call their own, so when somebody hit on a guy's girlfriend, it threatened the guy's sole source of tenderness in the world. Fistfights escalated into knife fights, and knife fights led to massive gang fights, planned with the strategic intensity of battlefield operations.

The situation grew worse when the Puerto Rican gangs came in. "There were unwritten rules between the gangs if you were going to have a gang fight," Mike Zello says. "It was understood that certain weapons would not be used, like guns and razorblades. The Puerto Ricans changed that. They tore antennas from cars because they were the perfect size to make a 'zip gun,' using the hammer of a toy gun and some wood. The zip gun problem became so prevalent in New York that car manufacturers stopped making round antennas. They started making them flat, so they couldn't be used. Switchblade knives were very common too. It got so bad that the federal government passed a law banning switchblades. So then the Puerto Ricans brought in razorblades. They would stick them between their fingers to slice open someone's face."

One Puerto Rican gang member was feared more than any other: Nicky Cruz, who was already infamous in the newspapers. Second in command of the Mau Maus, he was known even by its leader, Israel Narvaez, as the most brutal soldier. And the Mau Maus were the fiercest gang by all accounts. They grew in power when they persuaded the local African American gang, the Chaplains, to join forces with them. It was the leaders of these two gangs who first encountered a nerdy white guy wearing huge glasses and a tie one day on a street corner near the projects. The guy obviously didn't belong there, and they let him know it. But when he opened his mouth and preached to them, on a sidewalk in front of St. Edwards Church, a seismic shift occurred. Their hearts — and the world — would not be the same.

My dad's encounter with Nicky Cruz is famously chronicled in *The*

Cross and the Switchblade, a book published in 1963 that deservedly has never gone out of print. It is a marvel of economy in its powerful narrative and the equally powerful truths it conveys in a swift two hundred pages. Nicky's transformation into a messenger of God's love is told in his own bestselling book, *Run Baby Run*. And the worldwide drug-rehabilitation ministry born from that encounter — Teen Challenge — was only in its nascent stages when my dad's book was published. What has yet to be told with sufficient scope is how that ministry exploded in the sixties and has grown exponentially throughout the world ever since. In retrospect, the world needed Teen Challenge, because today there are more than eleven hundred centers in ninety-four countries, with thirty-three other nations on a waiting list. "And the countries that don't have Teen Challenge want it," asserts Dr. Donald Argue, who travels the globe representing the United States Commission on International Religious Freedom. Teen Challenge has expanded into countries that never would have considered it — including Muslim nations — based solely on its success in transforming the most hopeless addicts into joyful, productive, service-oriented citizens. My uncle Don has written a handful of books that track the ongoing story, but it's too vast to keep up with.

Meanwhile, what *The Cross and the Switchblade* did so effectively was to report the incredible works of God in the unlikeliest of places, enacted by the unlikeliest vessel. Yet that classic book has a very limited point of view — my dad's. As eager as he was to report the miracles he saw God perform on the streets, the world saw very little of what it took for my dad himself to keep going.

◆──◆

WHEN MY FATHER FIRST SHOWED up at Glad Tidings Tabernacle in midtown Manhattan, Reverend Stanley Berg didn't know what to make of him. "I've got a poor pastor here," he whispered into the phone to a trusted elder. "He thinks he's got a solution for dope addicts. I don't know anything about him, and he doesn't know a soul in New York."

Reverend Berg might have been baffled by the skinny, serious-minded minister sitting in his office, but he trusted what he saw for two reasons. First, my dad was referred to him by a pastor in New Jersey they both knew. Second, New York's police department had begun plead-ing with churches to help with the city's drug problem; it had grown too overwhelming for them to handle. Of course, most churches had no idea how to help, so they had been praying. But that day in Pastor Berg's office, my dad didn't look like anyone's answer to prayer.

The elder on the other end of the phone was a boisterous Ital-ian American, Paul Dilena. Paul knew firsthand about the city's drug problems, because he was a New York City policeman with the Transit Authority. An outsized personality, he was also the song leader at Glad Tidings Tabernacle. "I've called around and we're trying to set up a board for him," Pastor Berg told Paul. "I want you to be his treasurer."

"Great. Give me the books and I'll have a look."

"There aren't any books. He can't afford to buy one."

These were the days when Dad was sleeping in his car in Harlem week after week. He didn't even know what Harlem was, much less its dangers, which alarmed Pastor Berg. But my dad did know that Glad Tid-ings was the Assemblies of God's flagship church in New York and that Pastor Berg was respected. He was in the right place. For four months my father had been canvassing New York's slums and projects on weekly trips from Philipsburg. Reverend Berg was about to do him the great favor of calling together some city pastors to hear Dad's vision to reach gang members and addicts, young people whose trust he had inexplica-bly gained. Through that fledgling network of ministers and churches, support for Dad's work began.

"I thought he was some kind of kook," says Mike Zello, a teenager when my dad arrived at his church in Queens to share his vision. "I mean, nobody goes into a courtroom, holds up a Bible, and says, 'Judge, I want to talk to you.'"

The whole city had seen the headline in the *New York Daily News* as well as the infamous photo of my father. Dad hadn't been allowed to visit the seven boys on trial for murder, so he went to court one day to attend the trial proceedings. Just as the judge was adjourning, Dad impulsively rushed to the bench, hoping to gain his ear on behalf of the boys. Instead, he was manhandled and tossed out of the courtroom, and flashbulbs began popping.

Like everyone else in the pews that night, Mike Zello knew about this, and he was curious. His family had just moved from Carlton Avenue in Fort Greene and now attended the charismatic Lutheran church where Dad was speaking. "He tried to speak street lingo, but he used it out of context," Mike remembers. "The young people in the church were kind of laughing at him. Everybody thought, 'This guy's from out in the sticks of Pennsylvania, and he's trying to act cool.' But he preached with brokenness. It was as if that were the last sermon he was ever going to preach. And he believed Jesus was coming at any moment."

Dad's end-times message that night would have had a certain resonance. It was the Cold War era, when schoolchildren were doing duck-and-cover drills in school, and a lot of churches had turned to gospel songs about the second coming. "There was a sense of urgency," Mike says, "of being ready, being holy, of sharing the gospel with as many people as you could."

At some point, my dad took a detour in the sermon to talk about ministering to the gangs in the Fort Greene Housing Projects. Suddenly Mike sat bolt upright. He looked around at the other kids, who seemed nonchalant. He was one of the few who knew firsthand what my dad was talking about. His grandparents still lived back on Carlton Avenue. And this skinny little guy was going into that place?

Mike made a point after the service to talk to my dad. "That's my old neighborhood, Pastor," he told him. "I appreciate what you're trying to do." He offered this curiously, seeking some insight into why Dad would venture into that kind of danger.

Dad didn't hesitate in his response. "I need your help," he said. "Do you have a car?"

◆────◆

My dad's courtroom incident hadn't gone down well at his father's church in Scranton. As the story goes in *The Cross and the Switchblade*, his father was mostly silent when Dad showed up at the parsonage after an all-night drive from Manhattan. According to that account, his mother was encouraging; she had always liked the boldness in her son, even if it summoned the specter of a certain flamboyant showman.

Uncle Don was attending Bible college when he heard about the courtroom fiasco. A classmate had rushed up asking, "Did you hear what your brother did?" Uncle Don laughed at the news. "Oh no," he thought, "here he goes again." He couldn't be sure if this was the old Davie or the new David. "We didn't know until the circumstances demonstrated that God was leading him in all this," he says.

The fact is, my dad did retreat a bit after being tossed from the courtroom. Some sympathetic pastors in southern states heard what had happened in the Babylon of New York City and invited Dad to hold children's crusades in twelve of their churches. So my father hit the road with Red again, perhaps to lick his wounds.

Yet a few months later, Uncle Don and Aunt Ruth found out firsthand that God was indeed leading their brother. That was the night in July of 1958 when Dad held a citywide rally for the gangs he had been reaching. It was scheduled for St. Nicholas Arena, on 66th Street on Manhattan's West Side. If you've ever seen the movie *The Warriors*, where all the gangs in New York travel by subway to gather in one place, that's the kind of night my dad envisioned it to be, only as a confrontation with Jesus. It was the culmination of four months of footwork and prayer. He wrote of that period, "Fighting, sex, drug addiction: these were dramatic manifestations of the needs of New York's teenage gang members.... Gradually, from all the visits, a pattern emerged. It was a pattern of need, starting with loneliness and extending through the gang wars, the sex parties, the dope addiction, and ending in an early and ignominious grave. To check my own impressions, I visited police stations, talked with social workers and parole officers, and spent many hours in the public library."

Those four months on the streets involved more than study and observation. They demanded trust in God. "We would see him coming and be worried for him," says Sonny Arguinzoni, a heroin addict at the time. Today, Sonny is the founder and director of Victory Outreach, a network of fourteen hundred churches with ministries to recovering addicts and their families. He first met my father in his Williamsburg, Brooklyn, neighborhood as Dad reached out to people with the gospel. "People on the street would tell him, 'Preacher, we know you mean to do good, but you're in the wrong place. You could get hurt,'" Sonny says.

"He would answer, 'My God is able to take care of me. He's the one who sent me here to talk to you.'"

Dad made these claims with a palpable authority. "He had a special anointing upon him," Sonny remembers clearly. "When he spoke, you felt like God was talking directly to you. And he was bold. Dave didn't hold anything back. He would tell it like it is." To Sonny and his friends, Dad's forthrightness translated into care, and that gained their trust. "We respected him when we saw him coming," Sonny says. "He had the guts, the boldness to go to the streets. And he was willing to receive us. That made a big difference, because some of the Pentecostal churches would look down on us, and not even want us to come to their services because they thought we might corrupt them. Dave was different. When I met him, I saw the genuine compassion he had for inner-city people. Even though he didn't come from that background, he was able to relate."

During those months, Dad also had his first encounters with Nicky Cruz, as detailed in *The Cross and the Switchblade*. Despite his mounting hatred for my father, Nicky also discerned Dad's caring compassion. "Jesus took many detours for one person — the woman in Samaria, the blind man, the leper," Nicky reflects today. "He didn't need a crusade director telling him, 'Go here, go there.' He just said, 'Let's cross over to the other side.' That's the way it happened for Dave Wilkerson. He had the eyes of Christ, and he went for one person."

Dad also had to trust God to provide for his needs during that time. *The Cross and the Switchblade* contains an iconic scene in which my father offered his shoes to a teenager who had none. "It's all right," he urged the kid, "God will provide me with another pair." Some readers saw the gesture as innocent to the point of quaint. More accurate, it was an early indication of how unattached my dad was to material things. Yet my father did mean those words literally; he truly did rely on God to take care of all his needs. "Sometimes he didn't have a nickel for the subway," says Sonia Dilena. Her husband, Paul, the Transit Authority cop and elder at Glad Tidings Tabernacle, would have to provide him with one.

Nicky and Sonny offer a picture of confidence in my dad that fueled him through those grueling months. That doesn't mean he wasn't discouraged. He wrote, "In the end, my total impression of the problems of New York teenagers was so staggering that I almost quit." I cannot picture my father quitting, and thankfully he didn't. With the series of evangelistic meetings now set for St. Nicholas Arena, he was expectant. His journal reads:

July 8, 1958. Hamilton Place — Manhattan!
I will not ever forget this hour — nor this day. Here I sit — 3 o'clock in the afternoon — just four hours away from the opening night of the St. Nicholas mtg.
Storm clouds are gathering over the city. It is lightning — peals of thunder are rolling. Can this be an obvious warning of spiritual clouds & catastrophe enveloping this wicked city?
Four months of preparation! Four months of humility! Seeking God hours on end! Weeping, praying — fasting.
There are fears inside of me in the natural man — but the spiritual man grows in faith! What will we see the first night? What has God prepared? Are we prepared to believe God now for a genuine stirring of the masses of young teenagers — so far from God?
Now it has begun to rain hard. Oh God! Send heavenly rain upon the arena this night!
I am sold out to God. At home sits my expectant wife — wondering why her husband cannot be with her at her hour of delivery! But God is first!
My message seems so inadequate — I must depend totally on God's Holy Spirit. He has truly called me — He will not fail me now.
It hath not entered into the mind of man — what God has prepared for His own!
"God is good to those that wait upon Him!"

Dad wasn't the only person who was expectant. So was my mother. That's me who's mentioned in the journal entry, the one about to be delivered into the world. Our family was back in Philipsburg, and, yes, many fathers in the 1950s missed their children's births, a fact that baffles some of us today. But that was just the times, and in my parents' case, the decision was magnified by a sense of mission.

Dad made one other sacrifice leading up to the St. Nicholas crusade: his dignity. Flyers posted around the city featured the *Daily News* photo of Dad when he was thrown out of court, innocently holding up his Bible. It read, "This Country Preacher Is Coming Again to New York City." It had the appearance of buffoonery, but it was strategic. When Dad had first reached out to gangs on the streets, they recognized him from the photo. "You must be one of us," they said. The powers that be had rejected Dad, and that immediately bonded him to those who saw themselves as outcasts.

"That phrase, 'You must be on our side,' I call a redemptive analogy," says Uncle Don. "Jesus came to this earth to dwell among us as flesh. David didn't know it at the time, but he was there as a spokesperson to that subculture, to those gangs and those drug addicts. They always saw him as there to help."

———

THE FIRST SEVERAL NIGHTS AT St. Nicholas did not go well. The arena alternately sagged with the gangs' disinterest and then erupted in catcalls and chaos. Dad's parents may or may not have known about this, but his siblings, on a lark, decided to attend the final night of the crusade. Uncle Don was in Scranton, home from Bible college, when his sister Ruth and her husband, Don Harris, showed up. "David's having a crusade for gangs," Ruth said. "Want to go with us?"

"I was too ignorant to have any idea what it would be like," Uncle Don remembers. "If I knew back then what I know now, I never would have gone."

They made the long drive into Manhattan and stopped to ask a policeman for directions to St. Nicholas Arena. "He just stared at us," Uncle Don says. "Then he realized, 'Oh, you're going to that gang event,' and he laughed." It must have been an absurd sight to a New York City cop — a carload of grinning, country church kids coming to witness what the entire department was preparing for as a powder keg. My uncles and aunt had no idea what they were walking into.

"The place was ready to explode," Nicky Cruz says. "There were other gangs there, and the Mau Maus were ready to fight." It was a hair trigger away from happening, because once again Dad had lost control of the meeting.

Yet Nicky Cruz had come for another reason. As much hatred as he had toward my dad, he was powerfully drawn to him. "This guy had knowledge," says Nicky, whose parents had been involved in the occult. "He had insight into what can happen. At times I thought, eh! Here's another witch coming. But I didn't know anything about the mighty holiness of God.

"Social workers would come around, and we took advantage of them because we knew how the system worked. We knew they were there only because the mayor and the governor were panicked. They said, 'It's time to stop the blood of young people from running like rivers in the street.' The difference with Dave Wilkerson was he didn't come with anything but his Bible. You have to give credit to the Christians who prayed for him, because nobody came here to do what he did.

"He told me on the street, 'I'm here to give you a message from heaven: "Jesus loves you."' A boldness came over him, and for me to see a transformation like that, I knew it was a spiritual change, a beautiful one, and it rapidly controlled the situation. That's when he told me, 'You can kill me, cut me in a thousand pieces, and throw them into the street, and every little piece will arise and cry out, "Jesus loves you."' That was when Wilkerson beat the devil right there. And he got me."

That was the draw, the intrigue that led Nicky and Israel to bring the Mau Maus that night. But now, as the service wound down, the place was on the brink of violence. "It was the last two minutes," Nicky remembers. "People were making noise, kicking a photographer's camera around the floor, all this chaos. We thought, 'This guy has crossed the line to stupid. He's an embarrassment to every minister in this place. How in the world is he so calm? Where does he get the thoughts not to be afraid?'"

Then, according to Nicky, a sudden change came over Dad, the same change he had seen in his street encounter with him. "There was a tremendous change in Dave. The atmosphere was different, and everybody felt it. It was like Dave decided, 'I'm going to finish what I came here to do.' Even the gangs knew it, that there was something strange happening with this guy, but a good type of strange."

Dad was preaching on the crucifixion, a sermon that had taken shape in his mind over four months. The message struck Nicky at his core. "I thought, 'I wish I was there two thousand years ago. This man deserved life. I deserve the electric chair.' Bam, Wilkerson came in, 'He is resurrected from the dead, and he's here in this place right now. You don't see him, but you can feel him.'"

As millions of readers know, Nicky gave his life to Jesus that night. As for my dad, Nicky says, "This was not just a relief for him. He was not scared about going home emptyhanded. When I responded to Jesus, Dave was crying for me. He was drinking in every moment of salvation that he had earned." It was a glorious moment, and it overshadowed the fact that a near riot had been averted.

It was all lost on young Uncle Don, who had no idea of the drama taking place. "We went backstage, and I saw Nicky and the gang," he recalls, marveling at his own naivete. "I was six-foot-one, and to me they all looked so nonthreatening." He shakes his head today at what little he knew. What little they all knew.

5
—
OUTSIDE
FOUR WALLS

"It was revival," Sonny Arguinzoni says. He was the first to see the amazing stirrings among his friends, junkies from his old neighborhood, but it all began with Sonny himself. He thinks he may have been the first addict in my father's program, and I believe he was. What started for him as a torturous night of withdrawals and despair became a supernaturally instantaneous deliverance from heroin addiction. That miraculous intervention happened at a house my dad had rented in Bedford-Stuyvesant, one of Brooklyn's dangerous sections.

Sonny had first met my father on the streets two years before, but before any real connection was made, he was arrested for heroin possession. Paul Dilena accompanied Sonny to court and spoke on his behalf, urging the judge to send Sonny to one of the nation's two existing drug rehabilitation facilities. Sonny landed in Lexington, Kentucky, inside a federal prison. "They had a section for the drug addicts, but you were still incarcerated," Sonny says. "You really were in prison." Being there reinforced to Sonny his understanding of how the world viewed him: as someone to be locked up, hidden from a society that had no use for him. It was why his friends back home hid heroin needles in their mouths — so they could swallow them if the cops showed up. If they were caught with anything drug related, they would be treated like hardened criminals who deserved life sentences.

Now Sonny was back on the streets, working alongside Nicky Cruz to evangelize every neighborhood in New York City known as a gang hangout. They invited any kid who was interested to come to a weekly service my dad held specifically for gangs. These took place in a Brooklyn building called "the 3:16 church" — a converted van warehouse that was home to a Spanish congregation. Nicky, Sonny, and other young volunteers — mostly teenagers from area churches, including Mike Zello — drove a van into all the boroughs, gathered up kids, and brought them to the service. This all happened late at night, when gang members and addicts were just emerging into the streets to do business.

For my dad, the final night at St. Nicholas hadn't been the end of a campaign. It was the beginning, a spark that confirmed to him God wanted to reach the city's gangs. Typical of my father in those days, he saw Nicky's conversion as a "complete" event. God had worked an instantaneous change in his life; therefore, he was ready to go out as an evangelist. Overnight, Nicky was made leader over the evangelism teams, a role he seemed born for. As a leader of the Mau Maus, he had powerful charisma, and now that gift would be powered by the Holy Spirit.

The services at the 3:16 church started at 11:00 p.m. They were brief, tailored to gang members' attention spans, with sermons no longer than ten minutes. That brevity was also necessary because opposing gangs sat next to each other, and violence could erupt at any point. Dad made his messages for them simple, direct, and confrontational. Sometimes he preached from an evangelistic tract he had written called "Chicken," based on the dangerous game portrayed in the James Dean movie *Rebel without a Cause*. To help with the services, Dad enlisted a young African American Bible school graduate named Thurman Faison. He also drew together a small worship team of teenagers from area churches.

"Dave didn't know anybody," Mike Zello says. "The only contacts he had were some of the pastors. He relied heavily on volunteers, and in those days it was kids because we were the only ones with any real time." That was fine with Dad too. My father had received a mandate to reach gangs, and he saw no reason to wait around for a conventional adult ministry to develop. He trusted God's ability to work in young people and in the spiritual gifts he placed in them, something Dad had seen happen in Philipsburg. Now he would go to the streets with young people as his ministry leaders.

"I was very, very drawn to Dave Wilkerson's spirit," Mike Zello says. "There were churches around, good churches, but this was something different. This was taking the gospel out of the building, and nobody was doing that at the time. Everybody was trying to get the sinners into their church on a Sunday night. That's why we were attracted to him — he had a heart for young people, and we wanted to see people come to Christ."

Those experiences set the course for Mike Zello's life. "I went to Bible college a year or two later," he says. "But way before that, I was seeing people get saved. I saw how it could happen. We actually took Dave's vision and his burden, and somehow it became ours." It's still his today. Mike is Global Teen Challenge's Regional Representative for Africa.

As support grew for the ministry — then called Teen-Age Evangelism — my father began traveling to Bible colleges, recruiting students to come to New York as summer volunteers. "He could communicate his vision like few people," says Dr. Donald Argue, then a student at Central Bible College in Springfield, Missouri, who later served as president of the National Association of Evangelicals. "Of course, the students were deeply moved." More important, "he had credibility," says Dr. Stanley Burgess, who also heard my father speak at Central.

"I had never seen a man so utterly, totally consumed with his mission and calling," says Dr. Vinson Synan, who taught at Emmanuel College in Franklin Springs, Georgia, when Dad spoke there. "He overwhelmed the students with his vision, and some of our top students went to work with him in the very beginning."

Those students descended on New York in droves, and the house in Bedford-Stuyvesant became the nerve center of a humble yet powerful street evangelism effort. Teenage ministry teams canvassed every muddy, weed-filled playground in the Fort Greene Housing Projects, witnessing about Jesus to everyone they came across. They spread out to other tenement neighborhoods throughout New York City, passing out thousands of copies of tracts my dad had written. They worked as prayer counselors at open-air evangelism services where my dad preached. And they accompanied him to nearby churches, where Dad told pastors he would direct young converts their way, so would they please be willing to disciple them?

Gangs in the city had learned to trust those bold young evangelism teams. They knew they came to help, because they kept coming back to the neighborhoods with the same caring love. The gangs cared enough in return to warn the teams when something dangerous was about to happen. A few times Dad had to shut down a street evangelism service when a gang fight was about to take place. At one service in the Bronx, the team saw a teenager from the neighborhood get stabbed in a knife fight, stagger down the block, and collapse.

Yet those teams — mostly Pentecostal church kids from Middle America — maintained their bold, confident, trusting spirit. At times Mike Zello feared for them. "These were all kids from the Midwest, and they were on the subway, laughing and looking at people and smiling," he says. "When you're raised in the city, you don't do that. If you stare at somebody, it means you're looking for trouble. I said to Dave, 'Please talk to them and get them to stop doing that.' He said, 'They don't know any better. We're just not going to tell them.'

"You talk about God's grace," Mike adds. "He took us into places where angels fear to tread. But he made sure we were 'prayed up.' We were going into those communities prepared to die. That was the attitude — 'We're going out tonight, filled with the Holy Ghost, and we're prepared to leave our lives on the street.'"

Donald Argue was one of my dad's first hires as ministry support staff. Dr. Argue, now chancellor of Northwest University in Kirkland, Washington, remembers preaching at a gang service when rival gangs were ready to explode. To avert the violence, he read from Dad's "Chicken" tract, confronting them with the challenge to follow Jesus. One night he found himself using a garden hose to wash blood off the ministry center's front porch after a stabbing. "People said to me, 'You prayed a lot when you were with Teen Challenge, didn't you?'" Dr. Argue says. "I answered that we weren't just praying for God's presence in the work. It was to protect our lives. We were praying for survival."

It was tough, difficult work, and not just because of the dangers. Through all those dedicated efforts, not many gang members came to Christ. "There was only a short window before the drug problem hit," my uncle Don says. "That's when everything changed."

———

Sonny Arguinzoni saw a potential harvest field among his old friends. "I told Nicky, 'Man, let's go to the addicts,'" he says. He knew the territory better than anyone, especially in his home turf of Williamsburg. "That's when we began to see revival."

Heroin addicts at that time were given no hope. They were told they had a life sentence, that there was no cure for their addiction. Many of them just kept using, convinced their fate was to one day overdose and die. To accept my dad's claim that hope could be found in God, they had to see a reality behind it. Uncle Don had joined the work by then and was told by teenagers on the streets, "Your Jesus, he's all right for little kids and ladies dressed up on Sunday, but he doesn't work out here, where you can really use him."

Yet Sonny Arguinzoni was the proof of God's reality. "The drug addict who had been delivered and changed and was full of joy was an infallible proof," Uncle Don says. "He was a picture of the whole gospel for the whole person, and that's what society recognized. All these addicted people were written off, and David had true compassion for them."

The floodgates to minister Christ's powerful love to addicts began to open. Street junkies heard that someone cared and was offering hope, so they began showing up at the house in Bedford-Stuyvesant. *The Cross and the Switchblade* details what those days were like. Some addicts spent days going through withdrawals, with staff and volunteers praying for them and holding vigil. But many were immediately delivered from their addiction, instantaneously shaken from its grip through the baptism of the Holy Spirit. Dad called this "the thirty-second cure."

Meanwhile, the people who lived in drug-plagued neighborhoods knew the proof when they saw it. The former addicts they knew as virtual zombies came back to their neighborhoods as different people — they were alive again, with good news to share. As word spread, more and more addicts were dropped off at the ministry's doorstep. One was an emaciated young Jewish man named Harvey Kuflik, whose mother had driven up in a Cadillac and pushed him out of the car. Dressed only in an undershirt and boxers, Harvey bore hundreds of needle tracks on his arms and legs from heroin injections. "I don't believe in this Jesus Christ," his mother told the worker on the doorstep. "But whatever you can do with Harvey, he's yours." She sped off.

Harvey didn't speak for two weeks. He remained in a haze. Then one day in a chapel service, he knelt and gave his heart to Jesus. "Harvey never stopped talking after that," says John Kenzy, a young volunteer worker from a Nebraska farm. "Harvey knew the Old Testament Scriptures, and he became a powerhouse evangelist."

My dad was compelled to show these amazing proofs to the church. The world he had entered — of heroin shooting galleries in burned-out buildings, occupied by ghostly figures bereft of their humanity — could not be fully described in words. He had to make a film. When he finished shooting *Teenage Drug Addiction*, he dispatched Uncle Don to churches all along the Atlantic seaboard to exhibit the film. "This was brand-new stuff to people," Uncle Don says. "It had shocked David and it had shocked me. When I was a kid, I heard reports of dope dens in China. Now here it was in America."

That film signaled the resurgence of my dad's innovative gifts. Next he arranged for a gospel recording by a teenage choir made up of the volunteer workers, former gang members, and newly delivered addicts. Donald Argue's wife, Pat, a gifted musician trained at the University of Minnesota, led the group into RCA Victor's Studio B in Manhattan to record one side of an LP. On the flip side of their performance was an evangelistic message from my dad. The record was used by the evangelism teams to follow up with new converts' families in their homes.

It was only the beginning. Dad wrote a series of tracts called The Library of Life, encasing them in flip-top boxes designed to look like cigarette packs. He even got permission to have the packs placed on classroom desks in some high schools. Later he produced a newspaper called *The Last Days News*, with articles written as if Christ had already returned. Evangelism teams passed out thousands of copies on Wall Street, on subway platforms, and on buses and ferries. All of these innovations were meant to engage people in their world with the relevance of Christ's gospel.

Perhaps inevitably, it led to a TV program in the New York City area, showcasing the one-of-a-kind teen choir. Broadcast from Manhattan, the show mirrored the LP, with the young people singing and my dad preaching. In between, Dad interviewed one of the teenagers about his or her testimony. The program aired until one kid testified that God had delivered him from a smoking habit. That didn't go over well with a station sponsor, a major tobacco company. The show got canceled.

But the renown of the drug rehabilitation program that became Teen Challenge kept growing. Cures for addiction were still relatively unknown, while Teen Challenge's success continued to astound. It even gained an exhibit at the 1964 World's Fair in New York, where the central proof of the "thirty-second cure" was Harvey Kuflik in the flesh.

———

WHILE ALL THESE DEVELOPMENTS TOOK place, Dad lived in a tiny, government-sponsored apartment in Staten Island, on Victory Boulevard. His work in the city during the flurried days and nights had become full time, and inevitably he had to resign the Philipsburg pastorate. Meanwhile, Mom and we kids moved in with her parents, the Carossos, back in Turtle Creek — a temporary setup that was less than ideal until Dad could get things established for us to move to the city.

His life in New York was spartan. Everything for my father — every minute, every thought, every dime — was centered on God's work. He used the apartment as both an office and a place to sleep. His brother Jerry, who had joined the marines, had kept up on Dad through the family grapevine and decided to visit him on his next leave. My uncle was shocked by what he found.

"He had a cot and a burner, and that was it," Jerry says. "I thought he might be in a nice, plush place, but he didn't have any money. I didn't say a word to him about it, but I thought, 'This guy is crazy. What in the world is he doing?' I really thought there was something wrong with him."

Back in Scranton, their father might have had the same thoughts. "Maybe I heard our dad say he was nuts, I don't know," Jerry muses. "I vaguely remember him saying, 'I don't know what he's getting into.' I do know that when Dave launched out, our dad didn't understand it. And I didn't."

Before Uncle Don joined the ministry, he had visited Dad there too. "I would come in for a weekend from Bible college and spend time with him," he recalls. "There was a pullout couch in his office, with room for two people to sleep. We'd be lying in bed and Dave would say, 'Don, I think I'm going to die at an early age.' I have no idea where that came from. It might have just been that part of his personality, I don't know."

That thought was one my father never fully escaped, and it grew deeper over time. He became even more convinced of it some twenty years later, when he told his staff that he thought he would die within three years.

"He never took care of himself," Uncle Don notes. "He didn't eat well, and he just picked at his food." More than once during those fledgling days, Dad worked himself to exhaustion. He would just collapse, sometimes in midsermon, and have to be taken to the hospital. "If something had to be done, you just did it," Uncle Don explains about the family's work ethic. "Mother had to preach at the Scranton church all the time when Dad was laid low by the ulcers. There was no one else to do it — that's just the way it was. And a pioneering effort like David's was 24/7."

Uncle Don found that out for himself in just a few years' time. Once my father began traveling more, he appointed his brother the new director of Teen Challenge. Uncle Don approached exhaustion several times as he tried to run a difficult ministry for which there was no manual.

I want to note that other dedicated ministries like Teen Challenge were also getting off the ground in New York City, but without the same notoriety. One was in Hell's Kitchen and another was run by Damascus Christian Church with an outreach mainly to Hispanics. All were fledgling, and all involved grueling, inglorious work. At Teen Challenge, many days were more tragic than victorious. My aunt Cindy, Uncle Don's young bride, remembers a young woman convulsing from an overdose and later dying at a hospital. She recalls another female addict arriving in a drug haze with a baby in her arms. She handed the baby to Cindy and climbed onto a table, completely out of her head. Donald Argue once fielded a call from a New York City detective who had discovered a lifeless body on a rooftop with no identification. Clutched in the deceased young man's hand was a Teen Challenge card.

———

"ALMOST EVERYTHING DAVID DID IN those days was revival to the church," says Winkie Pratney, bestselling author of *Youth Aflame*. As a young convert from New Zealand, Winkie spent a summer at Teen Challenge in Brooklyn. "If David had only been an evangelist, he wouldn't have had the same impact. Without those visitations of God, there would have been no Teen Challenge. It would have just been a nice guy trying to help some people. I mean, this was an ordinary guy who nobody even remembered in Bible college. All those miraculous things that happened in New York came out of genuine revival. And all of the men and women who were attracted to David's work saw more than just evangelism taking place."

Dick Simmons agrees. The praying pastor in Dad's Brooklyn neighborhood became a resident director of Teen Challenge. "Dave knew the way of the Lord," Dick says. "He wasn't interested in just giving testimonies about what was accomplished. Dave was a pulpiteer — 'I'm a man of God; listen to me' — and that is needed. He saw how God works powerfully, and that's why he had such confidence."

My father was more comfortable with the mantle of evangelist than that of a revivalist. In later years he acknowledged his calling in a prophetic role, though he never publicly said so. My uncle Don sees that prophetic aspect as one more part of Teen Challenge's appeal. "People were hungry for a demonstration of God's power," he says. "David and I were raised during a healing wave — Oral Roberts, A. A. Allen — and there was a whole long list of those that went sour. People are always desperate to see healings, and most of those are very subjective. But here was a demonstration of God's healing power in a different way. It did involve physical healing, sometimes with an instantaneous deliverance, but the healing was also internal, from a habit that was not just physical but psychological. It was a demonstration of God's supernatural power, yet something that people could relate to."

It was also holistic. The miracle of God's intervention in addicts' lives

continued beyond instantaneous healing. A whole segment of society—
a despairing, written-off people who had been criminalized for their
addictions—was being prepared to reenter society to do good works.
To put it another way: they were coming back to serve a world that had
wanted to lock them away.

To the astonishment of many, it was all happening through the
church—and that was radical. "Churches didn't want to come out of
their four walls," Donald Argue says. That perception was generally held
about Pentecostal churches in particular. Vinson Synan says of Dad's
work, "David had a burden and vision for the truly down and out, and
that showed a social conscience. Pentecostals were accused of not having
that kind of care for people." My uncle Don concurs: "Historically it was
mainline denominations and Catholics who did 'social ministry,' running hospitals and feeding the poor. Along comes a Pentecostal who's
helping not only to cure and feed them but to prepare them for society."

Even before publication of *The Cross and the Switchblade*, an article
in *Christian Life* magazine alerted Christians to the miraculous works
God was performing in New York City. Soon a steady stream of people
came to the house in Brooklyn to witness it for themselves. As one young
worker said cheekily, "People expected to see Nicky Cruz getting saved
every hour on the hour."

At first those visitors came from a growing network of supporters
in New York City. Pat Robertson came to observe from the Brooklyn
church he was pastoring. Others showed up from afar, including David
du Plessis, the acknowledged leader of the growing charismatic movement. Known as "Mr. Pentecost," he had just had an audience with the
pope. Then one figure in particular, a minister whose entire calling was
to proclaim God's healing power, arrived with great interest. Kathryn
Kuhlman was moved beyond words at what she saw taking place in
the house in Bedford-Stuyvesant. Going from room to room—seeing
the looks of desperation on addicts' faces as they endured withdrawals,
alternating with cries of joy from others who were instantly freed—she
turned to my dad tearfully. "David," she said, pressing a roll of money
into his hand, "use this to help those boys."

Eventually the work drew the interest of an Englishman named

Leonard Ravenhill, the revered author of *Why Revival Tarries*. In decades to come, Leonard became one of my father's dearest friends and had a significant impact on his life. A distinguished gentleman with a devotion equal to my dad's, he had been a preacher for A. W. Tozer's ministry, based in the British Isles. More recently he had served with Bethany Fellowship in Minneapolis when he heard of my dad's outreach in New York.

"Leonard Ravenill wouldn't have gone to just hang out with somebody who's dealing with drug addicts," notes Winkie Pratney. Leonard had long prayed for revival. He was also one of the "pulpiteers" described by Dick Simmons. He loved preaching on the streets, as England had a long tradition of open-air ministry. In Brooklyn, Leonard was a firsthand witness to what a wide-eyed Sonny Arguinzoni could only call revival.

"What Leonard saw there was the dealings of God with people," Winkie Pratney says. "That's revival. It's what happened with David, when he picked up *Life* magazine at one o'clock in the morning and started weeping without knowing why. I saw it myself in those meetings at Teen Challenge. These were visitations from God."

Leonard Ravenhill didn't mince words when it came to the work of God, and that was a trait Dad trusted. He also knew of Leonard's reputation for holiness preaching and his pursuit of the "deeper life" espoused by Tozer. Eventually, my dad offered Leonard a position at Teen Challenge, to teach and preach.

"David didn't trust other people to do things as he did," Winkie says. "He didn't trust them to tell the truth as he would. That was important to him. Everybody thinks of revival as a nice time with people getting saved, but there's an element to revival that was revealed in David's ministry. That is a gut-level, wrenching discovery that you are really screwed. It's when you discover how deeply wrong you are, and it lasts for hours. I saw kids sobbing their guts out, and these were the toughest kids. Then the incredible joy comes, and it's from nowhere in your life — not your experience, not your circumstances, but from God. It's something only he can give you. You can't pretend to have it. If you haven't got it, you don't — it's as simple as that."

In that respect, Leonard Ravenhill was a match for my father in ministry. "An evangelist or a revivalist isn't looking for the normal, common thing," Winkie says. "They're looking for what needs to happen. That's why they'll say to you the tough thing, and they don't really care whether you like it."

———

THERE MAY HAVE BEEN ANOTHER REASON why Dad wanted an older, seasoned minister like Leonard Ravenhill around Teen Challenge. Dad's father, Kenneth, had just died. After all of my grandfather's battles with ulcers and the terrible toll they took on his body, he succumbed to a stroke.

"Our father didn't live long enough to see David vindicated," Uncle Don says. "Ruth and I have gone back and forth on whether he ever would have approved of David's work. It might have bothered him that this was a parachurch ministry, even though that wasn't a term back then. But I do know David would have found a place for Dad. He and Mom would have been living in the house we eventually bought at 416 Clinton Avenue, the original Teen Challenge building. David would have had him preaching to the students, and he would have drawn on our father's wisdom."

Decades passed before my dad opened up to me with his feelings from that period. "I know this is going to sound fleshly," he said, framing his emotions, characteristically, in spiritual terms, "but I always wish my father had seen more of the success in my life."

That statement might appear to be a son's longing for his father's approval, but it wasn't just that. My dad had already settled that issue in his heart, long before his father's death. It's what enabled him to keep going back to New York after being thrown out of court. Ultimately, it didn't matter if he kept being humiliated or if his actions might be embarrassing. He had determined then that the only approval he needed was God's.

What my dad disclosed to me in that statement wasn't a longing; it was a regret for his father. My grandfather had never tasted the freedom to serve God that my dad was now enjoying — to see God's reality manifested beyond the four walls of a church. It was a regret that came, very simply, from my father's heart of flesh. And there is nothing wrong with that.

6
—
THREE LEPERS KNOCKING

I WONDER IF MY FATHER had begun to notice the stars over Staten Island. Probably not; on the ferry ride home from Manhattan, his mind most likely still raced with the demands of the day. Maybe he noticed the stars as he paced up the walk to our house, since life was much better now that his family was with him. Dad couldn't be with us for supper most evenings, but at least he was comforted knowing his three children slept soundly through the night, and that his wife would wait up for him if she could keep her eyes open. This was not one of those nights. As I picture him quietly closing the door to his study to pray, I imagine him in a more settled frame of mind than before.

On these late nights, a Bible story kept coming to his mind. It was from 2 Kings, the tale of some lepers living outside the walls of Samaria. The city was under siege by a powerful enemy, and inside, the people were starving. Then one night, while everyone slept, God caused the surrounding enemy to flee. The next morning, the Samaritan lepers stumbled into the enemy camp and discovered a vast treasury their tormentors had left behind. They recognized right away that this was a gift from God meant to save them. Excited, they took the treasure back to their starving brothers and sisters inside the city walls.

In my dad's mind, the lepers' story took the shape of his own: a lone figure on the outskirts of the world stumbling upon a miraculous work of God. Meanwhile, a fearful church trembles inside its four walls, unable to see that God is powerfully at work manifesting his reality in a broken, hope-starved world.

The story that God had given my dad was a treasure, and he knew it. Now he had to share it, not just with his brothers and sisters but with the larger world. It offered answers to the questions every human being has about the reality of God: He can transform anyone. He can use anyone. And He wants everyone.

It took an unlikely collision of worlds for my father's story to be told.

———

I can't imagine that Dad wasn't skeptical when he met John and Elizabeth Sherrill. The Sherrills were nominal Episcopalians who lived in Westchester County, among the wealthy suburbs north of New York City, and the world they inhabited was intellectual and ultrarational. Until recently they didn't have a practicing faith, despite the fact they were writers for *Guideposts*, the inspirational magazine founded by Norman Vincent Peale, famous for his bestselling book *The Power of Positive Thinking*. *Guideposts* specialized in stories of people whose faith helped them through crises in their lives. It had a circulation of twelve million, and many of its first-person stories were those of celebrities.

None of this would have appealed to my dad. At some level, he had to be put off by *Guideposts'* ecumenical, inspirational approach. I can imagine the words that might have passed through his mind about the gospel it espoused: watered down, compromised, powerless. The Jesus he knew was a Savior of action, a living God who intervened daily, even miraculously, in people's lives. Dad didn't find that Jesus in *Guideposts*. So when my father met the Sherrills, "We were a shock to him," Elizabeth says. "Our whole lifestyle was something he equated with evil."

In turn, the Sherrills would have had every reason to be just as skeptical of my father. "By our way of thinking, we were meeting someone who was not educated, was narrow-minded and judgmental — all the wrongheaded cliches about certain people who had a primitive way of thinking," Elizabeth says.

As journalists the Sherrills had been trained to be skeptical of cliches, including their own. Likewise, my father's sharp discernment stirred him to look past appearances. Maybe it shouldn't have surprised either of them that when they met, "We liked one another — very, very much," Elizabeth says. My father felt an ease and kinship with John and Elizabeth that lasted their lifetime. A deep friendship was cemented at that very first meeting.

Dad would have recognized God's work in the Sherrills' lives right away, because they were on a journey just as improbable as his. Following their journalistic instincts, they had begun investigating what would come to be identified as one of the major Christian events of the twentieth century: the Charismatic Renewal. "There was something in the air," John says of the Pentecostal "outpourings" taking place all over the world — in Scandinavia, South America, even in Communist China — all independent of each other. "These people had no contact with each other," John says, "and the events were all happening within roughly the same time frame. That's what was exciting about it. There was no Billy Graham to lead this. You could actually see that something was going on."

John took notes for a book on the subject, and he and Elizabeth started researching more in depth. They absorbed the history of Pentecostals in previous centuries, up to the modern movement in the early twentieth century, which flourished with the Azusa Street Revival in Los Angeles. Now, at the dawn of the sixties, something similar was emerging on a global scale, "a spiritual event," as John calls it. As he tracked it, he saw the world experiencing pangs of a contemporary Pentecost.

It was a story John felt he had to pursue if only for its journalistic value. Yet he and Elizabeth also had been following their own spiritual stirrings. The story tugged at John for reasons he couldn't quite explain, and by the time they met my dad, the Sherrills had begun to call themselves Christians. Still, they knew nothing about the Holy-Spirit-empowered world they were on the cusp of entering.

Both John and Elizabeth were at work in *Guideposts*' Manhattan offices one morning when Reverend Peale's wife, Ruth, burst in. "I just heard the most astonishing thing," she announced. A dinner guest at the Peales' home had mentioned the phenomenon of speaking in tongues. It was no longer a cloistered practice among Pentecostal believers but now was spreading through mainline churches. "I just can't imagine that's going on," Mrs. Peale said. Her dinner guest had also mentioned David Wilkerson and the amazing work he was doing among gangs and drug addicts in Brooklyn, and that *he* spoke in tongues. The Sherrills' antennas shot up. "That was the impetus for us to go and meet David," Elizabeth says.

The dinner guest, it turned out, was a man named Harald Bredesen, a Lutheran minister who had been baptized in the Holy Spirit. He had become a friend of my dad's, coming alongside him to help with Teen Challenge. As John and Elizabeth learned more about Dad's story, they sensed it was the perfect demonstration of the birth pangs of the powerful worldwide movement of God. Dad's story wasn't just about the phenomenon of speaking in tongues. It was about the power of God's Spirit to transform lives — damaged, broken, hopeless lives — in an instant.

"His work had an influence on the larger story we were pursuing," Elizabeth says. "It helped to give it an authenticity and a fleshing out. David was a great encouragement to us to keep digging and finding out more and more about this phenomenon. He was a tremendous door opener for us, a window opener onto another world. It was a world very different from our own, and one we knew nothing about."

My father's fame didn't just happen one morning. When he met the Sherrills, he was still struggling from day to day, driving himself to exhaustion, sacrificing family time in a pioneering work, and nursing ulcers he had developed from the stress of his work. Likewise, the Sherrills weren't famous when they met my dad. They were magazine writers working in the niche publishing world of religious faith. They were good at what they did and highly respected, but they hadn't written books and their faith was still relatively unformed.

My point is this: Sometimes, before good things happen, it's hard to imagine they ever will. The series of magazine stories that later gave birth to *The Cross and the Switchblade* was as unlikely to interest a reader in 1960 as any other publishing crapshoot. Here was a preacher no one knew, with no credibility, claiming his recovery program for drug addicts was being run supernaturally by God. And his story was about to be told by a couple who had no idea what he was talking about.

It was collective blind faith. *Guideposts* — specifically its editor, Len LeSourd — would have to be convinced of this fantastic tale the Sherrills had brought to him. A magazine with twelve million readers couldn't accept at face value a story with as many questions as my dad's raised.

———

DESPITE ITS ECUMENICAL APPROACH, *GUIDEPOSTS*' origins would have been close to my dad's heart. Dr. Peale had founded it during World War II as a leaflet to encourage US soldiers returning home. Evidently, America was hungry for the kinds of stories it published, because its circulation skyrocketed. Dr. Peale soon shifted his aim: he wanted *Guideposts* on the desk of every American businessman on Monday morning. That meant spiritual truths had to be communicated in the plain language of the average American.

To accomplish this, *Guideposts* had to change "the quality of Christian magazine writing," Elizabeth says. Most journals, she notes, were mired in church jargon, language that meant something to believers but nothing to the average person. "Before *Guideposts* came on the scene, it was all either didactic or pompous or both, or boring or too sweet and saccharine. Our role was to be translators. We had to think of the reader who wouldn't necessarily know what is meant by, 'Are you saved?'"

The Sherrills' fledgling faith actually helped in that process. "Neither of us had had a personal conversion," Elizabeth says. "We did some of our best writing then because we took nothing for granted. When people said to us, 'God told me ...,' we said, 'Wait a minute, what do you mean? How did you know it was God?' We asked questions that any nonbeliever has, because *Guideposts*' target reader was not the devout Christian."

That was the Sherrills' challenge with my dad. "David talked then in what we think of as 'Christianese,'" John says. "It was a natural language for him, and it had an authenticity about it."

"He was from a particular background, and certain phrases were sacred to him," Elizabeth notes. "They meant everything to him, because he knew what they meant. But they would not communicate to people from other backgrounds."

At first that challenge was a struggle for Dad. "When we suggested there was another way to say a phrase — 'by the blood of the Lamb,' for example — it was as though we were proposing another savior to him. He thought, 'Never, over my dead body.' Luckily, there were two of us and one of him, and it turned into browbeating the poor man. But we respected David, and he came to respect us, and eventually he let us get away with things. He yielded to us in that way, when other subjects of ours did not. It's because he wanted to be heard."

The Sherrills were still on a learning curve of their own. They were just discovering theological matters that my father had taken for granted his whole life. "There were things we didn't understand," John says. "David would talk about Jesus representing the Godhead, and we'd shake our heads and say, 'What in the world are you talking about?' We'd have to stop for a minute so he could help us out, which he did with great patience."

Then there was the challenge of Dad's story itself, the substance of his faith experience. "David was so interesting," John says. "He was a good storyteller, and the stories he told were extravagant. But he told them in a very natural way, as if he had never told them before. He was so swept up in them that it was as if they were brand new."

"The stories were hard to believe," Elizabeth remembers. "And yet as we got to know David, we found him so very believable, just a deeply honest person, rigorous with his facts." As seasoned journalists, the Sherrills were used to verifying their subjects' claims. They knew by experience not to trust everything they were told. "Some would exaggerate to try to give God a little boost," Elizabeth says.

In Dad's case, the opposite was true. The Sherrills learned that my father tended to underplay his experiences. Early on, they discussed one of his first trips to Brooklyn, when he and a trumpet-player friend held an impromptu street meeting. Dozens of people came to Christ that day, a fact that impressed the Sherrills immediately. Naturally, they asked how many people had been at the gathering. "About three hundred," Dad said. That raised the couple's eyebrows. "We each thought, 'Three hundred people on a street corner?' That would have created congestion, stopped traffic, blocked the sidewalk," Elizabeth says. "The police would have noticed. So we went to the precinct and asked them if there was a record of any such crowd having gathered on that particular day. They looked it up and found it. 'Yes,' they said, 'there were about *five hundred* people on that street corner.' "

The stories that Dad told them were also tough, not the usual *Guideposts* fare. He related the horrific tales of teenagers and preteens engaging in group sex and bestiality. The Sherrills realized they could go only so far in detailing what Dad had witnessed. "Yet without telling how bad it was, it was hard to tell how powerful his ministry was," Elizabeth says. "You couldn't gloss over the horror of it."

The Sherrills were not strangers to the darker side of human nature. Elizabeth's father had been a private detective. "I had known about that world, about prostitution and drugs," she says. Even so, what she and John experienced on their first visit to my dad's center was a shock to their systems. "We went to visit his place in Bedford-Stuyvesant where he brought the young people, children, really," she recalls with a shiver. "As we approached, we could hear screams such as I have never heard coming from upstairs. Someone was going cold turkey. That was our introduction to heroin at a personal level. We had known about it, but we'd never been close to it, cheek by jowl."

Equally eye-opening were the miraculous deliverances those young addicts experienced, sparing them the agonies and risks of cold-turkey withdrawals. Noting it all, the Sherrills then trailed Dad to the streets as he evangelized addicts and gang members. They saw firsthand an aspect of Pentecost that tends to get overlooked: boldness to witness for Christ. "His eyes, his personality, his commitment, his intense love for the people he was talking to — the word that keeps coming to mind is *fearless*," Elizabeth recalls. "He confronted gang members and other unsavory types with great courage. He just read them the riot act, telling them that God loved them, and that *he* would love them."

As it turned out, the biggest challenge for the Sherrills was all the miracles that had taken place in Dad's work. They had to check these out too, with the people who had been with him when miraculous things occurred. One by one, the outlandish coincidences, the awe-inspiring conversions, the physical deliverances and instantly transformed lives — every account was verified. It led to an important discovery for John about my father. "That is actually the heart of David's story," John notes, "the power of the Holy Spirit to move into the world *right now* and change things."

The Sherrills concluded that Dad's word was as good as gold. "We eventually got to the point where we accepted his stories the way he told them," John adds. "Then we had the job of making those same stories believable and understandable to the reader. You have to assume that the reader is not going to believe it — that it's nonsense, that things don't happen that way." Dad understood the challenge. "He would have gone through that as a child, having to analyze the truthfulness of miracle stories in Pentecostal circles," John points out.

Yet even after all the verifying, another problem arose. Once the Sherrills had finished their research, they realized the sheer number of miracles in Dad's story was a problem. "It was just one miracle after another, and it got to be overwhelming," John says, remembering *Guideposts*' readers. "We decided we would not tell as many of these stories as we had in our inventory. We just couldn't. It wouldn't work."

Despite their cautiousness, the Sherrills encountered resistance from skeptics at the *Guideposts* offices. "One person didn't like David because it was all too mysterious for her," John says. "She came storming in saying, 'I told you so, this is all fake.'" The woman tossed down a copy of a newspaper. Dad claimed that that edition contained a story about him on the front page. "Look, there's the front page, and it's not there," the woman said.

She stomped out, leaving John and Elizabeth bewildered. They began thumbing through the edition and, sure enough, there was no article. Then they came across the newspaper's Sunday magazine, published separately. "There it was, on the cover of the magazine section, a full-blast story," John says. "It was an interesting case of people's reactions to David."

Since it first began publishing in 1945, *Guideposts* had never published a multipart story. My father's would be the first. The Sherrills knew it couldn't be contained in the usual way, and it took all their powers of persuasion to convince their editor, Len LeSourd, to run it in three parts. He agreed, and readers' responses were overwhelming.

People from all walks of life wrote in — mothers, teachers, school officials, police officers, teenagers, businessmen. The story had hit a nerve. "Reader mail was heavy with it," Elizabeth recalls. "But nobody said, 'We're shocked, we'll no longer give *Guideposts* to our children,' or anything like that. We didn't have that kind of reaction."

The snowballing response confirmed what the Sherrills had been thinking throughout the whole process. "The three-part series began to feel like a book as we worked on it," Elizabeth says. "There was so much to it."

For a book to emerge, more unlikely worlds had to collide.

———

THE OFFICES OF BERNARD GEIS and Associates Publishing were located in a former firehouse. When my father and the Sherrills entered the upper-floor office, they noticed the firepole was still in place. It led down a hole in the floor just a few paces away from the oak desk where Bernard Geis himself sat at work. If he had wanted, he could have hopped onto the pole and slid down to the first floor.

Normally my dad or John Sherrill might have mentioned this, just to break the ice, but they were too intimidated. Geis had barely glanced at them since they entered. He was busy at his final task of the day — writing out checks — and he seemed in a hurry to finish.

Geis's company was on the cusp of releasing *Sex and the Single Girl* by Helen Gurley Brown. It sold two million copies in its first three weeks. Geis followed that with *Valley of the Dolls*, surpassing those numbers by millions more. He already had Art Linkletter in his stable of authors, reaping millions from the Kids Say the Darndest Things book series.

When my father and the Sherrills visited his offices that day, they may not have known Bernard Geis was one of the pioneers of sensational publishing. He had gained a toehold on a brand of book just beginning to take off in the early sixties. His publicity director was instructed to stage stunts to move sales, no matter how controversially. In one of these, a scaffold was erected in Times Square and an aspiring young actress partially stripped for the crowd below, in order to promote a new novel, *The Voyeur.*

"You've got ten minutes," Geis announced, scribbling away.

They had come on a recommendation by a fellow writer at *Guide-posts*. Surprisingly, Dad had no objections to a secular publisher, even this one. "David's only concern was guidance," John says. To know for sure whether God was leading them, Dad had suggested to the Sherrills, "Let's put a fleece before the Lord."

"Hold it, a *what?*" John asked. Dad explained to them the concept of a "fleece" in the Old Testament story of Gideon, as interpreted by some Pentecostals. If a believer wanted to know God's will on a certain matter, he could set certain practical conditions and ask the Lord to meet them. God's response, whether by meeting the conditions or not, would indicate his will on the matter. I think only the Sherrills' investigative instincts would have persuaded them to go along with Dad on something like this.

Together, they decided to make the fleece so difficult there would be no mistaking God's response. They came up with two conditions: (1) that Geis would be able to meet them that very day, late on Friday afternoon, and (2) that Geis would meet their need for a five-thousand-dollar advance. "That doesn't sound like much, but back then you could buy a house with it," John says. Much of it would have to go toward expenses. The Sherrills estimated it would take three full years to research and write the book.

So the first part of the fleece had been met. Geis had agreed to meet with them if they made it to the office before closing time, and they arrived at 4:30. Now for the second part.

John shouldered the task of pitching the book idea. If ever there was a sharp-witted, well-spoken man, it's John Sherrill. But now, under the pressure of a ten-minute pitch, he had to scramble to compress everything in his head. As Geis scribbled away, John launched into the ministry's phenomenal success rate. He quoted statistics that never failed to gain a listener's attention. Geis didn't raise his head. He just scribbled away. He did look up once to glance at the firepole.

John shifted gears. He described the rescue and rehabilitation of gang members, stories that usually caused gasps of disbelief. Geis just kept scribbling and once again glanced at the firepole. John suddenly realized

what Geis had in mind: he was about to make his exit for the weekend —
right down that firepole.

Time was slipping away. It became clear to both my dad and the Sherrills that Bernard Geis wanted a bestseller. They only wanted to share
a godly treasure. Judging by Geis's nonplussed reaction, Dad's treasure
didn't translate into the world of sensational book publishing.

With the few minutes he had left, John took a different tack. "Okay,
forget all that, Mr. Geis," he said. "Let me tell you about this preacher who
came to Bedford-Stuyvesant from the mountains." John then unfolded
my father's story, from the late night in a Pennsylvania farm town when
Dad flipped opened the pages of *Life* magazine; to the white-knuckle service at St. Nicholas Arena and Nicky Cruz's radical transformation; to the
current neighbors' complaints about all the loud singing in that big house
on Clinton Avenue that glows with life each night.

Geis stopped scribbling. He was rapt. Something had grabbed this son
of a cigar manufacturer, a self-made man who had had no connections to
the publishing world. "Other publishers were very buttoned-down and
believed it was a gentleman's profession," a Geis associate once said. A
"gentleman's profession" never would have entertained my dad's story.

Geis was leaning back now, listening. From time to time he glanced
at Dad as John talked, as if to gauge whether the story was real. Gang
members, rapists, heroin addicts — all getting religion, all turning their
lives around to help others. And this little guy from the country had
made all of that happen. I wonder how my father must have appeared to
Geis, whether the skinny, silent figure sitting across from him matched
up to the stories he was hearing. I like to think that Geis, a common man
who had started his own publishing company in Manhattan, New York
City, had one word in mind as John talked about my father: guts.

Geis pushed back his chair and stood up. "I've heard enough," he said.
"Write up a proposal." He threaded his arms into the sleeves of his jacket.
"If it's a go, I'll give you five thousand dollars." With that, he strode to the
firepole, wrapped himself around it, and dropped out of sight.

Ten minutes. Five thousand dollars.

So *that* was a fleece.

———

"THE TIMING WAS JUST EXACTLY right for David's story," John says. "It was a time when, to use the Christian word for it, the 'personal witness story' was being read all over the Christian world. That's what we were trained to do at *Guideposts*. All of a sudden, this fell into place. I think the same books written today would not become bestsellers, even though everything that went into them would be the same. We were there, by the grace of God, at that time."

Week by week, sales of *The Cross and the Switchblade* kept going up. "It just took off right away," Elizabeth says. "It was nothing we could have foreseen."

"I don't think books take off and do well, or don't do well, depending just on the quality of the writing," John adds. "I think it depends on catching something that's in the air, something that people need."

The timing was right for other reasons too. A huge segment of the church was ready to take the book's message to the world, to send congregations beyond their four walls to proclaim Jesus' wonder-working love. A great swath of believers — both within Pentecostal denominations and those from the larger Christian church — wanted to know that in the rapidly changing world of the sixties, the God they believed in was real. *The Cross and the Switchblade* provided a catalyst for multitudes who were hungry to see God prove his reality. In my dad's story, they could read for themselves how God demonstrated his love, a la the book of Acts, in their own era and world.

"The reaction of young people encountering something in the book was just fascinating," Elizabeth says. "Our favorite kind of letter was from teachers who assigned their students to write to us, asking questions or making a comment or objection."

The timing for a book like *The Cross and the Switchblade* had been right for another reason. It coincided with the global outpouring of the Holy Spirit that the Sherrills had been tracking. The baptism of the Holy Spirit played a central role in Teen Challenge's successes, yet my dad had been hesitant about including it in the book. He reflected:

> I had trouble with the last chapter. In it John and Elizabeth had written about the Pentecostal side of our work. Suddenly there

it was, ready to go into print, that we spoke in tongues.... I had spent years trying to get the social agencies in New York to accept us as a proper house of therapy, years trying to get the courts and the jails to cooperate with us. And now I was afraid we would become the laughingstock of these same institutions. The charismatic renewal had not yet become acceptable; we were still living in a day when Pentecostals were considered Holy Ghost bumpkins. If we told it like it was, I was worried: If we talked about how our young people raised their hands and praised the Lord and spoke in languages which were not their own — would this hurt us?

Dad called the Sherrills. After some concerted prayer, they all decided to leave the matter in Bernard Geis's hands. As expected, when the publisher responded, he was critical of the final chapter, but not because they had included the Holy Spirit; they hadn't included *enough*. Geis wanted more. Besides, he said, they wrote about the subject as if they were afraid of it. He asked them to rewrite the last chapter and expand it into two.

Who knows, maybe that was the sensational side of Bernard Geis. In any case, the Sherrills rewrote the ending, and Dad reflected again, "This time we put ourselves on the line. We talked pointedly about the source of power we were working with.... I saw now why the Lord had chosen Bernard Geis, who is Jewish, to publish this Christ-centered book. The reason was very simple. If we had taken the story to almost any Christian publisher in those days, their reaction to that last chapter would have been the opposite of Bernard Geis's. 'Tongues are too controversial,' they would have said."

Dad's hunch about this was confirmed. Once the book went international, an unusual sales report came in: it was a bestseller in every Scandinavian country — except one. Dad wondered why. After some digging, he found out the publisher there had deleted the last two chapters from their edition. Dad insisted that they reinstate the chapters, and once they did, sales took off, matching those in other countries.

At one time, my father had turned away from a healing ministry because of its sensational attraction. It had brought him a name he didn't want. Now every healing he saw taking place spoke of another name, the rightful one: Jesus.

The book also turned out to be prophetic. "Who knew that in a little while, the drug scene was going to be in the suburbs," Elizabeth says. "At the time we worked on David's story, drugs were an inner-city phenomenon, a gang phenomenon. But in our little suburb there would soon be drug abuse. A boy on our own street would die of an overdose. The book had a lot of resonance because people like us had children who were beginning to do the same things. Other parents would have been completely as ignorant as we were."

———

WHAT MAY SURPRISE SOME IS that the book never made anyone rich. As royalties came in, Dad plowed the initial income back into the ministry. Then unexpectedly, Bernard Geis Publishers went belly up. Its reputation for sensationalism had backfired. The novels it published featured more and more sex, with thinner and thinner veils over the actual celebrities they depicted. Geis's investing partners backed off, and he filed for bankruptcy in 1971.

That bankruptcy stalled *The Cross and the Switchblade*'s income for years. Dad had to work harder than ever to raise funds for the ministry. But years later, once the bankruptcy was settled, the rights reverted to my father and the Sherrills. To this day, John and Elizabeth don't know — and make a point not to know — how many copies of *The Cross and the Switchblade* have sold. (It's in the range of sixteen million and has been translated into thirty languages.) Like my dad, they saw the telling of the story as a sacred endeavor. They would always be three lepers knocking at the city gate, offering wondrous treasure to a people starved for hope.

Part Three

REACH

When the drug problem started to spread, he saw what was coming. But people simply would not, could not, believe it.

— *Dallas Holm*

7
—
A WILDERNESS OF YOUTH

At one time the most vile sinners were innocent children, full of the gift of life. Jesus says of children, "Of such is the kingdom of God." And it is their precious life Satan goes hunting for. He seeks to wound and deceive them, to turn them away from God and into slavery to sin.

I once was approached by a young man who for years had been a witch. Now he told me he wanted Christ. He had just had a horrible dream in which demons tried to possess him. Frightened, he cried out in the dream, "Jesus!" and the demons shrank back. But they rallied their forces and came toward him again. Louder than before, he cried out, "Jesus!" and again the demons fled. "That's why I want Christ," he told me. "I know Satan wants me." I gladly prayed with him.

Did Satan try to possess this young man because he was inherently bad? What about this young man attracted the devil? What caused Satan to gather his forces to try to possess his life?

I believe it was because at a very young age this man had such potential for the kingdom of God that the adulteress came after him, hunting him down and deceiving him. But now the devil's greatest fear was coming to pass. As I prayed with the young man, I sensed he would be a powerful witness for the gospel. And his life would be a testimony of the power of Christ to transform even the possessed.

— EXCERPT FROM THE SERMON "THE HUNTER FROM HELL"

—■—

DALLAS HOLM WAS A TWENTY-YEAR-OLD youth minister at Rosen Heights Church in Fort Worth when he received an unusual phone call late one night in the summer of 1969. "This is David Wilkerson," the voice on the other end said abruptly.

"Everything with Brother Dave was immediate," Dallas says today. "Looking back, he was on a mission. I knew who he was, because he'd come to my church in St. Paul when I was a teenager." Yet Dallas had no idea why my father would be calling him now.

"I'm looking for somebody to travel with me to minister in music," Dad said. That phrase — "minister in music" — had a limited meaning in 1969. It spoke of choral groups and gospel singers, and that wasn't Dallas. My father added this kicker: "I'd like someone who's more contemporary."

Dad was calling him from Eugene, Oregon, where he had just concluded an evangelistic youth crusade at a high school auditorium. Meetings like this were what my dad had been doing full time for three years, on the road for roughly six months each year. When he called Dallas Holm, he was sitting in the living room of the host pastor in Eugene. The pastor's son had known Dallas in college and had just played one of Dallas's LPs for my father. The needle was halfway through the second song when Dad asked to use the phone.

"We'll be at Oak Cliff Assembly in Dallas, Texas, next month for a youth crusade," my dad told the singer. "Would you come and do a few songs for us?"

As he spoke, Dallas was still trying to get his bearings. Images flashed through his head of switchblades and heroin needles. That was all he knew of David Wilkerson, and he wasn't quite sure what a "youth crusade" was.

Besides, Dallas liked his work at Rosen Heights. It was rewarding to see young people mature in their faith under his watch. As a bonus, Dallas's mentor, the pastor at Rosen Heights, was Ira Stanphill, the renowned gospel songwriter. Reverend Stanphill's songs comprised a good portion of the evangelical hymnals used throughout the English-speaking world.

Yet my dad's offer had some appeal. Music was Dallas Holm's passion; it was what he wanted to do with his life. He had been writing songs
since he'd come to Christ at age sixteen but had no role models then. In
1965 his musical influences were Ricky Nelson and Elvis Presley. All he
knew to do was to take his electric guitar and small amp with him to
churches, jails, anyplace that would have him, and sing the songs he'd
been writing about Jesus.

"Those of us who had gotten saved were taking our music out as a
vehicle for the gospel," he says. "But we were taking a lot of abuse. That's
not a complaint; it's just the way it was. A pastor would walk me into
his office and tell me why I needed to cut my hair and why I should get
an acoustic guitar to replace my electric. Those ministers honestly felt
they had grounds to stand on. We, on the other hand, thought, 'This is
what kids listen to. They're not going to walk into your church and sing
a hymn. They'd be totally disinterested. But they will listen to this style
of music. Why can't we just sing about Jesus?'"

Dallas didn't know then how careful my father was about whom
he associated with his ministry. "He was a very spiritually discerning
man," Dallas says. "That's a component you can't measure. He was not
impressed with notoriety; he wasn't impressed with talent necessarily.
What he was looking for was the right combination — someone with
integrity in ministry and who had a walk with the Lord."

The album that Dallas's college friend had just played for my dad
wasn't a technical masterpiece. "It was one of those times when you pay
the engineer twenty-five bucks just to roll tape," Dallas says. "I suppose
Brother Dave heard something in the music that made him think, 'This
could be my guy.'"

Throughout his life, Dad would speak of a certain "sound" he
heard in preachers, something that spoke to him of God's holiness. He
couldn't have known why at the time, but he intuited in Dallas's music
the intense training the musician had undergone in Scripture, theology, and a deep spiritual walk. Those practices had begun early on,
when Dallas, clearly a musical talent as a teenager, found himself being
booked to perform every weekend. Receiving invitations to perform
original music for appreciative audiences was any singer-songwriter's

dream. But when Dallas's discerning pastor saw this happening, he gently took the teenager aside and gave him advice that would benefit him the rest of his days.

"You've got your whole life to do what you're gifted to do," the pastor said. "But you only have now to train for it." Dallas heard the wisdom in this, so he buckled down and did the groundwork to walk knowledgeably and faithfully as a Christian. I think my father heard that integrity between the crackles on Dallas's humble record.

There was another reason why Dallas would indeed be Dad's guy: he was his own man. Dallas was completely himself, unintimidated by anyone's intensity. Maybe even more important, Dallas had a sense of humor that cut through seriousness, laying bare a situation with a single comment or observation. A quip from Dallas could cut through baloney the same way my father's spiritual gravitas did.

"Dallas had demonstrated a profound heart for God before Brother Dave ever met him," notes Paul Annan, the design artist who crafted the graphic look of Dad's ministry materials over several decades. "I think that formed the context of how Brother Dave looked at Dallas. There was something real there, and it was real before Brother Dave ever met him. He and Dallas had a very foundational affection for each other that was virtually unshakable. That allowed Dallas to be a comedian in a way Brother Dave would have accepted from no one else."

Two months later, Dallas and Dad got to know each other after the crusade service at Oak Cliff Assembly. "I sang a couple of songs, and he ministered," Dallas recalls. "Great meeting. I saw the results of the impact of his ministry and was very impressed, of course. We went out to eat afterward. I had a '65 Barracuda with a lift kit in the back and loud mufflers, and it rode like an army truck. Brother Dave crawled in there. Back then I drove a little faster than I should have, and I remember him saying, 'We're in no hurry here. You can slow down if you like.'"

I picture them facing each other at some restaurant and Dad getting right to the point. "He said, 'I'll only ask this one time. I'll never ask you again,'" Dallas recalls. My father blurted this so abruptly that it took Dallas aback. "Suddenly I was trying to remember if I'd committed some sin," Dallas says. "What was he going to ask? 'Have you ever killed anybody?'"

"Do you have a devotional life?" Dad asked him. "Do you spend time with the Lord every day?" Dallas grins at the memory. "My mind was way down the road somewhere else. Now I was backing up, reeling all those thoughts in. He probably thought, 'Oh, I've caught him here.' So I said, 'Do you mean like, reading the Bible and praying and spending time with the Lord?'" Dad nodded with intensity. Dallas replied, "Well, that's kind of the whole point, isn't it?"

His response contained everything my father needed to know. "It put his mind at ease," Dallas says. "But looking back, I had been a Christian for only a little more than three years. I shouldn't have even been a youth pastor. Twenty years old, single, hadn't been saved that long—I would never have hired me." Yet Dad could see exactly whom he was getting.

———

MOVING FROM A DRUG REHABILITATION ministry to evangelistic crusades might have seemed an unlikely leap to those who knew my dad from *The Cross and the Switchblade*, but it was a perfectly natural extension. In Dad's travels for Teen Challenge, host family after host family had asked him to talk to their son or daughter, whom they suspected of experimenting with drugs. These were godly, upstanding, middle-class families, and as Dad spoke with their kids, a chilling picture emerged: The drug wave was no longer relegated to the inner cities. It was trickling into the suburbs—and it was about to become a flood.

Dad was incredulous that these parents were in denial about it. They didn't think their kids would get hooked and become "druggies" like inner-city kids. My father never said so outright, but he was angered by the class discrepancy. Aside from that, he was alarmed by the parents' blindness to the power of addiction. A tidal wave of drug abuse was about to engulf a generation of youth, and the turning tide of the culture supported their experiments.

Dad had already seen pushers pouring into poor neighborhoods in New York City, hooking kids with addictions, who in turn got their friends hooked. It was a pyramid scheme with horrific consequences, and it was implemented by a new breed of pusher: organized crime. It made Dad respect the good deeds of the Brown Berets, the neighborhood patrols of Chicano men who sought to push back against the dealers. But those foot soldiers were no match for mafia money. Neither were the suburban kids who thought themselves immune to addiction.

By the time Dad started David Wilkerson Youth Crusades in 1967, he had already been speaking to large audiences, primarily to raise money for Teen Challenge. Along with sales of *The Cross and the Switchblade*, the success of Teen Challenge had made him an in-demand drug expert, a tag that baffled him. Suddenly he was a guest on national TV shows, interviewed by Mike Douglas and Art Linkletter. "David was thrust into national prominence at a very early age," notes Uncle Don. "We knew that the cross was mightier than the switchblade. What we hadn't known was that it was mightier than the narcotic needle." A study had been conducted by the National Opinion Research Center at the University of Chicago, involving long-term follow-up with Teen Challenge graduates seven years after they had left the program. The study revealed an eighty-six percent cure rate, a standard that holds up today. By comparison, government programs at the time had success in the single-digit range. Demand for Teen Challenge centers across the country grew so fast that in 1965 Dad turned over the ministry to the Assemblies of God's Home Missions department.

"When the drug problem started to spread, he saw what was coming," Dallas Holm says. "He warned about it coming to the suburbs, saying, 'This is going to spread like a cancer, and it's coming to a town near you.' But people simply would not, could not, believe it."

Dad began crisscrossing the country, speaking anywhere he was invited, from auditorium crowds to small-town Midwest churches of less than a hundred. As he traveled, he discovered a silent majority of kids he called "goodniks," those who didn't do drugs but despaired of ever finding purpose or meaning in life. Many of them were church kids. From this heartbreaking discovery Dad founded a movement called CURE Corps — Collegiate Urban Renewal Effort. It was a Christian version of the Peace Corps, enlisting college graduates to offer education to inner-city children and assist their impoverished families. Dad had already seen through Teen Challenge how crucial it was to reach urban kids at an early age, before they could fall prey to addiction. As CURE Corps got off the ground in a handful of cities, the invitations to speak to young people kept pouring in.

———

THE THIRD MEMBER OF DAD'S traveling team was David Patterson, whom Dad had hired in 1967 as his first full-time crusade director. David was only in his twenties then and had first encountered my father as a student at Bethany Bible College in Santa Cruz. "Brother Dave was speaking at an Assemblies of God convention in northern California," David recalls. "I went to hear him, and it was revelatory. It was so totally different, even for a Spirit-filled person. There was such a commanding sense of the conviction of the Lord."

Soon after David signed on, he saw the reemergence of a gift in my dad that had lain dormant for several years. "We were primarily doing evangelistic services sponsored by evangelical pastors," David says. "Sometimes in the counseling area, with people who had responded to the altar call, Brother Dave would catch himself because he'd start to operate in the gifts of the Spirit. He would tell them what was going on in their lives, and it scared the wits out of them. They didn't understand it."

David was impressed by how Dad handled those demonstrative gifts — with a wisdom informed by his devotional life. "Early on, my wife, Carol, and I experienced something with him that was a great comfort to us," David says. "Our apartment was right above his office in Massapequa, Long Island. In the wee hours of the morning, long after we'd gone to bed, we would hear the office door open below and he would start praying." David Patterson has known and worked for several recognizable names in ministry over the decades. "I've been around the world of Christian celebrity most of my life," he says. "I've had the privilege of knowing and being pastored by some really wonderful, significant men of God. Very few men walk in the same integrity that Brother Dave had."

That was the only way my dad knew how to walk. Besides, he had to have integrity if he expected to reach young people. "When I joined him, it was in the middle of the psychedelic revolution," Dallas Holm says. "We had an assembly at a place in Oakland that seated about eight thousand people. Many of those kids had just come in off the street and were stoned out of their minds. When Brother Dave gave the invitation after his sermon, hundreds of them came forward to receive Christ. They were throwing bags full of drugs onto the platform. Those kids didn't necessarily know who David Wilkerson was, but they knew something was going on related to Jesus. It was such a phenomenon. In those crusades, it was nothing to see a thousand or fifteen hundred young people come forward."

———

TO BORROW A PHRASE FROM John Sherrill, once again "something was in the air." "California was a great draw to young people back then," Dallas Holm says. "They were checking out of their communities to go to the beaches, do drugs, find 'free love.' It was the nature of the culture, and Brother Dave targeted that area very effectively."

"David was so relevant," says Ralph Wilkerson, pastor of a southern California congregation at the epicenter of the Jesus Movement. He invited Dad to speak at his church because drugs were already a problem among the disaffected youth flooding into the region. "Half of our congregation was twenty-five or under," Ralph says, "so I decided we would put half of our budget into youth rallies." Those rallies featured my father once a month for five straight years.

Up till then, my dad had spent a lot of time in the Bay Area. He had started a Teen Challenge center in San Francisco years before, and he went back regularly to do street evangelism in the Haight-Ashbury district. He set his sights there because so much happened that set the tone for America's youth culture, from the drug scene to the psychedelic "San Francisco sound" of musicians like the Jefferson Airplane and Janis Joplin. In 1967, Haight-Ashbury became ground zero for the Summer of Love. Yet it was southern California where Dad's ministry struck a profound chord.

Crowds of young people overflowed out the doors of Melodyland, the thirty-two-hundred-seat theater in the round that Ralph Wilkerson rented for youth rallies. "The services were packed out," notes David Patterson, and when Dad preached, "hundreds of kids were getting saved." Even those close to my father find it hard to describe the spiritual canopy that enveloped those meetings. Paul Annan was a brand-new convert when he attended a rally. "I was barely cognizant during that time," Paul says. "When I went, I had no idea who he was or even what was going on. I just remember that it was captivating. It would have been impossible for me to define at the time what it was about this guy that made him even interesting. I had no context to put it into. But then he gave an altar call, and there was this overwhelming need to flock forward. I was not sufficiently sophisticated to know why I felt the way I did. There was an overwhelming but indefinable presence, and it was absolutely, one hundred percent all-consuming. No other thought was possible."

Dad would give a brief altar call — his were always brief, lasting only a few minutes — and then he would step back, hand on chin, and stand in silence. The crowd response in those meetings could last up to twenty minutes or more. Sometimes it took that long for a young person coming forward just to make contact with a prayer counselor.

Those powerful moments were not the effect of my dad's oratorical skills, because he basically read his sermons from his script. As Ralph Wilkerson observes, "He was like some of the old revivalists. There was so much prayer behind his sermons that there was a powerful anointing on the reading, and people were converted."

"*Christianity Today* called him 'the wooden-tongued preacher,'" says David Patterson. "But that statement was made in a context. They were saying, 'This man is a phenomenon.' When he gave an altar call, it was not unusual to see fifteen percent of the entire gathering stand up and come forward."

Those meetings drew so many young people that Ralph Wilkerson decided to hold a quarterly "super rally" at the Anaheim Convention Center, which seated eight thousand. Even those meetings could barely hold the crowds they drew. Ralph and his wife, Allene, remember freeway traffic being backed up for two hours.

"He was so uniquely specific to cultural topics," Dallas says. "You would think suicide might apply to only a handful of people in an auditorium of several thousand, but it was on everybody's minds. 'What about my kids? What about my friends, my family?' Brother Dave wasn't the prototypical gospel evangelist who gave a three-point sermon. He had ample scriptural support to make his point presentable. But here was a guy who was not like anybody else. And whether or not you agreed with him, he held your attention."

Ralph Wilkerson's ministry made LPs of some of Dad's sermons: "I'm Not Mad at God," "Are You a Phony?" "Suicide." "He wasn't just talking theoretically," Ralph says. "He knew where the young people were hurting, and he knew the answers they needed. He knew their language and how to communicate with them, and he would tell it like it is. The kids received it because they knew he was telling them the truth."

David Patterson points out that Dad did something unorthodox during those Melodyland rallies. "One of his favorite messages to young people was 'The Call of God,'" David says. "He would finish with a call not for salvation but for young people to give their lives in service to the Lord. That's not the normal thing you do in an evangelistic crusade. By the end, there would be three, four, five hundred teenagers up at the front, praying and reaching out to the Lord, making themselves available to serve him."

One of those young people was a southern California teenager named Bob Rogers. Like many earnest Assemblies of God kids, Bob had responded to dozens of altar calls. "I was the guaranteed altar-call kid for every evangelist who came to town," Bob says. "I cried and I prayed. I tried to be saved. But on that night, he laid out the case, 'This is what it means to be a Christian.'" It was real for Bob that night — so real that Bob succeeded David Patterson a few years later as my dad's crusade director.

"The first half of the meeting was music, and it was all very current and contemporary," Bob says of the group that opened the rally. "But the minute David stood up, everything changed. When this guy spoke, it was the Word of God. I don't mean Scriptures, because back then he didn't use that much. He had a knowledge of God."

●━━━●

FOR ALL THE POWERFUL WAYS God used him with young people, my father needed to grow in a significant area. He had a hard time shaking off his old-time Pentecostal view of holiness, and that view included appearances.

"At one point, David drove the long-haired hippies out of our church,"

Ralph Wilkerson says. "It was from the extreme teachings of what's called holiness. That's one area where David wasn't relevant. Later on he got over it, and eventually those kids came back, but for a while, his attitude was, 'You smelly, long-haired young people need to get straightened out.'"

A visionary young pastor named Chuck Smith confronted my dad about it. Chuck was making great inroads with hippies as pastor of Calvary Chapel in nearby Costa Mesa. After he heard my dad preach a harsh message about having a godly appearance, Chuck made a point to talk to him. Sonny Arguinzoni was with my dad at Melodyland that day.

"Dave was preaching about guys that don't cut their hair," Sonny says. "After the service, Chuck Smith approached him with a couple of his brand-new converts. He said, 'Dave, how could you say what you did? You have your way of doing things, and I have my way.' Dave said to Chuck, 'Look at your converts, the way they appear. There's no change in them. Now, look at Sonny here. He *looks* like he's really changed.' I thought, 'Oh, Lord.' That was the first time I'd met Chuck Smith."

Shortly after that, Dad had a moving encounter with a down-and-out hippie that broke his heart and caused him to soften his messages. But even then he occasionally reverted to his old stance. "David wasn't consistent," Ralph says. "He would flip-flop. One month he would preach that they could have long hair, and the next month he was down on it again." As progressive as Dad was in so many areas, this was one area where he struggled hard. For some reason, when it came to appearances he couldn't let go of his parents' religion.

Even for Dallas Holm, whom Dad respected, there was a fine line to walk with the type of music he chose to play. "There was a sense with him of what was 'worldly,' and that's what I wanted to avoid," Dallas says. "But he also was very progressive in what he did. That was the line I walked with him for ten and a half years."

Dallas had it pretty easy compared with a guy who wanted to get my dad into movies.

———

IN 1968, PAT BOONE WAS on an airplane to Mexico City, booked for a two-week singing gig in an upscale supper club. He and his wife, Shirley, had been struggling in their marriage, and he was relieved to be going. "The business of Hollywood had gotten into my head," Pat says, and the resulting tensions had caused him to look for solace in the faith he'd grown up with. He had a strict Church of Christ upbringing, with legalistic tenets that forbade a lot of things, including dancing and even musical instruments in church. That latter prohibition had been a blessing in disguise: it emphasized vocal power, which had helped shape Pat into the multi-million album-selling crooner he became in the fifties and sixties.

His telegenic popularity had catapulted Pat into films. A decade earlier, he had costarred in *Journey to the Center of the Earth*, a box office success that had helped save Twentieth Century Fox from financial ruin. But none of that was a help to him in 1968. Now he was just looking forward to the singing gig and taking some time to clear his head. But for the moment, he needed a distraction for the long flight from LA to Mexico City, so before boarding he browsed the paperback racks for something to hold his attention. He decided on a small book that promised a story of faith told in the most realistic terms.

"My Church of Christ dogma held that God had quit performing miracles," Pat says. "But when I read about what God did on the streets of New York City in the life of Dave Wilkerson, I got goose bumps." He was mesmerized by the small-town minister who had his tires stolen as he slept in his car, whose life was threatened at knifepoint, and who fearlessly challenged gang members with the message of God's love.

Something about the story spoke to the hunger stirring in Pat. Its testimonies of transformed lives transcended doctrine, sending a reader headlong into the palpable reality of God. "A story like this should be made into a movie," Pat thought. The more he read, the greater his conviction grew to bring that story to the screen.

Little did Pat know that the story's central figure might be the biggest obstacle. "David was very businesslike on the phone," Pat says of his first conversation with my dad. "He knew who I was, and he was not impressed. He asked, 'What can I do for you?' I said, 'Well, sir, I've read your book. First, I just have to ask you, did all those things happen just the way you wrote them?' I could almost hear him bristling. He asked, 'Do you think I'm lying?' I answered, 'No, sir. I didn't know God did this kind of thing today.' Dave said, 'If God didn't perform miracles all the time, I'd be dead. *Of course* everything I wrote was the way it happened.'"

Pat explained his interest in making a movie version. "I had no idea I was talking to a guy who grew up being taught it was wrong to go to movies," he says. "I was in midsentence when Dave jumped in and started praying. He just started talking to Jesus while we were on the phone." My father's prayer with Pat was simple and direct: "Jesus, my life is your life. My story is your story. You know Pat Boone; I don't know him. But if this is something you want, then do it. If not, bring it to an end." Then he said, "Is that it, Pat?"

"I just stammered out, 'Well, I guess so,'" Pat says. "It was over that quickly."

Thankfully, Pat Boone took the prospect of a film more seriously than my dad did. As he sought funding, a friend suggested that Pat ought to play my dad in the film. Up till then, Pat had assumed only Dad could play himself. But when he asked my father about it, Dad squashed the idea, still skeptical that a film should even be made.

So Pat went forward researching the role and decided to attend one of Dad's crusades at Melodyland, where he saw my father in action for the first time. "Dave was talking to this big, big crowd of young people, and he was very blunt, no-nonsense. He was laying it on them, saying, 'You've got to get right with Jesus. You can't get off drugs by yourself.'"

When Dad gave the altar call, hundreds of people flooded forward to the altar. Pat decided to slip backstage to the counseling area. "One guy, probably in his twenties, was really out of it," Pat recalls. "He was clutching at his face. You could tell something was really wrong, that he was trying to get something out of his head. One of the counselors told me he was having a bad drug trip."

Two prayer counselors gently led the man to a chair, placed their hands on his shoulders, and began praying. "The guy's head suddenly dropped onto his chest, relaxed, and he seemed to go to sleep," Pat says. It astonished him. "One minute, there was a physical, chemical reaction going on in this guy's brain. It was really assaulting him. Then these people prayed, and immediately that whole tornado in his head just hushed."

When Pat met my father afterward, he asked him about it. "Look," Dad said, "these things happen all the time or I wouldn't be here. The kingdom of God is all powerful, and I have to depend on that."

———

A YEAR LATER, PAT FOUND himself trailing my dad through some of New York City's roughest areas in firsthand preparation for his role as David Wilkerson. A production was finally financed, scheduled, and set to roll. Funding had come through a prominent group of American Baptists, and even Kathryn Kuhlman, ever a supporter of my dad, had made an investment.

My father and his board would have been comfortable with the production team Pat had put together. Dick Ross was well known as the producer of Billy Graham's films at World Wide Pictures. The director, Don Murray, was a trusted friend of Pat's who had already made his name as an acclaimed actor. He was a committed Christian with a hand in several Hollywood films with themes of faith. In short, everyone had signed up for the right reasons.

But as shooting approached, Pat was having trouble getting a handle on how to play my father. "Obviously, as an actor, I studied him," Pat says, but he quickly discovered that he and Dad couldn't have been more different. "By nature I'm a lot more laid back compared with Dave. He was kinetic, crisp, fast-moving. He was succinct in his talk and not casual. And, of course, there was already an aura of the prophet. So for me to try to portray him, all I could think to do was to come into New York early and let him take me around. I wanted to see what he saw, experience the things that motivated him and made him cry."

It helped that shooting would be on location, where the story's events had occurred. "Dave took me into the places he frequented to reach the drug addicts — the shooting galleries, the empty, decaying buildings where dealers met and dispensed the drugs," Pat says. "While we were in those places, we saw limos and fancy cars come up from Manhattan. Some stockbroker would get out, make his purchase, climb back in, and take off."

After that, Dad took Pat to the tenements, where the actor was

stunned by the poverty. "Dave took me up some stairs, and we saw con-
doms and drug paraphernalia on the stairwells. There were bars over
every door. We looked down into the alleys, and garbage was piled shoulder high, with rats the size of dogs crawling through it."

By this time, the story that had been told in *The Cross and the Switchblade* was ten years old. But the conditions — the desperate human
need — had not changed. Pat's soul slumped at what he heard next. "Dave
said, 'No teenage girl here will escape being a "gang girl." If she doesn't
join up with the gangs, she's open to rape. Her only protection will be to
join.'"

Pat thought of his own four daughters at home in Beverly Hills. "I
told Dave, 'How could you possibly try to raise kids in this environment?
I'd leave the city, even if it meant sleeping under a tree somewhere in New
Jersey.'"

Dad shook his head. "You wouldn't leave," he said. "Not if you came
from Puerto Rico. You'd want to be among people who know your language, your customs. Out in the world they're ridiculed and misunder-
stood. Even though they live in the midst of all this horror, they feel more
secure than if they were to strike out on their own."

That was Pat's first insight into what made my dad tick, and it told
him everything he needed to know. "I was feeling the empathy for all
these people that Dave had," he says. "That's what prepared me to portray
him."

Meanwhile, the crew faced practical problems. Police said they
couldn't protect them during the location shoots, because the neighborhoods were so dangerous. "I'd get in a cab in Midtown Manhattan and
tell the driver where we were shooting that day," Pat recalls. "It was either
Harlem or the Bronx or Fort Greene. Every one of those cabbies said, 'Are
you crazy? When we get there, I won't stop; I'll just slow down. When you
open the door, be ready to get out fast, because I'll be gone. I don't want
to be there for three seconds.'"

During the climactic shoot at St. Nicholas Arena, Pat found himself
preaching to actual gang members who had been hired as extras. "There
was going to be a real gang fight that night," Pat recalls with clarity. "I
looked up into the second balcony and saw some of them shooting up.

That gave me additional fervor as I gave the sermon. Even though I was shooting a scene for the movie, I was really preaching to those guys in the balcony. My wife was sitting in the audience on the arena floor, praying in the Spirit the whole time I was delivering Dave's sermon."

Walking in Dad's shoes during that film shoot gave Pat unique insight into my father. "I've known a lot of dedicated Christian leaders," he says, "but I've never known anybody who was so totally committed to what God wanted him to do with every ounce of his being and every minute of his life. Dave Wilkerson was like the apostle Peter — impulsive, spontaneous, in your face a lot. Dave was someone who would jump out of the boat after the Lord and walk on water. Like Peter, he was not a man without faults, but he was a man whom Jesus particularly loved."

■———◄

THE MOVIE VERSION OF *THE Cross and the Switchblade* was a low-budget production, but it had grit and a heart that were genuine to its source. Predictably, my dad was bothered by the scene with Erik Estrada, as Nicky Cruz, appearing in his underwear. A few people around the ministry grumbled that the "rumble" in the opening sequence had never taken place. And someone complained about one character's use of the word *bastard*. But the finished movie had the power to move an audience.

"It was not a slick Hollywood production by any means," Pat says. "But everybody was involved because we believed in it. And it had a supernatural power. Dick Ross knew that."

Once production wrapped, the movie needed a distributor. Somehow, a screening was held for one of Hollywood's most powerful figures — Joseph E. Levine, founder of Embassy Pictures, which had just released *The Graduate*. "Joe was watching the film, and his associates were snickering, thinking he would come out laughing at this low-budget Christian movie," Pat says. "But when the lights came up, he said, 'I like this film. I think it will do something. Let's distribute it.' He saw the quality, and he had the sense that millions of people would be moved by it."

Pat shakes his head over what happened next. "Dick Ross and the American Baptists refused," he says. "They didn't want to be associated with Joe Levine, the big cigar-chomping, Jewish producer known for putting out *The Graduate*." He still feels frustrated over what might have been. "Joe would have put the movie into big theaters all over the country. It would have had regular distribution and promotion. But they didn't do it. So Dick Ross had to figure out how to get it into theaters and get some low-cost promotion. It did okay, but it could have been a much bigger, more successful film, possibly spawning others."

According to imdb.com, the go-to website for movies, *The Cross and the Switchblade* "was dismissed by secular critics as 'uninteresting.' However, it has been viewed by an estimated fifty million people in over thirty languages in 150 countries, according to World Film Crusade. They also report that it is one of the most viewed films in the world and is credited with drawing millions to Christ."

"I was amazed to hear it had a particularly big reception in Iran, in Farsi," Pat says. "I was puzzled, because that's such a heavily Muslim country. Why would Muslims want this strongly Christian film to be translated into their language and seen in theaters all over Iran? It's because they saw it as an antidrug film. They were trying to discourage drug use, even though they are very much involved in the international drug trade. They didn't want their own young people on drugs, so they were willing to let the film be seen." And, he adds, "We kept getting reports about people who were coming to the Lord." That was the truest sign that God was working through the movie.

While the film did well in Iran, it didn't go over well in Springfield, Missouri. That's where the denominational headquarters of the Assemblies of God is located. Dad was called on the carpet by the governing body to explain why he allowed a movie to be made of his book when moviegoing wasn't encouraged in the denomination.

"You're going to Springfield with me," Dad told David Patterson. David said he didn't want to go. "You're going anyway," Dad said.

"I realized he wanted a witness," David says.

Presiding over the meeting was Thomas Zimmerman, the General Superintendent who back in the day had been aware of the quite flamboyant, very showmanlike J. A. Wilkerson. "Thomas Zimmerman was a good man, but there was a lot of pressure coming from the rank and file in churches across the country," David Patterson says. "We went into the meeting, and some of the men were angry, some were complacent. One started accusing Brother Dave of contributing to the waywardness of young people by encouraging them to go to movies.

"Brother Dave stopped him. He said, 'You can't be that naive to think your kids aren't going to the theater. They were going to movies before this one came out. Besides, when I signed the contract, I relinquished my rights to the movie. I have no control over it.'"

The meeting got rancorous. At one point, Dad removed his ministerial credential card from his wallet and slid it across the table to Thomas Zimmerman. "Here, Tom, take this," he said. "I'm fine with it."

Thomas Zimmerman pressed a finger onto the card. The room fell silent. The superintendent looked into the eyes of the grandson of J. A. Wilkerson and slid the card back across the table. "We're not taking your card," he said. "This meeting is over."

———

"DAVID WILKERSON HAD AN INCREDIBLE influence in those years," says historian Vinson Synan. "He was a prophet to his generation in planting seeds for the great renewal among hippies and the downtrodden. I remember him at the World Pentecostal Conference in Dallas in 1970, talking about the Jesus People. His movie with Pat Boone and the book *The Cross and the Switchblade* really were key in the beginning of the Jesus revolution. I think he helped start the Jesus Movement. Then he had a role in the Charismatic Renewal in all the churches and among Catholics."

Dad's work had crossed denominational lines in ways he couldn't have foreseen. *The Cross and the Switchblade* book was seminal in the growth of the Catholic charismatic movement. Historians and writers point to a specific event that sparked that great renewal.

In 1967 an informal gathering took place in Pittsburgh that became known as "the Duquesne Weekend." A group of students at that Catholic university convened at a place called the Ark of the Dove Retreat house to explore the growing charismatic phenomenon. The reading list for the weekend consisted of *The Cross and the Switchblade*, John Sherrill's seminal book *They Speak with Other Tongues*, and the first four chapters of the book of Acts. That weekend event effectively launched the Catholic charismatic movement. Students and university leaders were baptized in the Holy Spirit, a phenomenon that quickly spread through Catholic congregations.

"After a while, it wasn't unusual for us to have a contingent of nuns and priests on our local crusade boards," says David Patterson. "Brother Dave's ministry was breaking loose all these things. At times it seemed to me he was uneasy with it. He thought, 'I didn't know all this was going to happen.'"

Dad received an invitation from a group of nuns in New Orleans who asked him to hold a citywide crusade. According to David Patterson, most ministries didn't hold conferences or crusades in New Orleans at the time. "It was known as kind of a hard place," David says. "People would go to Mobile or to Houston, but not to New Orleans. But Brother Dave did it. We held it at the Riverfront Coliseum. The response to his preaching was so strong, we knew it was God's blessing. We looked around and thought, 'This is just so right.' Those Catholic leaders who were involved with the churches were appreciative and so embracing of David. It was one of our best experiences."

Later, Dad made a trip to Mexico at the request of a Catholic diocese when the Charismatic Renewal began spreading through its churches. By that point, "Dave Wilkerson had become a kind of latter David du Plessis," says Dr. Stanley Burgess. "He was a leading light in that area." John Sherrill marveled at Dad's role. "If people are facing in the same direction, involved with other people at an intercessory level," John says, "well, David acted that out as well as anyone I will ever know." There was no turning back now.

8
—
FAITHFUL UNORTHODOXY

MY FIRST CRUSADE TRIP WITH MY FATHER didn't happen the way any of us would have planned it. I was seven years old and standing next to Dad in our house in Massapequa Park, Long Island, as he demanded into the telephone, "Where are you?... What?... Then meet me at the airport." He slammed down the receiver and grabbed his suit coat, his briefcase, and my hand. "You're coming with me," he said.

I don't recall where my siblings were at the time, but my mother was out shopping. Dad was booked to preach for Kathryn Kuhlman in Pittsburgh, and Mom hadn't made it home in time before he had to leave.

At the airport concourse, Dad tapped his foot. He paced; he grumbled. No sign of Mom. Soon people started boarding the flight. Finally, he sprang to the counter and bought a ticket for me. "You're coming with me," he said again.

I was kind of excited. I'd heard Dad talk about Kathryn Kuhlman and looked forward to seeing her for the first time. As I stared out the airplane window, eager for the propellers to start cranking, Dad fumed in the seat next to mine. An hour or so later, we landed and exited, and he led me to the airline counter, where he bought me a ticket home on the next flight. He pointed to the stewardess near the boarding ramp. "She'll take care of you, son, don't worry," he said. "Mom will be waiting for you at the other end." He waited with me until it was time for me to board. As the stewardess took my hand, Dad forced a smile and waved goodbye.

The pilot visited me in my seat next to the stewardess. "Here's something for you," he said, handing me a lapel pin with the airline logo. The stewardess pinned it onto my striped T-shirt. I watched the propellers crank up again. As the plane rumbled down the runway and lifted into the air, the stewardess lit a cigarette and leaned back for the flight.

I tapped her arm. "Ma'am," I said, "did you know if you smoke you'll go to hell?"

It was turning out to be a momentous trip. Not only had I just gone on my first crusade with my dad, but I'd also made my first attempt at evangelism. Hey, this is easy!

＊——＊

I DON'T KNOW WHETHER MY mom's failure to show up that day — twice, in fact — was an early sign of passive-aggression. But it certainly fit the picture of Dad's demanding schedule in our lives. Given how often he had to travel, I'm surprised that kind of snafu didn't occur more often.

I admired my mom as a boy. I thought she looked like Jackie Onassis, because she dressed like the First Lady and even had a similar smile. And my mother was a great hostess, with a gift for hospitality that was off the charts. She was kind to strangers and loved cooking for her friends and having all of us around the table for dinner. Even when Dad wasn't home, her rule was, "No trays in front of the TV. Come sit around the table. Let's be together."

Hospitality is the broad term I use to describe her gifts. I think the better phrase might be "sheer joy of people." She loved being around them. Whenever someone tried to reach my dad, she offered, "He won't be available today. Why don't I help you with that?"

My parents loved each other — I had no doubt about that. Yet their marriage could be tempestuous even apart from Dad's constant travel. Still, over the years they maintained a romance that, to their credit, endured obstacles they could not have foreseen. That romance rose and fell amid those challenges, always enduring to rise again. My dad's ministry demands were the first obstacle they had to contend with, but in some ways it ended up being the least of what my mother had to wrestle with. She faced a lot of physical problems throughout her life, one affliction after another that never seemed to cease. They began with an early cancer when she was pregnant with my younger brother, Greg. Aunt Cindy, Uncle Don's wife, remembers the pressure that doctors put on my mother to abort. We're all thankful Mom refused. But other cancers developed, more than a dozen times, in fact, with more than one that we thought would be fatal.

Mom wrote about her journey in a 1978 memoir, *In His Strength*. She spoke openly of the toll taken on her body by those cancers, and by an early hysterectomy and the hormonal problems that followed. Through it all came healings that had to be seen as miraculous because she was given a death sentence more than once. Yet her life was never without difficulties. Growing up, we witnessed a polarity in our mother — a spirit so gracious, loving, and kind that could turn on a dime into despair or sometimes rage. It's hard to sustain a giving, hospitable demeanor when your body and mind are under assault, and more than once I saw my mom torn by thoughts she surely had: "I want to love people. It seems so easy to do at times. Why do I end up yelling at them?" When that happened, my sisters were most often in her line of fire.

None of us four kids was wise enough — nor should we have needed to be — to know how a person's physical battle can lead to a spiritual one, or to know the difference between the two. I often thought, "How could she be so godly at times, and then throw a pot across the kitchen?" We didn't know how to read her moods, and they could last awhile. At the same time, we discerned a fight being waged in her, as if she were telling herself, "I've got to come out of this."

By contrast, my father was rarely as nurturing as my mom. Yet when he got mad at us, it was over in a flash. Moments later he was asking, "Hey, are things okay between us?"

All children project Godlike qualities onto their parents. As Christian kids observe their mothers and fathers, they wonder, "What is Christlikeness?" and in trying to figure it out, they may try to balance the spiritual traits between them. In my dad, I saw godliness in evangelism and soul-winning and dedicated Bible study and prayer. But he didn't connect with people one-on-one in love. As for my mom, she didn't like to go to street rallies, and she didn't read the Bible in much depth. When she did read it, she admitted, "Sometimes I don't get a lot out of the Scriptures." I wondered, "Really? Dad reads the Bible three hours a day, and he goes all around the world saving souls. But sometimes he's not very loving. So where do you get all of your love for God?"

Mom was never a step behind my dad in intellect or wit. She had a kind of observational intelligence, as did Dad—his piercing eye cut through matters all too clearly—but Mom's gift had a social dimension, whereas Dad's was purely spiritual discernment. He never had anything to do with my friends Kevin and Patrick, for example; he just didn't relate to them. However, he did play basketball with me whenever he was home. I think he was determined to do with me what his father never did with him. Once in a while he even took me into the city to see a Knicks game at Madison Square Garden, and beforehand we would eat at Willis Reed's hamburger joint, Beef 'n Bun. Those were special times because I had Dad alone to myself.

When Dad was home—when he was really with us, and we had his attention—he was tender and kind. And always generous. If we saw his hand go into his pocket, we knew a green bill was coming out, with permission to ride our bikes to the movie theater. Moviegoing wasn't an issue for our parents back then. Entertainment was fine as long as it didn't dishonor God, and *The Love Bug* or a John Wayne movie wouldn't offend much. In terms of fashion, Dad wanted his wife and his daughters to be the antithesis of Pentecostal legalism. My sisters not only got to cut their hair and wear pants and shorts, but they did it in the latest styles. Dad even liked taking them shopping to help pick out their wardrobes.

Being home for him seemed a respite and a joy, though he constantly seemed distracted. What amazes me now is that I never once heard my dad raise his voice with us kids. One time I got so frustrated with him I yelled, "You're a stupid idiot, and I can't stand you!" He didn't bat an eye. He just listened to my rant until I wound down, and then suggested, "Let's sit down and talk. What's wrong? Tell me what's bothering you." His response changed my whole demeanor. Suddenly I thought my dad was cool for treating me that way.

He also trained us to pray in a very natural way. At bedtime he would come into each of our rooms and kneel with us beside our beds to pray.

Every night, from the time I was four until I was eleven, Dad told me, "Don't forget to pray for your uncle Jerry." Those were the years of my uncle's alcoholism. He was separated from my aunt Eve and their kids, and no one knew where Uncle Jerry was much of the time.

Years later, when my uncle became sober, he told my dad he wondered if he had ever cared about him while he was addicted. To him, my father was out changing the lives of thousands of addicts without any real concern for his brother. Dad admitted he was distracted and didn't know why he didn't reach out more. In a sense, Uncle Jerry could have been speaking for us kids: our father was spending half of each year away from us while conducting *youth crusades*. Each of us handled it in our own way, but there's no getting around the fact that it was hard on us all.

Cracks first appeared when my oldest sibling, Debi, began to rebel at orders from our nanny. Dad had hired a young woman to live with us once he saw the load Mom had to shoulder while he was away. The nanny was nice and we were glad to have her around, but after a while, whenever she asked Debi to do something, my sister snapped back, "You're not my mother."

Anyone who's ever known Debi acknowledges she's the gentlest, most accommodating person around. It's easy to see what she was reacting to back then: she wanted both of her parents to be present to give the orders, but one of them wasn't around half the time. And the other was sometimes debilitated beyond her ability to control it. It wasn't easy having our father away so much of the time.

I got my first inkling that Dad was famous when he took me to an event where he was scheduled to speak. The mayor of the town introduced him, and after Dad's speech people rushed up to get his autograph. I thought, "Wow, these people treat him like a superstar. My dad must be really doing something." It made me proud.

I learned more about his work when he began taking me into Brooklyn to spend the day at the Teen Challenge Center at 416 Clinton Avenue. He and I played basketball with the teenagers in residence — Puerto Ricans, Hispanics, Anglos, and African Americans. I got to sit in on Dad's conversations with his ministry leaders — also brown, white, and black — men whom he appointed based on no other qualification than their walk with God. Sometimes Dad sent me down to the basement to help the volunteer workers staple together evangelistic tracts to be passed out in neighborhoods. I rubber-stamped the Teen Challenge address onto thousands of those tracts, some of which made their way back to the center months or even years later, in the pockets of addicts looking for help. It was in that basement that I first heard a Dallas Holm album play all the way through and thought it was pretty cool.

During those grade school years my best friend was Orlando, who was black, and whose father was a Pentecostal minister who knew my dad. He and I were always in each other's homes. I remember my father telling me how proud he was because I didn't let division come into my friendships on account of color. I just shrugged and said, "I learned it from you, Dad."

And, eventually, I got to meet Kathryn Kuhlman. A couple of years after my whirlwind visit to Pittsburgh, I went with Dad again as he preached at one of her services. Afterward, I watched from the wings as Kathryn prayed for the people who came forward. She had already seemed eccentric to me, appearing onstage in flowing robes and breathily announcing to the audience, "You've been *waiting* for me!" It seemed showy and ostentatious, and now, as she touched the people who asked for prayer, they either fainted or died, I couldn't tell which. When Dad brought her over to meet me, I backed away in fear. But she ended up being as nice as could be.

For many years I wondered why my dad kept his friendship with her. Only over time did it become clearer. Like him, she had had to wage her own battles with Pentecostal-holiness legalism, especially after she'd endured a bad early marriage and had to buck doctrine to proceed with a divorce. To my dad, those weren't the things that defined her. A person's past did matter to him, but he knew it wasn't the whole story; to him, what mattered was the heart. If he sensed God was at work in someone, he would stand by them.

"There was a deep mutual respect between the two of them," says David Patterson. "Brother Dave preached for Kathryn once a month, in Pittsburgh and in Youngstown, Ohio, for a year or more. And she was very supportive of him."

I give my dad credit where I might not have shown the same grace. His gift for discernment worked both ways: He saw past godly appearances to discern sin, and he saw beyond ostentation to discern substance.

———

"He loved the one-nighters," David Patterson says. "Go into town, hit them hard, see what God has in store, then maybe go back in a couple of years and do it again. We did hundreds of those — in big cities, in little towns, all over the country."

For six years, Dad's traveling team for David Wilkerson Youth Crusades was small — just himself, David Patterson, and Dallas Holm. "That team worked like a Swiss watch," Dallas says. "We knew each other at a personal level. I could sense what Brother Dave wanted — what he was thinking, when to be light, when to give him space — and he knew me. He never told me what to sing or to share. Very few ministers at his level would allow someone in my position to have the freedom he gave me."

Dallas would open a service with twenty minutes or so of singing, sharing anecdotes, and testifying. "Knowing Brother Dave — his drive and passion to get out there, preach the Word, and get these kids to Christ — those twenty minutes could have been an eternity to him. But it wasn't as if I just did my segment and then he did his. It was all one thing. Music is its own force in ministry, but I was always conscious of, 'How can I best prepare the way for him?' He was like a thoroughbred racehorse in the gate, 'Just let me out; let me preach.'"

What Dallas provided during those brief openings was remarkable, according to David Patterson. The audiences were mostly teenagers, full of energy, noise, and attitude. Yet from the moment Dallas stepped up and started singing, David says, "You could hear a pin drop." Dallas's gift onstage didn't just settle people; it made them receptive. It cleared the path for Dad to do what he relished doing most — preaching Christ.

My father was never more at home than he was in the pulpit. It was the one place that allowed him to fulfill what he saw as his purpose in life: to deliver, with holy reverence, what he had seen and heard from God.

"I called him 'the Reluctant Evangelist,'" David Patterson says. "He was not enamored of the bright lights and the big time. He was enamored of being in the place that God wanted him to be and doing what God wanted him to do. On many levels, Brother Dave was a retiring person. He never wanted to have to do the kinds of things that evangelists do — the promotion, the interviews. At times he was quite happy to be on a platform with other people or to meet other leaders, but at other times, he'd rather go off and be by himself."

Beyond those spiritual dimensions of crusade life, the ministry involved a lot of hard, grueling work. "At first all our travel was by air and by rental car, from 1967 to '71," David Patterson says. "I can't tell you how many times in the early days we'd be in Lakeland, Florida, on Friday night, then in Los Angeles all day Sunday, then in Fargo, North Dakota, on Monday night, and then home. We probably did that a hundred times."

Add to this that my father was exacting about certain things, most especially timeliness. Dallas once showed up ten minutes late when the team was supposed to leave for a crusade trip. Dad didn't say anything. He just took off his wristwatch and tossed it to Dallas. "He got the message," David Patterson says.

David himself was called on the carpet more than once. "Brother Dave hated going into an auditorium and seeing a lot of empty seats," David says. My dad usually attributed it to shoddy planning, but a lot of variables were beyond the control of a crusade director, and no one worked harder than David Patterson. "He wanted to preach to a full house, and I understood that," David says. "But sometimes he made a judgment on a situation before he knew what was going on. He would get on me about stuff, and I'm not exactly a shrinking violet. So at times our conversations were hot. But we loved each other, and when it was over, it was over.

"Those first three years it was just he and I on the road. I would pinch myself, thinking, 'I can't believe this is happening. This is my hero, and I'm traveling all over North America with him for the gospel.' We spent countless hours together, and of course his frailties came out. We would talk about the things of God, and I came to trust him in those things. I also came to understand that he put his pants on one leg at a time, just like everybody else. Brother Dave was just another man, but he was a man who loved God. And he was powerfully anointed of God. It gave me great confidence in seeing and understanding how God can use anyone."

As a skeleton crew, they carried their own sound equipment onto the planes for those crusades. Once they arrived at the event venue, David and Dallas spent the afternoon setting up and doing sound checks. Dad stayed at the hotel reviewing his sermon and praying.

"We were on the road constantly, sometimes a hundred and fifty nights a year," David says. "It was hard being away from home. There were perks to it — we were with people we liked, we ate well, and we stayed in pretty good hotels — but it was hard to be gone that much, away from our wives and kids. But Brother Dave's popularity was at its peak, crowds were coming, and the harvest was coming in. That was the reward, and it was why we were traveling."

That satisfaction provided all the fuel they needed. "On many of those nights, as we were loading things close to midnight, we would laugh and say, 'This is the big time,'" David says. "You're tired, you're sweaty, it's late, everybody else is at home in bed — and this was the big time. Then it was on to the next town and we'd start all over again."

———

BY THE LATE SIXTIES, EVANGELISTIC crusades had become commonplace in American culture. But an aspect of Dad's ministry made his unique, according to David. "In the middle to late sixties there were basically two major streams of Christian speakers traveling," he says. "There were the TV evangelists, like Rex Humbard, who went to cities where their program aired and essentially put on a public version of their televised show. They worked the circuit, going to the same places every year — Dallas, Oklahoma City, Denver. They never went to Waco or Temple, Texas, or Colorado Springs.

"Then there were major evangelists like Billy Graham and healing evangelists like Kathryn Kuhlman. They went to big cities where they could draw big crowds. I don't mean any disrespect at all when I say this, but those were massive machines coming to town. They organized all the churches, hired professional advertising agencies, and raised hundreds of thousands of dollars. Dr. Graham would come in, preach the gospel, and a wonderful harvest would take place.

"Along comes a guy like Brother Dave, whose fame has skyrocketed because of *The Cross and the Switchblade*, which by then had sold millions of copies, and yet David went *everywhere*. He had a heart for the small towns as well as the big cities. That was pretty unorthodox for crusade evangelism. He didn't want any part of 'traveling the circuit.' To him, that was not being responsive to how the Spirit of God leads."

When a speaking invitation came, David Patterson wrote down the information on a three-by-five notecard. "I would give it to Brother Dave and he would pray over it," David says. "A week or two would pass, and he would give the card back to me and say either yes or no. He really didn't care whether it was a big town or a little town. If he felt that God wanted him to go, we went. And there were certain areas where his ministry was unusually received, where the Holy Spirit just opened the door. California and a lot of the West Coast were extremely receptive to his ministry. Rockford, Illinois. I think there's hardly a town in Kansas that he didn't preach in — Hutchinson, Clay Center, Salina, Pittsburg. He didn't miss very many."

Book sales, fame, TV appearances, even a movie hadn't changed anything. Prayer for guidance still determined my dad's every decision. That had been his way ever since Philipsburg, and it continued to inform Dad's actions, even the ones that looked spontaneous. John Sherrill observes, "David had a personality trait that wasn't what it appeared to be. He would have an abrupt change of direction that gave the impression of being spontaneous. But it was prayer that gave him a foundation to stand on for making what appeared to be sudden decisions." As my father first got to know the Sherrills, he confided to them that he "tithed" his time to God in prayer — meaning he set aside ten percent of his day to pray. That's more than two hours a day, and my dad did that almost every day of his life. "My own prayer life includes a constant, rolling relationship with God," John says. "But that's not what I'm referring to with David. He literally was down on his knees often, praying, interceding, listening. He would listen for direction rather than plan."

Dad's decisions over where to go — or not to go — were almost always fruitful, according to David. "I've marveled at the plan of God," he says. "We'd go to a place like New Orleans, where nobody goes, and the response would be wonderful. Then we'd go to Kansas City, where there are all kinds of evangelical churches, and we would come out feeling ten years older. It was the supernatural element — Brother Dave getting the mind of the Lord — that made all the difference."

That element applied equally in small towns. "We had just held a crusade in Denver and were driving through Colorado," David recalls. "A group from Sterling, in the eastern part of the state, asked if we would stop and do an event for them on our way home. They rented the football stadium for us on a Saturday night, and Brother Dave preached to about five thousand people. Then we were in Goodland, Kansas, the next day, which had a population of about five thousand people. *Six* thousand people showed up to hear him on a Sunday afternoon."

Dad was still known as the gang preacher from New York, which could explain the big crowds in small towns. But once those people heard him preach, they immediately sensed his respect for them. "Remember, he had pastored in a small town," David says. "He never said this to me, but I honestly think he felt more at home sharing the gospel in those towns than he did in the big cities." I do know that when Dad preached "The Call of God" to teenagers in Dodge City, it was with the same conviction and compassion that he preached to gang members at St. Nicholas Arena.

"His love for the little towns was reciprocated by the people," David notes. "They saw this well-known person coming to their town, and a lot of them got on his mailing list. Those people prayed for Brother Dave and supported his ministry through the years." By the end of the sixties, David Patterson was booking crusades up to eighteen months in advance. "I would have to tell people, 'We haven't forgotten you. We're working on the calendar, and we'll get back to you with some dates as soon as we can.'"

While crusades were popular during that period, the ministry didn't make a lot of income from them. David Wilkerson Youth Crusades was unusual in that it always covered its own travel expenses and didn't ask for a fee. All that it asked of local committees was to cover the cost of the venue and to place a small ad in the local newspaper. "We kept the budget miniscule," David says. "If churches weren't able to raise all that was needed for local expenses, we saw to it that every bill was paid by Brother Dave's ministry." David remembers setting up an event with pastors in Jacksonville, Florida, who still owed seventy-five thousand dollars in bills a year after a crusade by a Methodist evangelist. "Brother Dave was appalled that evangelists would leave unpaid bills in towns where they had preached," he says.

The crusade ministry's only financial request was to be allowed to take an offering during the service. But Dad didn't like doing even that, because the audiences were mainly teenagers. "He was determined that the crusades not be fundraising events," David says. "We could encourage people to give and hope we would get a dollar or two per person if we're lucky. Book sales might be significant, but that's it."

Dad even undercut his own book sales. "When he saw the impact that *The Cross and the Switchblade* was having, he came up with the idea of an unroyaltied edition," David says. "It was an el-cheapo version, with the cover printed in one color, blue. Brother Dave didn't get royalties from it, nor did John Sherrill or the publisher. We sold them in bulk, and churches could buy one thousand copies for two hundred dollars. We encouraged them to have an impact in their community by giving them away."

David credits that version of the book with augmenting the Charismatic Renewal in Jacksonville, Florida. "Southside Assembly in Jacksonville bought over fifty thousand copies," he says. "That may have done more to birth the charismatic movement in that area than anything else. The church just gave them away. The pastor would call me and say, 'I've raised five hundred more dollars. How many more books can you send?'"

———

IF THE MINISTRY OPERATED ON a shoestring budget, how did Dad keep the crusades going through those early days? Mostly, he had to write books. "He was producing one to three books a year," says Barbara Mackery, who had just signed on as Dad's personal secretary. "That was all precomputer days."

David Patterson's wife, Carol, had been Dad's secretary until she had their first child. Carol called her younger sister, Barbara, in California to see if she was interested in the job. That phone call ended up being a monumental moment in my dad's ministry — and in our family. Barb Mackery would become my father's virtual right hand, de facto brain on certain matters, and an extended family member over the next forty-two years. Actually, she was more than that — she *was* family. People all over the world today ask how Barb is doing, because they made friends with her through the ministry. We kids remember her for more, like teaching a few of us to tie our shoelaces.

As I look back, I see in Barb several traits that fitted her perfectly for the role. Like my dad, she came from a large family whose father was a Pentecostal minister. In that family, however, every child was encouraged to voice an opinion. That dinner-table practice formed in Barb the second crucial trait she brought with her: she was loyal and respectful, but she was her own person.

Barb had already been the executive secretary to a vice president of an oil company on Wilshire Boulevard in Beverly Hills. "I had worked with some movers and shakers, so I wasn't intimidated by Brother Dave," she says. "I never hero-worshiped him, but I knew my place with him. And also with Gwen. I worked for Brother Dave; I befriended Gwen. That also lasted for over forty years. Gwen and I never once had a harsh glance, much less a harsh word. It was because she knew I loved her and had her back, and Brother Dave knew I had his back." That kind of discretion is an invaluable gift to a family like ours that's forced to live in a fishbowl. Barb's vigilance on our behalf over the years simply can't be measured.

Also like my Dad, Barb had learned the value of hard work and tenacity in childhood. She had known tragedy, having seen her younger brother die when hit by a car. Yet none of these things came up in my dad's interview with her. Instead, Dad would have simply discerned in Barb the same things he'd discerned in Dallas Holm, and known immediately she was the right person.

"Brother Dave contracted books, and that was the ministry's source of income, basically," Barb says. "We did not have a list of large donors.

He was building up his mailing list from the travels, but that was slowly. He had a growing staff, and on occasion we did go without paychecks. So he was under the gun to write those books."

Barb would receive book chapters from my dad in parcels. "He was a yellow-notepad writer," she says. "Everything was in longhand, in complete sentences and paragraphs. Nothing was outlined. I'd type it, and he would cut and paste with Scotch tape. He worked from a skeleton and then added the meat to the bones. Many of those books went through five complete retypings."

So when did my father find time to write up to three books a year? It happened on airplanes, in hotel rooms, in the passenger seats of rental cars. It happened when he was at home and excused himself early from the dinner table to go into his study. And he was writing just as often in his head, when, say, he was in midconversation with one of his children and his gaze drifted off into the distance.

———

MY BEDROOM WAS ON THE second floor of our split-level house in Massapequa Park, and one night I was awakened by noises downstairs. As I looked out the window, I saw my father on a stretcher being wheeled into an ambulance.

"He had called me at two o'clock in the morning," says David Patterson. "He said, 'Dave, I've got blood in my stool. Can you come get me?' There was panic in his voice. By the time I arrived, the ambulance was already there. It was a bleeding ulcer."

Dad had held in the stress for years. He worried over finances, he worried about the strain on us from his travels, and on top of it all he had a deathly fear of flying. When I was old enough to fly with him on a crusade tour, I remember seeing him grip the seat handles, his face white. "Dad, are you okay?" I asked. "Yeah, why?" he answered, trying not to alarm me. But after a half dozen flights between various cities, he finally told the team, "I can't take it anymore." They rented a van and drove the rest of the way.

As I ponder it now, nothing seemed to be able to slow our dad down. His emergency trips to the hospital must have reminded him of his father's shortened life, and the work that Dad felt he still needed to accomplish. Ironically, it pushed him even harder. In fact, his work intensified when he moved the entire ministry — and our family — to southern California in the summer of 1970.

"Melodyland was already like a second home to him," Barb Mackery says. "He knew about Chuck Smith and the baptisms in the ocean, and Brother Dave had the highest respect for him. He started thinking, 'I have to see what's going on in the minds of those radical young hippies. What is God doing there? And what does he want from me?'"

Before we moved, I flew out with Dad for one of the Melodyland rallies. I was fascinated by it. I had been exposed to the hippie movement in New York, but it wasn't pervasive like what I saw that night: thousands of long-haired, bead-wearing kids with headbands, tie-dyes, and fringe.

Yet what fascinated me most was my dad. He came to the stage wearing wide-flare pants and an open-collar shirt, unbuttoned a rung lower than usual. He may also have been wearing gold chains. I thought, "That's not his New York attire." He was still in his thirties then, so he was young enough to get away with it. He had always had a sense of style, but at Melodyland I think he was trying to relate.

Dad sat on a stool that night, and he didn't deliver his sermon in the usual way. It was more casual, more conversational, and he told stories. Yet what was not different that night was the palpable presence of God. When Dad gave the altar call, hundreds of kids came forward almost en masse, some of them surrendering their drugs onto the stage. Dad lowered the microphone into the crowd to interview them. "Why did you come forward?" "I'm hooked on heroin." "Are you ready to be free?" "Yes." "Then let's pray."

Soon he began to operate in the prophetic gifts. He would point to kids in the crowd and say, "Come up here, I want to talk to you." Their friends would lift them onto the stage, and Dad would tell them things about their lives, struggles they were going through — specific things, never vague. "Your father just left your mom." "You've been contemplating suicide." "You're tempted to start using heroin." He was careful not to expose them to any embarrassment or shame, but these were the kinds of exchanges one would hear in a psychologist's office. Dad was fatherly in the way he went about it, and those teenage hippies heaved with sobs as he prayed for them.

———•

WE WERE ONLY RESIDENTS of southern California for nine months, the exact length of one horrible school year. Our life there coincided with the most intense time of my dad's crusade ministry. He was away a lot and we didn't see much of him at all that year. His absence hit each of us hard, but it was the beginning of a particularly lonely stretch for me.

We had settled in a tract-home development in Irvine, which at the time was a brand-new town of about ten thousand people. The hacienda-style house was small, with three bedrooms and a tiny yard, nothing like our roomy split-level back on Long Island. My sisters, who were teenagers by then, seemed to land on their feet. I remember the day they came home from the beach, where they'd been with a hundred and fifty other kids. They had spent the afternoon baptizing new converts, singing choruses, sharing their testimonies, and leading other teenagers to Christ.

I was less lonely once I met Mark Schulz, the son of my dad's new business manager, Richard Schulz. Mark introduced me to his friends, and I spent a lot of time at his house. But school was horrible. All my classmates in Irvine were taking drugs and having sex. They were disrespectful, foulmouthed, and got into fights all the time — all in gleaming Orange County. The irony wasn't lost on me, a New York kid, where supposedly the schools were bad.

Dallas Holm probably wasn't aware of how important his presence was to me during that time. He drove me around in his Plymouth Duster, which he had outfitted for hot rod racing. Later he introduced me to motorcycles and I got involved in motocross. We raced on Saddleback Mountain, the site of the now famous community church pastored by Rick Warren.

Meanwhile, my dad bought a leather jacket and a Vespa motor scooter (not all that cool in an age of Triumphs and Harleys), and he hit the beaches to talk to kids. He also hit the music festivals taking place in open fields and on farms, where groups like the Grateful Dead performed. He had jumped back into the fray in a new way, and out of it came an enduring book Dad wrote for young converts, *The Jesus Person Maturity Manual*. It contained frank talk about all the temptations I'd seen my classmates succumb to: drugs, sex, alcohol — not the typical subjects you'd hear about in your church youth group in 1970. Typical of Dad, he addressed topics others wouldn't touch, and it helped to disciple a great number of kids during the Jesus Movement.

Somewhat less successful was the poetry Dad had begun to produce. I don't know how to categorize it, but it was popularized at the time by figures like Rod McKuen. I remember a gathering in our living room as Dad read from it, with lines like:

> *Life   freedom   flowing hair*
> *should have used that move with coolness.*

I actually just made that up. But if that's the kind of thing that remains in my memory from the evening, your imagination can fill in the rest. All I can say is when the time came for World Challenge to reprint some of my dad's older work, that volume didn't make the cut.

———

ONE OTHER LASTING BLESSING from that year came in a friendship my parents formed with some neighbors in Irvine, Barry and Karen Meguiar. My mom had met Karen at the swimming pool near our house and became tight friends with her. Barry was a young executive expanding his family's car product business to the consumer marketplace. He and Karen both were spiritually hungry Christians when they met my mom and dad, and it turned out to be a friendship both couples needed. My parents could laugh and have a good time with the Meguiars, something they hadn't done since saying goodbye to Paul and Sonia Dilena back in Long Island. "Dave was hilarious," Barry says. "He would be silly, because he could with us. And all four laughed so hard it was painful. We just had an affinity."

For the Meguiars, the friendship offered a spiritual depth they had been looking for. "Dave is the only friend I've ever had who I could never talk into anything," Barry says.

Dad never needed the warmth of friendship more. That year, his ulcers exploded, taking him to the brink of death. "He underwent surgery to have the vagus nerve in his stomach severed to control the production of acid," Barb Mackery says. He would have to slow down now, no matter how much responsibility he thought his Father wanted him to carry.

Part Four

JUDGMENT

He wasn't the CEO. God was the CEO.

—*Barry Meguiar*

Young David with siblings

Gwen as a teenager

Newlyweds in Pennsylvania

The church in Phillipsburg, PA

Art Whittaker/New York Daily News

The famous picture of a country preacher being thrown from a murder trial

Nicky and Israel of the Mau Maus trading bats for Bibles

Credit: © Bettmann/CORBIS

Gang members charged with murdering polio victim Michael Farmer

Nicky, Dave and Israel.

MASS MURDER TRIAL OF A TEEN-AGE GANG

Life magazine article that prompted David to go to New York City

Students and volunteers at first Teen Challenge in Brooklyn

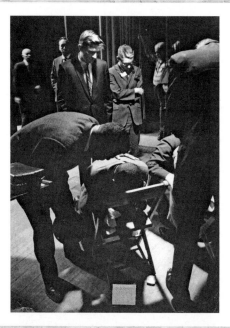

Some of the first drug addicts who entered Teen Challenge

Greenwich Village coffeehouse

Brother "Davie" and his Messerschmitt KR200

PLEASE REMEMBER ME IN YOUR PRAYERS

The HOUR OF DELIVERANCE
RADIO & TELEVISION
Brother Davie Wilkerson

"...the Prince of the world commeth and hath nothing in me..."   (John 14:30)

Early outreaches

Conference on drug addiction

Family photo in the early days of ministry

Street preaching in Ft. Greene Projects

Beginning of international ministry

The Cross and the Switchblade

The Cross and the Switchblade
translated into many languages

July 8, 1958.   Hamilton Place—Manhattan!
I will not ever forget this hour—nor this day. Here I sit—3 o'clock in the afternoon—just four hours away from the opening rites of the St. Nicholas mtg.

Storm clouds are gathering over the city. It is lightning—peals of thunder are rolling. Can this be an ominous evening of spiritual clouds & catastrophe enveloping this wicked city?

Four months of preparation! Four months of humility! Seeking God hours on end! Weeping—Praying, fasting.

There are fears in side of me in the natural man—but the spiritual man grows in faith! What will we see the first night? What has God prepared? We are prepared & believe God now for a genuine stirring of the masses of young teen-agers—So far from God?

Now it has begun to rain hard. Oh God! Send heavenly rain upon the Arena this night!

I am sold out to God. At home sits my dear expectant wife—wondering why her husband cannot be with her at her hour of delivery! But God is first!

My message seems so inadequate—I must depend totally on God's Holy Spirit. He has truly called me—He will not fail me now.

It hath not entered into the mind of man what God hath prepared for his own!
"God is good to them that wait upon Him!"

Father and son (Gary)
at Teen Challenge farm

Family photo in
the late 1960s

Youth rally

Pat Boone, Don Murray (director), and David discuss
the making of *The Cross and the Switchblade* movie

Erik Estrada and Pat Boone during filming
of *The Cross and the Switchblade*

President Ford with Don Wilkerson, discussing Teen Challenge

David Wilkerson in the 1970s

Street rally at Central Park

Street preaching in Detroit

Grandmother Wilkerson (left) at Greenwich Village coffeehouse

David with children from CURE Corps

Youth crusades

Packed houses coming to hear the gospel

Ministry to those in need

David's parish in New York City

Taking the good news to the streets

International pastors' conference

David and Gary in Europe at a pastors' conference

Thousands of pastors gathered
for encouragement

Pastors' conference

David ministered to pastors in sixty countries.

Gary and David ministering in South Africa

Gary and David with bishops in Mathare Valley slum of Kenya

Please Pass the Bread feeding ministry
touches children around the world.

David's passionate preaching
marked his ministry.

David and Gwen were married nearly sixty years.

Times Square Church on Broadway and 51st in New York City

Preaching in Times Square

Nicky and David sharing the pulpit

David preaching at Times Square Church

9
—
A PROPHET

Don Haney stared out the picture window of his parents' west Texas home, peering down the sun-baked street. It was 1973 and he was back in Big Spring, on the flat high plains, having just graduated from Oral Roberts University. Don was a talented musician who had traveled coast to coast with the college's acclaimed singing group, an experience that was both eye-opening and world-expanding. It gave him a taste of what it meant to serve God with his artistic gifts, and he decided that if he could, that's what he'd like to do.

Now, as Don waited expectantly, a massive Continental Trailways bus rounded the corner. It was right on time, just as Don had been instructed to be. It pulled up to the curb in front of the house, air brakes sighing, motor chugging, and Don grabbed his suitcase. As he strode across the lawn, the bus doors flung open and a voice called out, "Hop in, you're driving."

For the next three years, Don steered that bus across the majority of American states, playing a rented organ each night at David Wilkerson Youth Crusades. A half hour before every service, he softly pumped out a prelude as people filed into brightly lit city arenas, college auditoriums, and tiny, fluorescent-lit church halls. On occasion, at his boss's request, he would play again at the close of a service, accompanying Dallas Holm on a hymn, perhaps "Amazing Grace" or whatever suited my father's sense for the moment when people gave their lives to Jesus.

As Don stepped onto the bus that first time, my father met him with an extended hand. "Welcome," he said. Don was then greeted by the rest of the traveling team — Dallas Holm, David Patterson, and Richard Schulz. The bus's interior was plush, with couches, chairs, a television, a sound system, and a kitchenette. At the back was a closed mini-apartment that allowed the boss privacy for writing, studying, or napping.

As Don shook the last extended hand, my father cleared his throat. "Well," Dad said abruptly, "let's get going," and gestured to the driver's seat.

———

MOST PEOPLE ON THE GROWING crusade staff were happy to have resettled in Dallas, Texas. Dad had picked the booming city as home base for his ministry after some precipitous events in California. In 1971, after nine months there, an earthquake hit. The crusade team was on the road at the time, and some of the women on staff had held a slumber party at the Pattersons' house in Irvine. Barb Mackery remembers waking in the night to the sound of china and crystal rattling and books tumbling out of bookcases. Her sister Carol had a new baby at the time and rushed to check on her.

When Dad learned about it, he felt terrible. The quake was the tipping point for him. "He thought it just wasn't working from California," Dallas Holm says. The crusade team still flew across three time zones, and Dad had agonized through several turbulent flights. Relocating more centrally made sense, as did the choice of bus travel.

With the ministry now rooted in north Dallas and the intensity of his California outreaches behind him, a new side of my father emerged. "He was a jokester," Barb says. "He wasn't that way by personality, but he loved to entertain." Dad hosted a Christmas party for the staff each year, and he loved enacting Johnny Carson's "Carnac" routine. This was a positive change in our father, whose depth of "social shyness" had surprised Barb when she first met him. Dad was notorious in our family for attempting jokes that ended up silencing the room. But as a host, he was without peer, and he loved it whenever jokes were played on him.

By now the crusade ministry had expanded to more than a dozen staff members. The newest was Ken Berg, a young photographer and graphic artist who produced my father's monthly magazine, *The Cross and the Switchblade*. The magazine served as the main artery to ministry supporters who signed up for Dad's mailing list at his crusades, and that list had grown to more than one hundred thousand readers.

Within a year of relocating to Dallas, Dad plunged into an opportunity presented by Explo '72, a massive international youth gathering in the city orchestrated by Campus Crusade for Christ. Dad wrote special tracts to be passed out there, addressing "previously taboo subjects that young people were just then exploring," Barb says. Dad also mass-produced a bumper sticker — "God Has Everything Under Control" — that became somewhat popular during the period. Less successful, however, was his attempt to institute a "Jesus handshake," a greeting in the style of the soul handshake. He and Dallas Holm demonstrated it at the crusades, but, as Dallas remarks with a grin, it didn't quite catch on.

Ken Berg could appreciate it all. As an art school graduate with a heart to serve God, working for Dad provided a creative outlet like no other. "I don't think Brother Dave had any peers in terms of what he was doing with young people," Ken says. "I was working for an ad agency on Sunset Boulevard in Hollywood during the Jesus Movement, and I saw the outreaches to youth on the Strip. It was pretty much localized to that area. Dave took the same emphasis into a national vacuum of sorts. When he wrote to young people, he didn't tiptoe around things. He was very pointed, and they appreciated that."

Ken was already aware of my dad's ministry. He's the son of Reverend Stanley Berg, the late pastor of Glad Tidings Tabernacle in Manhattan who had welcomed my dad to the city. Ken was in junior high when Dad spoke to his youth group. "He wanted us involved with his projects," Ken remembers. "No one else would think of evangelizing with a flip-top box that looked like a cigarette pack. He spoke our language, not from some theological approach. His heart for young people was God given."

Ken remembered Dad's passion and innovation when my father asked him to work for the crusade ministry. "I knew he was a step ahead of everybody in terms of visual communication," Ken says. He jumped at the chance.

———

THE NEW ADDITIONS TO the crusade staff were desperately needed. Doors to further ministry were opening, and not just to youth. Dad had begun traveling internationally, with invitations from all over the world. David Patterson's notes from a Brazil trip capture the amazing work God was doing:

> Brasilia was our first stop in Brazil. We had secured the use of a large gymnasium at a Catholic church for the rallies, and the first night was packed out (four to five thousand); the response was strong with hundreds of young people getting saved. We got word the next morning that the Catholics had kicked us out and would not allow us to use the facility for the second service.
>
> Next door to the Catholic church was a large Methodist church with a huge plaza-type area in front of it. The Methodist pastor made his church available. We used the front steps of the church as the stage and had the crowd stand on the plaza. Conservative estimates put the crowd at two to three times larger than the first night.
>
> –
>
> From Brasilia we went to Belo Horizonte for several days of meetings. By this time on the trip, the media in Brazil was starting to pick up on things that Brother Dave was saying about drugs, alcohol, and promiscuous sex among the young people. The ruling military junta in Brazil at that time censored the press and would not allow them to report on these issues among Brazilian young people.
>
> Since Brother Dave was a foreign evangelist, the media began to talk about these things by quoting the American. It became headline news with a feature article in *Manchete* magazine (the Brazilian equivalent of *Time* or *Life* magazines) and an appearance by David on one of the top-rated variety/guest interview TV shows.
>
> –
>
> From Belo we went to Rio. We did at least three crusade services in different parts of the city. One of the services was right next

to the 180,000-seat Maracana Soccer Stadium. We were in the 25,000-seat indoor arena, and it was packed — with a huge altar response....

While we were in Rio the censorship issue came up. One morning as our team was having breakfast, a military limousine pulled up in front of the hotel and an officer came to our table and asked us to "come with him." Brother Dave, along with the rest of the team and me, got into the limo, and we were taken to the office of the general in charge of security in the nation.

The general wanted to know how Brother Dave was getting his information about the youth of Brazil, specifically relating to drug and alcohol use. He said that he must have a leak in his office for Wilkerson to have such accurate information. Brother Dave asked the man, "Are you a Christian?" and the general replied that yes, he was a Baptist. Brother Dave then said to him, words to the effect, "Then you understand about prayer. You don't have a leak in your office. The Holy Spirit speaks to me when I pray, and He tells me about the needs of your youth."

—

At our hotel in Sao Paulo a group of pastors showed up from Campinas and asked if we could come for one service. We were scheduled to have a day off before we left for Porto Alegre in the south, but the team agreed to do the service in Campinas on that day. When we arrived at the arena, it was packed with about ten thousand (on only two days' notice). The service was great and there was a lot of excitement in the building. Brother Dave preached a salvation message and hundreds of people came forward.

Brother Dave always took a few minutes with those who had responded and talked to them about following Jesus and then led them in a sinner's prayer of repentance. After he had finished leading the group in the sinner's prayer, he said to them through the interpreter something like, "As a sign of your newfound faith in Jesus Christ, lift up your heads, look at me, and smile." This is something he did in all our crusades in the US, Canada, and Europe. I was standing just to the left of Brother Dave on the stage and watched as the whole crowd of responders lifted their heads and smiled — all except one young man right in front of us.

David said to the interpreter, "Tell that young man to lift up his head and smile." The interpreter spoke to the young man and then turned to David and said, "He says he has nothing to smile about; he was born blind."

I can only describe what happened next by trying to explain what I saw. It was as though a righteous indignation came on Brother Dave and he said to the interpreter, "You tell him to lift up his head and smile!" The interpreter told the young man just that. As the young man began to lift his head, suddenly he began to yell and scream, "I can see! I can see!" Both of his eyes were opened by the power of God! There had been no preaching about miracles or healing in the crusade service. We watched a sovereign miracle take place!

What happened next is not easy to understand from an American context. The crowd apparently had some awareness of who the boy was and that he was blind, because suddenly pandemonium broke out in the arena as people began to rush toward the stage. They didn't want to hurt anybody but just wanted to get close to where this miracle had happened. Earlier in the trip military police had been assigned to us for protection, and they quickly hustled all of us out of the building and into our cars and out of the area.

—

From Sao Paulo we went to Porto Alegre in the south of Brazil. About the time we got to Porto Alegre, David began to get sick. He was exhausted and the constant travel, the pressure of the media, and the lack of days off took a toll on him. After the first night of crusade in Porto Alegre, he collapsed back at the hotel. The interpreter and I met with his team and ours, and the decision was made that I should take Brother Dave back home and that the interpreter and his team, Dallas Holm (our singer), and Pastor Carl Alcorn (who was traveling with us) would do the remainder of the services in Fortaleza and Belem.

———

WITH EVENTFUL TRIPS LIKE this one happening, it's no wonder Dad seemed distracted at home. He loved being with his family, but try as he might, his mind would drift off while he was in midconversation with us. We would say, "Dad, where are you right now? You've slipped off to Asia or South America. Hello, I'm talking to you!"

He always tried to make up for it, though, both with Mom and with us. He was romantic with our mother — flowers were a constant — and he took my sisters on dates. In those respects, my dad modeled manhood well to my little brother, Greg, and me. But he still was prey to classic male issues such as bringing work home with him. He was fairly quiet during dinnertime when the rest of us showcased our humor. Greg would hide his peas and I would threaten to tell on him — everything seemed hilarious to us. Mom was usually smiling and happy during this, and when Dad was truly present, involved in the conversation, those were the best times. But he was always the first one up from the table.

I had heard my father preach a certain sermon to other pastors: "Don't give your whole life to ministry and neglect your children," he cautioned. I knew he had written that message as a sermon to himself. Yet I also began to see more clearly why Dad could be so distracted. He wasn't simply preoccupied with work. There really was another conversation going on, and he was attentive to it, but it was a conversation the rest of us never got to hear. Although it seemed to pull our father away from us, it was something we respected.

My siblings and I refer to a kind of switch that turned on and off within my dad. This happened at home quite a bit. Our mom would suddenly call us to the living room for a family meeting, which we knew was significant because we never had family devotions. Dad had something important to say to us, and when he spoke, we knew God's Spirit was present — no ifs, ands, or buts. In those moments, we sensed a gravitas, for lack of a better word — or *schmika*, as Hebrew theology identifies it, meaning "weightiness." These were my first experiences in understanding the phrase "holy ground," and they gave us all another reason to respect our father.

At other times, we just wished we had more of a normal dad, somebody who was present with us in the day-to-day. I remember wanting my father to tell me how to ask a girl for a date, but when I thought to ask him, he was never around. When he was present, Dad could go overboard trying to establish a normal relationship with us, such as the time he insisted on taking me on a bike ride. It turned out to be a superlong ride, and I finally told him, "Dad, I'm glad you want to spend time with me, but my friends and I are supposed to go to the skate park and trade baseball cards. Would you mind if I went to play with them?" He laughed at himself.

At other times he would sit me down and say, "Okay, tell me about your life." He truly wanted to have quality father-child time, but I could sense when he would rather be praying or studying. Sometimes I just wanted to tell him, "It's okay, Dad. I know you're really trying."

But there were other times when, in midconversation, our father just stood up and walked away. He did this to me once when I had a friend over. I was talking with my father when suddenly, without a word, Dad got up from the couch and walked out the front door. My friend asked, "Is he sick or something?"

Dad's distractedness made our three years in Dallas — my middle-school years — incredibly lonely for me. That loneliness began to shape the way I related to my younger brother. I've always felt close to Greg, though we're almost six years apart, but my feelings toward him during that period were more like a father's toward a son. I wanted to help and guide him. Of course, I was never a father to Greg in any real sense; I was projecting onto him my own longings for guidance. Years later, when my wife, Kelly, gave birth to our first child, the emotions that surged in me in the delivery room were very familiar. I recognized them as the same feelings I'd had toward Greg.

Loneliness turned into fear when I discovered a lump on one of my ribs. I thought it had to be cancer, and I had no one to talk to about it. Dad was away on a trip, and I could tell Mom had plenty going on herself. I worried every day, "Could I be dying?" It turned out to be nothing, but I remember that time as one of the darkest of my life.

I'm sure Dad thought he could make things better with my Christmas present that year. As I opened the box I saw a set of car keys. "Go look in the garage," he told me eagerly. I did and saw a gleaming new Toyota Corolla. "Dad, thanks, this is great!" I said. "I'll be able to drive it next year."

"Next year?" he said.

"Yeah. I'm fifteen now. I can't drive yet." The car was a dream gift for any teenager, but it was sadly typical of Dad not to know how old his kids were. He was so embarrassed that he turned to Mom and said, "Gwen, why didn't you tell me?"

❧

DAD SPENT MUCH OF THOSE long crusade bus trips in his back compartment writing. And more and more he found himself critiquing the charismatic movement. He saw a growing excess when "demonstrations" of the Spirit became the focal point rather than Jesus.

"He was as thoroughly Pentecostal as anybody I've ever known, but he always seemed to have questions about what was going on in the charismatic movement," David Patterson says. "He didn't like a lot of things he saw. But leaders would keep reaching out to him as a spokesperson. He had some reservations about them, and they didn't quite know how to take him either."

During his outreaches in both northern and southern California, Dad had seen excesses among newly converted hippies turn into outright sin. Some of them continued using psychedelic drugs in misguided attempts to enhance their spiritual experience. Dad took a camera crew into one San Francisco circle to try to expose its use of pot. A few fringe groups became cults, like the Children of God, which used sex to win converts.

The charismatic movement wasn't practicing these kinds of sinful extremes. As Winkie Pratney says, the movement spread mainly through pantsuited women who played teaching cassettes for small gatherings in living rooms. But Dad sensed that the movement's growing emphasis on "freedom in the Spirit" led to sinful license that God in his holiness had never intended. He wrote a pamphlet about Christians who drank socially titled *Sipping Saints*. To David Patterson, it was an example of my dad's occasional reversion to old-line Pentecostalism. "At one time *Sipping Saints* was used at Fuller Theological Seminary as an example of faulty exegesis," he says.

At the same time he was critiquing charismatics, Dad cared very much about the Jesus Movement. When he thought it was beginning to fragment, he decided to publish a magazine to keep it thriving. "It was a one-shot publication, the size of *Time* magazine, with articles by key authors," says David Patterson. Among those contributors were Hal Lindsey, Kathryn Kuhlman, and Pat Boone.

The magazine was *Jesus Christ Solid Rock*, and its theme was the last days. Dad wrote articles about the second coming, pointing to the worldwide outpouring of the Holy Spirit as a sign of the times. Also included were articles about nuclear apocalypse, prophecy through the ages, and "phony Jesus people." With the other contributors helping to finance it, Dad printed a quarter of a million copies and gave most of them away.

Jesus Christ Solid Rock reflected the time: a young generation searching for answers, and concerned adult leaders hoping to reach them. The magazine was also more prophetic in nature than anything my dad had ever produced. It was a precursor to the book he was about to write, one that redefined him in the public mind more than anything else since *The Cross and the Switchblade*.

▬▬▬

IN 1973, MY DAD BEGAN to have stirrings he'd never felt before. He sensed a need to sequester himself in prayer to be able to hear from God. This was the beginning of his most controversial book, *The Vision*.

True to form, Dad didn't disclose to us what was going on inside him, but we could tell something was happening. My brother, Greg, and I would be in the living room with Dad, maybe watching a sports event, when we would notice him get up quietly and slip into the master bedroom, closing the door behind him. Years later Dad described to me what he was experiencing.

Off my parents' bedroom was a spacious master bathroom. He would go in, locking the door behind him. Then he simply lay on the floor, prayed, and listened. The first day was somber. Dad was overcome with a heavy angst. The emotions he felt seemed to come from outside himself, and they kept coming all day long. Dad emerged from his bedroom that day depressed.

Day after day, he would lie on the bathroom floor and listen. Soon images formed in his mind — not daydream images but clear pictures he couldn't have imagined. *What is that, Lord — a building?*

He was shaken. "I don't know what's happening," he let on to us occasionally. "This is all new. I don't get these kinds of messages from God." His conversations with the Lord became more pointed. "Take this away from me, Lord," he prayed. "I can't bear to look at it." He had the kind of soul-shattering experience we imagine happening to biblical prophets, such as Jeremiah in the Old Testament or John in Revelation. It continued for two or three weeks.

After a while, the various things Dad was seeing began to connect in his mind, taking shape as a whole. It was like a mural being painted, one portion at a time, with the full outline appearing very slowly. He could literally see what he was to write in the book. Soon he discerned that almost everything coming to him was related to current news events. In essence, the alarming images being impressed on him were a spiritual vision of what was already going on in the world. Almost every prediction my father makes in *The Vision* is tied to news events of the time — not just cataclysmic, headline news but in-depth economic and geopolitical events, industrial developments, weather shifts, cultural trends.

When he began writing, scribbling the images onto his yellow pad, it was the worst period of his life. Dad wasn't just depressed by what he wrote. He was discouraged. The weight was so heavy, he told himself, "This is crazy. I can't write this; it's too outlandish. People will think I'm an idiot. My staff is going to leave me. I'll lose the ministry. Gwen will think I've lost all my marbles."

He kept writing.

—▪—

DAD WAS IN CANADA WHEN he called to start dictating the book to Barb Mackery. "I don't want to scare you," he told her, but he didn't hold back as he read the first chapter over the phone.

As Barb took down the contents in shorthand, she thought, "This is the most alarming thing I've ever heard in my life." Every day, as Dad called to dictate a chapter, Barb thought, "Oh, Lord, this is all a great mystery. I've got to make big changes in my life." She noted a similar reaction in Dad. "There was a withdrawal from the mundane," she recalls. He decided to move his and Barb's offices to a private suite away from the business offices to distance them from day-to-day ministry matters. The chapter titles of *The Vision* reveal his deep preoccupations:

"Economic Confusion"
"Drastic Weather Changes and Earthquakes"
"A Flood of Filth"
"Persecution Madness"
"The Number One Youth Problem of the Future"
"God's Message to the Unprepared"
"Predictions and Prophecies of Bible Men"

Altogether, it sounded apocalyptic, but the chapters were grounded in thorough news analysis and events. While John Sherrill reported on worldwide moves of the Holy Spirit, Dad wrote of worldwide upheaval taking place, and the spiritual meaning it pointed to. He had always interpreted world events — indeed, life itself — through the patterns of human nature and history as revealed in Scripture. Now, with this vision, God had opened up the future to him all too clearly.

Dad was right about the fallout. When he showed the manuscript to his staff, the majority of them counseled him not to publish it. David Patterson advised, "This is not good for your ministry. People will think you've gone too far. They won't trust your spiritual judgment if you go out on a limb with this."

Dad considered their concerns, but he couldn't shake his conviction that *The Vision* had to go out to the world. "I don't remember any hesitation in him," Barb says.

A few of his staff ended up leaving, but Dad didn't blame them. Inevitably, other ministers got word of what Dad was writing and asked to read the manuscript. Most of them urged, "Please, don't publish this."

Some were Dad's friends and had his best interests at heart. Others had the church's reputation in mind and wanted to protect the gains that the Charismatic Renewal movement had made in mainline churches and in society.

Typically, Dad shouldered the burden himself. He didn't tell us about the pressures he felt and would only say, "A couple of my key leaders don't understand it." He understood their reactions, because he didn't understand the whole thing himself.

———

DAD HAD BEEN ENTRUSTED with something strange and powerful, so one might think he would want to test the waters with it. But for him, preaching to an audience was never about trying out new material. Every event was a sacred moment ordained by God, with nothing less than eternity at stake for everyone present. For that reason alone, he could never judge a sermon based on people's reactions to it. He had to judge himself on how faithful he was to speak the message God had impressed on him.

It was no different for him the night he unveiled his vision to an unsuspecting audience. He was scheduled to speak at a massive charismatic conference in Minneapolis, hosted by the acknowledged charismatic movement leader David du Plessis. His invitation to Dad gave my father's message an added weight.

The auditorium held about ten thousand people, mostly charismatic Lutherans, a gathering that David Patterson describes as "one big Sunday school class." The atmosphere was giddy, with throngs of happy Christians doing sit-down-stand-up songs. It was the sort of thing Dad abided until his turn came to speak. That night, when he stepped to the microphone, he got straight down to business. He detailed a vision of upheaval, chaos, tumult coming to America and the world. All of it would reveal God's judgment, and God's people would not be exempted.

All ten thousand listeners sat in silence. When Dad finished and the meeting closed, people filed out in shock. The experience wasn't just sobering; it was unnerving. Many in the audience had heard my dad preach difficult messages before, but this one was hard to swallow. David du Plessis approached my dad with a perplexed look. "Well, do you feel

better now?" he whispered. He didn't seem to know what to make of what
he had just heard.

The initial readers of Dad's book would have the same reaction, and
it polarized them.

"Several district superintendents in the Assemblies of God shut him
off," Barb says. "It was a horribly hard time for him, because he lost some
friends. Some just didn't want to be associated with him, probably to
preserve their reputations."

Discussion of *The Vision* was all over the airwaves on Christian
radio, and a lot of it wasn't positive: "David Wilkerson is speaking out
of his vain imagination." "He's having a midlife crisis." Barb lost track
of how many times she heard someone report that Dad was having a
nervous breakdown.

David Patterson had been right: Dad's ministry did suffer. "Brother
Dave had been the first Pentecostal ever to address the Texas State Baptist Convention," David notes. "They recognized him as a man God was
using to win young people to the Lord by the thousands. And we had a
wonderful reception from them. But when *The Vision* came out, they
pulled away as if they'd been scalded. Brother Dave understood that. I
think he knew it was going to happen."

Yet Dad couldn't help but absorb it personally. My sister Bonnie
remembers being in the room when our father got a phone call from a
minister friend within the denomination. As Dad hung up the receiver,
he was ashen. "So-and-so just told me off," he said.

Dad never told me who criticized him, but his close friends knew.
According to Paul Dilena, even a few people involved with Teen Challenge had turned against him. "When they started to hear about little
black boxes on TV sets turning homes into porno palaces," Paul said,
"they rejected him."

Those reactions were tempered somewhat as *The Vision*'s predictions started coming to pass. "I'm glad he didn't pay attention to me,"
David Patterson says. "Brother Dave brought a prophet's mantle into the
church, and people didn't know how to respond to it. His approach to the
prophetic word was like no one else's who had the same level of accep-
tance that he had."

David was always the one who introduced my father to audiences. "I used to introduce him as 'the author of *The Cross and the Switchblade*,'" David says. "Sometime after *The Vision* had been out, I asked him, 'Can I introduce you as a prophet of God?' 'No, no,' he said, 'never.'" David understood. My father wanted to avoid the baggage that came with the tag of prophet. "But I don't know of another spokesman for the Spirit-filled community who had a greater impact," David says. "He was a prophet."

———

DAD DIDN'T LIMIT HIS PROPHETIC vision to the book. Once again he was compelled to put his experiences onto film, and he had a ready-made producer in Ken Berg. "When he felt God had spoken to him, it was 'green light,' go ahead, do it," Ken says.

The first film Dad scripted was *The Road to Armageddon*, based on *The Vision*. "He took pieces of *The Vision* and worked it up as a script," Ken says. "I accessed stock footage for the current events he referred to as signs of the end times — earthquakes, famines, storms. We did it documentary style, with Dave commenting on those things in voiceover. On camera, he was just the way he was in the pulpit. He was comfortable, as if he felt God was speaking through him."

The Road to Armageddon was a quick half hour of prophesied events presented in rapid-fire succession. "He just read the headlines and saw it all as God's doing," Ken says. "His message was, 'Here's the news; here's what the Bible says; so put the pieces together, folks. We're in the end times.'"

When the film was finished, it found an eager audience. "There was an incredible appetite in those days for David's ministry in local churches," David Patterson says. Evidently, laypeople and local pastors were more accepting of Dad's vision than ecclesiastical leaders had been. "We hired six full-time guys who took the film out on the road to exhibit it," David says. "Little towns, big towns — they could book showings four or five nights a week. We'd give them a region and say, 'These five states are yours. Here's a list of all the churches we know. Now go for it.'"

One of those six film representatives was a young Bob Rogers. The teenager who had responded to my dad's altar call at Melodyland had ended up being a youth pastor at our church in Dallas. Dad hired him away to help with the film screenings — a fortuitous move, ultimately, because David Patterson soon left his post as crusade director, and Dad named Bob as his replacement. In the meantime, the film-rep job provided great preparation.

"Just about every pastor I called said yes to the movie, because *The Vision* had created such enormous interest," Bob says. That interest extended beyond Pentecostal churches into independent charismatic churches. "Audience reactions were insane," Bob says. "I was driving in central Wisconsin, in the middle of nowhere, when I rolled up to a little building at a crossroads. It wasn't even a town. I walked in and there were six hundred people there on a Monday night to watch *The Road to Armageddon*. After a month or two, I understood what was going on. I told pastors, 'Look, if this place is not filled, it'll be your fault. All you have to do is place a few newspaper ads. Forget television. Go to Christian radio and put on a commercial. If you just do that, it doesn't matter what night of the week it is. This place will be filled.' "

"The church was hungry for it," David Patterson says. "And it was a great soul-winning tool. Our reps gave an altar invitation after every showing, and people were getting saved. It added to local churches everywhere." The six film reps stayed busy on the road screening *Armageddon* for almost a year.

Dad and Ken produced a quick succession of films after that. One was *Return to Sodom*, an examination of what Dad identified as the rise of militant homosexuality, shot in New Orleans during Mardi Gras. Another was a second coming film that Dad titled *The Rapture*. "We filmed it as a fictitious newscast," Ken says. "We found a news set in a Dallas studio and hired a professional newscaster from one of the stations. It starts off like the six o'clock news, with the guy reading news reports, until a hand reaches in to give him an update."

The update, of course, consists of reports from all over the country of people disappearing, airplanes crashing, cars wrecking on the freeway — all because the rapture has taken place. One scene features a famous Christian recording artist — played by Dallas Holm — singing on *The Tonight Show* and vanishing on camera.

"Others have done films with the rapture theme, but Brother Dave was the first," Ken says, noting this was 1974. "People had never thought about what would really happen when the rapture takes place. Of course, he did."

Around that time, Dad decided to stop sending out film reps and just ship the films to churches directly. Included in the screening agreement was that *The Rapture* could not be shown on local television without a disclaimer, because of the confusion it might cause. "A church in Calgary had its own half-hour weekly telecast," David Patterson remembers. "Without telling us, they ran the movie in their slot, but without a disclaimer. Within minutes, the local police station was flooded with calls. 'People are disappearing. What's going on?' It was a mess. The Canadian equivalent of the FCC sanctioned the station."

Yet it wasn't *The Rapture* that ended my dad's film run. "It was *The Hiding Place*," Bob Rogers says. "It raised the bar of what a Christian film should look like. Billy Graham had done a lot of films through World Wide Pictures, but none of them really captured the nation until *The Hiding Place*. After that, churches didn't want to book ours anymore."

For a time, though, "Those films were a major part of the ministry's evangelistic thrust," Dallas Holm notes. Ken Berg reflects on the pioneer who conceived them and his purpose in producing them. "He heard from God and wasn't afraid to tell people about it," Ken says. "He was the boldest, the closest to the apostle Paul, of anyone I've ever met. You feel humbled to stand next to a person like that. I'll always appreciate that he said, 'Come on, Ken, and join our team. Let's go win the world for the Lord.'"

10

—

SOULS

"DON'T EVER ASK DAVID WHY he does something, because he'll always give you the wrong answer," said Bob Rogers, capturing a great truism about my dad's relationship to the Lord — notably, how Dad received direction from God.

"He wouldn't know why he was doing something," Bob explains. "If you forced him to give an answer, he would tell you something from his flesh, because he really didn't know. He just knew he'd heard from God. Whatever he was doing, it was because he was convinced the Lord wanted him to. But if you listened to David for an explanation, you'd be in trouble."

Bob's insight is helpful to anyone ever puzzled by my dad's tendency to give different reasons at different times for having done things. Bob is no mystic; he's as grounded and earthy as any pastor has to be, and he has led several churches since serving my dad. But in 1974, my father's next unorthodox move made a vivid impression on the young lay minister.

That year Dad uprooted the crusade ministry — his family, staff, and operations, which by then were considerable — and moved us into the isolated countryside two hours east of Dallas. It's an area where north Texas's flat pastures and broad lakes begin to undulate into east Texas's piney woods. The closest city to the property my dad was looking to buy was Tyler, forty minutes south; farther north was Mineola. The nearest town of any size was Lindale, ten miles away, which had a population of around one thousand. In short, we were going to the sticks.

Dad gave various reasons for this move, and none contradicts the other. Each reveals a different dimension of what weighed on his mind in those days.

Winkie Pratney was by then a well-known apologist-evangelist to college students. He says Dad told him the following story: "David was driving between Shreveport and Dallas when the Lord told him to stop and get out. This was near Highway 110, off the interstate. David looked around and there was nothing out there, just fields. The Lord told him, 'You will have a place here one day.' David noted it in his journal, and that was the very location he moved to later."

The pull of the countryside may also have tapped into Dad's roots. "He loved rural America," Barb Mackery notes. "He was a country boy at heart. His relaxation between all the traveling was to drive country roads." Dad's routes from our home in Dallas spoked outward in all directions from the Metroplex. Those drives not only relaxed him but also fed what had become a hobby. "Brother Dave loved real estate," says Barb, noting that while in Dallas the ministry moved its offices four times. "He was one of those unique men who loved the chase. He could spend two years looking for a ministry property and then develop it in six months."

On one of those drives, an hour west of Fort Worth, Dad came across a property he thought would make a perfect retreat for himself, our family, and the ministry staff. It was a lot on Possum Kingdom Lake, a vast blue body of water bordered on some sides by hundred-foot bluffs. Dad bought the lot, built a house on it, and, somewhat tongue in cheek, called it Camp David. He made great use of it, writing his books and film scripts there, urging the staff to use it, and offering it to visiting missionaries he had supported over the years. Still, Barb says, "He would always spiritualize acquisitions like that one." She put her finger on Dad's chronic inner case of push-pull. He had a guilt complex over anything related to the material.

Bob Rogers offers another angle on Dad's decision to move to the country: "David Wilkerson never preached anything he didn't believe one hundred and ten percent. He may have been dead wrong, but you can be sure he believed that puppy when he preached it. There was not an ounce of guile or sham in this human being, and he believed *The Vision's*

message, that the economy was going to collapse and disaster was coming. He wanted to move to east Texas because he wanted to escape the
city. We all were supposed to live on that property, and it was going to
be self-sustaining."

Winkie Pratney corroborates this. "There are five or six places in
America where if a bomb dropped on a major city, you would be safe,"
he says. "The property near Lindale sits on one of the largest water tables
in the United States. The wind currents there are such that if a bomb was
dropped on Dallas, it wouldn't affect the area further east."

This was not information that Dad wanted to announce to anyone,
but as Bob Rogers notes, my father acted on his beliefs. All I know is that
the move to east Texas was a great one for our family—at least for me,
mired as I was in middle-school misery. The only rationale I needed to
hear from Dad was the one he pitched to us: "We've bought four hundred
acres. Let's go have some fun in the country."

———

TWIN OAKS RANCH WAS A game-changer for me. The suburbs of
Orange County and Dallas had been bewildering. When we moved to
Lindale, I thought, "How have I missed this my whole life?"

The caretaker and his wife, E.L. and Claudia Proctor, showed me
around the property that Dad bought. E.L. must have seen how enamored I was with the place, because he asked, "I could use some help this
summer. How about coming to work for me?" I couldn't believe my ears.
Dad and Mom were all for it, so when ninth grade ended, I grabbed my
friend Mark Schulz and we sprang out to the open fields of Twin Oaks.

That fall, as Dad developed the ranch for offices and housing, some
of the staff moved into trailer homes along a dirt road off Highway 16.
"It was fun," says Barb. "Every afternoon the question was, 'What are you
guys having for supper tonight?' 'Oh, I just made baked apples; they'll be
ready at four.' It was like an open house among the trailers.'"

Nicky Cruz was curious about the move and decided to pay a visit.
By now he was traveling the globe with his own evangelistic ministry. A
New Yorker to the marrow, Nicky got antsy after dinner and started pac-
ing. "Come on, Davie, what do you guys do out here after dark?" he said.

Dad curled a good-humored grin. "What do *you* do after dark?"

What Nicky couldn't see was the fully developed image of the property that my father carried in his head. As Dad traversed the land each day, a bulldozer moved earth around. "We're putting a dam over there," Dad pointed out to me. "It'll make this pond ten times bigger."

"He was still busy," Barb says, as her boss shuttled back and forth to Dallas to oversee the move of ministry operations, "but he was so much more relaxed." In retrospect, I can see why. My father was in a kind of heaven. Twin Oaks was both a playground where he could indulge his talent for development, and a property with a fully spiritual use. It was one more conquest of a divide in his heart he'd been working to reconcile since childhood.

———

"THE CRUSADES WERE STILL POPULAR," Bob Rogers says of the period when he took over from David Patterson. Dad's longtime director, David, had resigned at what he felt was God's direction. He was moving his family to southern California to take a leadership position with an international missions agency. Dad and the Pattersons had spent eight years together, a history that reached back to Dad's recruitment of them as college students. Saying goodbye now, David and Carol marveled with Dad at all that the Lord had brought to fruition.

"In 1974 we still had a stack of invitations," Bob notes. "Anybody could have done my job, because crusades were still in the phenomenon stage then. Scheduling was a piece of cake. Brother Dave would just step onto the bus and ask, 'Where are we going?'"

As a teenager, I was old enough to tag along on crusade bus tours, and I acted as a roadie, lugging sound equipment and boxes of literature. Those long miles with my father were my favorite moments with him. He was naturally at ease on the bus because he was doing exactly what he loved to do, and our times together flowed more naturally there.

Dad was also more relaxed because another staff member had joined the crusade team: his brother Jerry. After a seven-year estrangement, my uncle had returned to Aunt Eve and my cousins in Pittsburgh. To put his alcohol habit behind him, he had undergone a Teen Challenge program at my dad's suggestion. When Jerry graduated, Dad invited him to join the ministry, and he moved his family to Lindale, where he ended up in charge of the ministry's literature sales.

I enjoyed helping at the literature tables, stacking books, tracts, eight-track tapes of Dallas Holm's music, and LPs of my dad's sermons. Answering people's questions, I got a better idea of the impact my dad's books were having. I also gained insight into Dad's larger purpose for them beyond income for the ministry. During a service at Fort Hood, Texas, a military officer informed my father he wasn't allowed to sell the literature on a government base. Dad didn't hesitate in his response, and simply told Uncle Jerry to give it all away. After the service, crowds of soldiers took home every last item on the tables; we were left packing empty boxes. Uncle Jerry had made his living in the grocery business, and he knew to a cent the value of the inventory Dad had just donated: more than fifteen thousand dollars.

The ministry would have felt the pinch in those days. But when a support team saw their boss making that kind of costly decision, they couldn't help but respect him. As tough a boss as my dad could be — and at times he could be very demanding — I saw the crusade team's respect for him grow.

He counted a different kind of cost on a trip to St. Louis. Dad was invited to address the Assemblies of God's General Council, its annual gathering of ministry leaders. "He was as nervous as a cat on the bus heading into St. Louis," recalls Jerry Nance, a hardworking young team member who helped on the organizational side. Dad always prayed to have a specific message for special audiences like this one, and he had been rattled by what God impressed on him to preach at General Council.

There were more than ten thousand ministers in the arena for Dad's sermon. Even before he could be introduced, Dad stepped forward and interrupted the host. "He just grabbed the mike away," Jerry Nance says. "Brother Dave hated long introductions anyway, so it wasn't the first time he'd done that. But he made the man get out of the way so he could start preaching. He just said, 'Open your Bibles to this passage,' and he preached hell hot that night. He spoke about compromise in pastors' lives and the things that separate them from God. Before it was over, pastors were running to the altar."

With other audiences, Dad was sometimes compelled to address darker issues that weren't being talked about but he knew were taking place. "A young person might come to the altar and say she was being sexually molested," Jerry says. "When that happened, there was a righteous indignation in Brother Dave. He would take the mike and go after it aggressively." He had never shrunk from the most difficult areas of life, taking the crusade team into prisons regularly, from Angola in Louisiana to several in Texas. The ministry received nothing for doing those outreaches. "He knew the bottom line, but he never looked at it," Uncle Jerry says. "Whenever he went overseas, he never took an offering. David just looked at souls."

When a team is being led by someone who gives with an open hand and takes risks in faith, it builds confidence. Confidence leads to trust, trust leads to camaraderie, and the camaraderie on the crusade bus was fantastic. As Dad worked in his compartment, the rest of the guys told jokes, listened to music, and parsed Bible passages. Dallas Holm's humor had matured by then, from a youthful impishness to the wry observations of a seasoned minister. At times that humor had a leveling effect on my dad whenever Dallas sensed he needed it.

"Dallas and I served on Dave's ministry's board," Uncle Jerry says. "My brother would discuss what he wanted in those meetings and nobody ever had any objections. It was just, 'Yes, yes, amen, amen.' One day Dave was wrapping up and asked, 'Everybody agreed?' Dallas said, 'No.' Dave looked at him surprised. Dallas said, 'I just wanted to hear what that sounds like.'"

Dallas was also present during an awkward moment when Dad was poised to preach at a large charismatic conference. Just as my father was ready to step to the podium, the host suggested a unity-building exercise. He wanted everyone to pass around an imaginary candle, beginning at the back of the auditorium and moving down every aisle, from person to person, till it reached the stage.

Of course, this took forever, and Dallas could sense my dad bristling. The "candle" was supposed to end with my father, but Dallas saw the exercise as one long fuse leading to a powder keg.

Finally, the "candle" reached Dallas. Taking it, he turned somberly to my dad, whispered, "Oops!" and pretended to fumble it. Dad allowed himself a grin as he stepped forward to speak.

My father didn't mind those jokes from Dallas because the trust — and even the humor — went both ways. During our years in Dallas, Texas, my dad had become a diehard Cowboys football fan, something few people knew. More than once, after an altar call at a Sunday crusade, my father would pass Dallas on the way to the counseling area and whisper, "How'd the Cowboys do?"

To me, it all seemed as fun and meaningful and fulfilling as a life in ministry could be. I know my dad loved it, and, by God's grace, he was able to provide enjoyable work for godly young people who were as passionate for the gospel as he was. Occasionally he emerged from his compartment on the bus to join them in laughter and spiritual discussion. He would pray with the guys, talk to them about the sermon he was working on, or show them what God was revealing to him from Scripture.

Meals in restaurants could be a bit chaotic on the road. Everyone knew to shovel down the food fast, because, like at home, Dad was always the first one up from the table. As soon as the meal arrived, he gobbled a few bites and pushed back his chair. His standard line at that point — "Take your time; I'll be on the bus" — became kind of a joke. Everyone knew this was their cue to follow him out.

The guys were good natured about it, and it probably helped that, apart from Uncle Jerry, they were all in their twenties. Dad had chosen them well. Although they respected my father, and maybe feared him a little, none were yes men. My dad loathed schmoozers and brownnosers. He wanted only people who were likeminded in their passion for Jesus. In turn, he wanted the ministry to be a place where they could flourish, and to that end, he took exceptional care of them.

"Brother Dave had an innate ability to attract young leaders," says Jerry Nance, who is cut from the same cloth as his brother-in-law, Bob Rogers. Both are the personification of organization — they're get-it-done guys — yet both are extremely down to earth, caring for people more than process. "Brother Dave's style was very authoritarian," Jerry says, "but he also had confidence in you. He was never afraid to delegate.

He would throw you into the deep end of the pool because he knew you could swim. He pulled that out of young leaders, and they would just get it done, or they would die trying because they didn't want to disappoint him."

"That was both good and bad," says Roger Jonker, the tall Texan who married my sister Debi. A business graduate of North Texas State University, my brother-in-law had been thrown into the deep end himself. Dad named Roger his business manager when the previous man in that role died of cancer. "One thing I missed was having a mentor," Roger says. "I never had anyone to show me the ropes. But it was spooky the amount of faith Brother Dave put in you as an individual. He had prayed about it and asked God for confirmations. So if he felt in his spirit you were right for the job, that had an effect on you. It motivated you to be just as diligent to seek God as he was."

Some of my dad's staff decisions came across as impulsive. Dad was at a restaurant once with a pastor and his youth minister when he said to the younger man, "I need you to come to work for me." The young guy's jaw dropped. The pastor must have felt like doing the same. "Can you come on Monday?" Dad pressed. "We can provide you with an apartment."

Moments like those seemed completely random, yet they were anything but that. "He was very methodical," says Craig Smith, a gifted music artist who joined Dad's ministry a few years later. "David would do a hairpin turn, and it would seem spontaneous. But then you found out it was something he'd been thinking about for a long time."

Staff meetings were short, usually no more than twenty minutes. There was never any reason to belabor an issue or to strategize. Dad had already done that work, in hours of prayer and by processing things in his head. He decided, delegated, and directed, and he didn't trust agendas, including his own. He constantly searched his heart to discern whether he was acting by his own will or by what he sensed as God's leading. He was convinced human agendas could derail the supernatural work of God. "That's the stuff that can ruin us," he always said. A godly leader's role, as he saw it, was to empty himself, not to assert himself.

———

Traveling on the bus was the best education a young man like me could have had. I was starting to feel my way into what I wanted to do in life, and I'm certain that observing my father on those trips informed God's call on my own life.

Dad called the pulpit "the sacred desk," meaning, after all the preparation, that was where the actual work got done. When he stepped into the pulpit, he had to move purely as a vessel of God, almost as if he himself didn't exist. To Dad, the moment in the pulpit was the hour of life or death for those in the audience. The power of God had to move through him to bring them to repentance and salvation, and for that reason, he had to be utterly prepared — and emptied.

"Early in a crusade season, he would be nervous about his new sermons," Jerry Nance says. "But when he walked to the pulpit, it was all business. He got right to the point. He stayed pretty close to his notes, but he was so focused and under the anointing of God that when he preached, instantly people submitted to what they were hearing. He had spent time in God's presence, and that gave him an authority when he delivered the message he'd received."

To a sixteen-year-old like me, watching Dad from the side of a stage was an incredible experience. I looked out and saw thousands of people, young and old, on the edges of their seats, taking in every word. Then came the part of his message I think of as a magical moment. My dad would stop preaching, sometimes before the end of his sermon. He would close his Bible and put his hands together in a little clap. My heart leapt as I thought, "This is it. Now the Holy Spirit will come, and we'll all do business with God."

His invitation for people to come forward never lasted long. "Here is why you need to come," he would say simply, and he would spend no more than three or four minutes giving the altar call. The rest he left to faith. In his mind, to plead with people was to short-circuit the power of God. "The more talking you do, the less faith you have," he told me. That ability to trust God was one of his greatest gifts.

He backed away from the pulpit at that point. He even had a stance — crossing an arm across his midsection, raising his free hand to his chin, and bowing his head. Every time I was with him on a crusade tour, the altars were packed. It was never a matter of facing a hard crowd and having only twenty people come forward. People always responded by the hundreds.

Bob Rogers knew for himself how powerful those moments could be. "I was a victim of the gift myself," he chuckles. "He brought a clarity. He wasn't after the masses; he spoke to the one life out there, and he laid the gospel out clearly. But the masses responded."

When Bob first began organizing the crusades, even he was surprised by the results. "I had organized a service in Fort Wayne," he says. "At that time we were mainly doing smaller places, auditoriums and college field houses. But this was held in the city arena, and there were eight thousand people in the building. My planning allowed for one thousand people at an altar-call area. I thought I'd done a good job, but when he gave the altar call, three thousand people came forward."

During those years, Dad was occasionally compelled to speak a word of knowledge to someone in the audience. He didn't do this often, but when he did it was with great purpose and conviction. With hundreds of people crowding the altar, one person in the arena would rocket out of his seat, thrust his arm skyward, and race to the altar crying, "It's me!" And while the masses were receiving salvation, one life would have been rescued from suicide.

———

BOB ROGERS RECALLS A MOMENT that reveals all about my father's reverent approach to the supernatural gifts. It happened on a quiet ride eastward across Pennsylvania toward New York City. Dad emerged from his quarters and asked, "Do we have time to take a detour?"

Bob glanced at his watch. "Of course," he said. "You're the boss."

"I'd like to make a stop in Philipsburg," Dad instructed.

As Bob recalls, the front doors of Gospel Tabernacle were unlocked when they arrived. The team followed Dad into the sanctuary, where he sat down in a pew at the back. My father started laughing.

"What is it?" Bob asked.

"See that mural behind the baptistery?" Dad pointed out. "I had that put there. It's been here ever since I left. Nothing has changed in this building."

"So, Brother Dave," Bob ventured to ask, "what was it like when you were here?"

Dad laughed again. "It was crazy," he said. "I started a healing service on Sunday afternoons. That was how my evangelism ministry got started."

This was the first any of the young guys had heard about it. Bob recalls Dad's story vividly: "He said the gifts of healing and word of knowledge were operating in his life then. In those Sunday services, he was just following what his role model, Kathryn Kuhlman, had done. He was doing what he'd seen, and it worked — and it was of God."

Dad then described that difficult Sunday afternoon service when everything changed. "I was on that stage," he pointed, "and I called out a healing in a person. Suddenly I heard the Holy Spirit say to me, 'Who told you that?' I had not been in tune with the Spirit. In fact, I wasn't operating in the Spirit at all. It was just me."

"It scared him to death," Bob says. "He realized he was speaking things that weren't from God but that came out of his own mind. He saw there was a part of him that could be false. And being false was the number one thing he detested."

Dad said he felt a depth of shame as never before. That night he prayed with fear and trembling. "I was tempted to continue doing it," Dad said, "so I prayed, 'Lord, this is a dangerous path, and I don't want to go down it. I'm afraid of it. Please, take these gifts from me.'"

The guys were astonished and a little perplexed. They had seen my dad minister with these gifts time after time. The blind boy in Brazil was just one instance of healing. And words of knowledge came frequently during Dad's altar calls. The team had seen Dad use that gift to touch thousands of broken people's lives.

"Then I heard the Lord say, 'David, what gift do you want?'" Dad said.

"Well," Bob asked, "what did you ask for?"

"I asked the Lord to give me faith for souls," Dad said.

Suddenly, everything clicked for Bob. It explained what he'd seen in every crusade service: The nervous pacing in prayer beforehand. The powerful delivery of an anointed word from God. The floods to the altar by crowds of weeping, broken people.

"That was the gift he operated in — the gift of faith for souls — unlike anyone I have ever known," Bob says. "It is the faith to believe for the salvation of souls, believing the Holy Spirit to draw people to Jesus when they would not have been drawn before. That's what had happened with me as a teenager. When he told us that, I finally understood. I had seen it in operation, and it blew my mind."

Bob marvels at that hinge moment in my dad's history with God. "Faith for souls," he says, "that's the success you see behind Teen Challenge. You see it playing out in every center all over the world. The DNA of Teen Challenge is *faith for souls*, and that comes from the gift that was in David Wilkerson. When the rehabilitation program becomes the key, everything is lost, because the program is just the mechanism. First and foremost is introducing people to Christ."

Bob muses on it all. "Who would have thought this little preacher from the hills of Pennsylvania would drop down spiritual DNA in the middle of China?" he says. "And yet there it is."

Part Five

CRUCIBLE

Before I was afflicted I went astray: but now have I kept thy word.

—*Psalm 119:67*

11
—
"YOU GET TO SUFFER"

In 1974, for reasons known only to himself, Dad decided it was time for the family to come together. His siblings hadn't all gathered since their father's funeral in 1960. The entire riotous decade of the sixties had passed, along with half of the languid seventies. Now, as my dad put the word out, everyone came — my grandmother, my aunts and uncles, even my aunt Juanita, who had mostly kept her distance from the family. "We had *fun*," says Aunt Eve.

Everyone stayed in houses or rooms near Camp David along Possum Kingdom Lake. With all my cousins around, we boated, water-skied, rode motorbikes, and ate like crazy. Aunt Ruth's husband, my uncle Don Harris, insisted on taking his first motorcycle ride. He hopped onto the seat of a bike, gunned the accelerator, and promptly crashed into a parked car. What's a family reunion without a trip to the emergency room?

Several of my cousins went to Six Flags amusement park in nearby Arlington, which left my aunts and uncles to do something they hadn't been allowed to do as kids: play cards. "We played Rook, and Mom Wilkerson had no sense of the game," says Aunt Eve. "She would have nothing in her hand, but she would bid high. It made us so mad. She didn't care if she lost. She just wanted to play — and bid."

From her earliest days in New York City, my grandmother and her friend Faye Mianulli had run a coffeehouse outreach in Greenwich Village called The Lost Coin. Over that period, my grandmother watched as beatniks morphed into hippies and later into disco hustlers. Through it all, she remained "the Village Square," as she was known to locals. She was as comfortable witnessing to transvestites as to drug addicts and hipsters. She just loved the lost, and she was an equal opportunist when it came to confronting them. Whenever she found drugs on anyone, she took them away and flushed them down the toilet. That maddened a lot of young people, but it earned their respect too.

I was once with my grandmother at a street outreach in San Francisco when an angry young guy got right in her face and started swearing a blue streak. Grandma didn't flinch. She just stood listening. When a gentlemanly bystander saw this, he tried to stop it. "You leave her alone," he threatened the screamer.

My grandmother turned a stern eye on the bystander. "Don't yell at him," she said. "You're just as much a sinner as he is. You both need Jesus. But I'm talking to him right now. You can wait your turn."

I laughed my head off. It reminded me that my dad's gumption wasn't just spiritually endowed. He had inherited Grandma's directness.

But a different side of my father emerged at the Possum Kingdom reunion. When the youngest cousins ventured near the water, Dad hovered over them tenderly. He scheduled an evening for a fireworks show he would put on. To everyone's delight, Dad skittered back and forth, giddily lighting rows of skyrockets. He was as loose and happy as anyone had ever seen him. It's a shame that weekend was the only time his whole family would be together.

Aunt Juanita seemed to enjoy it all while keeping spiritual matters at arm's length. One of my cousins remembered her as being warm and solicitous, another as acerbic and needling whenever faith came up. "I never liked it when she came to visit Mother in New York," says Uncle Don. "It was an opportunity for her to express her anger toward Mother. And Mother did not have the gift of diplomacy."

Dad had helped out Aunt Juanita when she went through a divorce. Later, when my aunt wanted to expand her horizons, Dad paid for her to be able to travel. He did all these things quietly, rarely mentioning them to anyone. Part of that was his humility; part of it may also have been a lifelong perplexity over how to relate to a sibling on the other side of faith.

He pursued his sister through a difficult, complex relationship, doing what he could to connect, which to him meant giving to her.

Dad scheduled one other event that truly made it a Wilkerson family reunion. He was friends with the pastor of a church in nearby Wichita Falls, and he arranged for all of us to attend a service there, with my grandmother scheduled to preach. That was only fitting; back in the day, church was the one place they'd felt most like family.

———

MY BROTHER, GREG, AND I used to joke that Dad had a severe case of Murphy's Law. His outlook was just not positive; he thought that if something could go wrong, it would. We teased him about this a lot. If Dad's team was playing on TV, we were guaranteed to hear him say, "He won't make this free throw," or, "They'll never be able to catch up."

It was a continual puzzler to us because our father had faith for everything else. He looked into the heart of the most strung-out addict and saw a future evangelist. Even in the prophetic books he wrote — such as *The Vision* and *Racing toward Judgment*, in which he predicted Middle East chaos, economies collapsing, utter bleakness, and disaster — he always brought a note of hope at the end. For him, there was a serious conviction behind even a bumper sticker slogan like "God Has Everything Under Control."

I see this now as a Depression-era mentality. As a child he had been conditioned by the worst of times, and in his mind those conditions could return at any time. Yet even with that outlook, my father wasn't going to allow bad times to triumph. He would acknowledge the worst possible scenario, if only to preach to himself about God's faithfulness and to silence any lingering doubt. This wasn't Pollyannaish; it was an ability to face any difficulty knowing he couldn't handle it on his own and that he needed God to see him through.

We saw that trait in our father when our mom faced another frightening cancer. It struck after our move to the country. "Your mother has cancer, and it doesn't look good," he told us. "We don't know if she's going to make it, so we need to prepare our hearts for that." He cast it in the worst light possible, and he didn't offer false promises about God's ability to heal Mom. Yet we believed him when he said, "The Lord is going to see us through."

We needed that note of uplift more than anything, because cancer had visited our home several times already, and we could never be sure whether it would come again. Back in Long Island, our parents had shielded us from it, but I remembered its onset. Normally Mom was happy as she cooked breakfast for us, but one morning she was unusually grumpy, then angry, then clattering pans around.

The next morning, our dad cooked breakfast. "Where's Mom?" we asked. "Oh, she's getting some rest," he said. He served up the worst French toast in history, with clumps of egg hanging from the dipped bread. He had probably been up late the night before, as usual, but had risen early to try to maintain our normal routine. The toast didn't matter; our father was an incredible caregiver. We were on our own for a lot of emotional needs, but in a crisis he was the first to take action. "He took Gwen to a Dallas hospital, and he would not leave her side," Barb Mackery remembers. "He was totally shaken. He made sure she had a room with a bedroom adjoining, so he could stay close beside her."

I admire my dad for all the ways he took care of us through those times. And I understand why he prepared us for the worst, because cancer back then could mean a death sentence. But the outcome wasn't always as he had presented it. Thankfully, in Mom's case, it never was. She survived every bout until she was eighty years old, with more than one supernatural assist. Through those trials, I learned I didn't always have to accept a message that the sky was falling, as my father saw it. But I also learned I had a dad who would do anything to see his loved ones through a trial.

———

DAD'S CAREGIVER ROLE EXTENDED WELL beyond our family. I can't put my finger on exactly when it began to happen, but at some point he became a sort of Christian godfather type to many who looked to him for guidance. There was always a long line of people waiting to meet with him. It was a role he seemed comfortable with; he was quick to take on another's burden and share the load. A sincere young preacher might show up needing funding to start a ministry. A distraught father's teenager had run away. A struggling mother with an alcoholic husband needed grocery money. I think they came because Dad conveyed in his preaching and writing an earthiness regarding God's care. As spiritually minded as my father was, his messages conveyed the painful struggles of everyday life.

Dad was a giver by nature, and with his newsletter mailing list now providing financial support, he could help needy people even more freely — maybe too freely. My mom used to tell David Patterson, "Don't be surprised if you come back from this trip and find our house gone." Musician Craig Smith remembers seeing a distraught Bob Rogers after a crusade event, pulling at his hair. "Brother Dave just signed away every cent in the budget for this trip," Bob said. "He gave it to a local ministry."

"There wasn't a missionary who came through who didn't get outfitted in a new set of clothes," David Patterson recalls. "A suit, shirts, slacks, underwear, the whole nine yards. And Brother Dave would *find* needs; God would lead him to them."

"I saw it happen a thousand times in a thousand different ways," says Roger Hayslip, the plainspoken Texan who married my sister Bonnie. "I've been with him at restaurants where a waitress might be putting herself through college to try to better her life. He'd tell her, 'We'll pay your tuition for a semester. Here's my secretary's number; she'll take care of it.' That happened time after time. If you were a young minister, and he sensed the Spirit at work in your calling, he threw his support behind you. He would say, 'Let's support this guy for a year while he gets off the ground.'"

At times, Dad's giving bordered on the absurd. Jerry Nance was driving away with a van full of students, headed for an outreach in Savannah, Georgia, when Dad ran out of the ministry offices waving for him to stop. A visiting missionary trailed behind him.

Jerry rolled down the window.

"I just gave the van to this missionary," Dad said between breaths.

Jerry was dumbfounded. He quickly sized up the situation. "Well, Brother Dave, we have meetings tonight in Savannah, Georgia," he said. "Do you think it would be okay if we used the van for this trip? And then gave it to him afterward?"

Dad turned to the missionary. "If that guy had said, 'No, we really need the van,' Brother Dave would have told me to get out," Jerry laughs. "Thankfully the man said, 'Sure, I guess so. Go ahead and use it.' Otherwise, we'd have been unloading all our stuff and scrambling to buy another van."

After long days of giving, I can see why my dad would want to go home at night and be with his wife or bury himself in reading. But my parents did take advantage of opportunities to socialize, especially with their neighbors Jack and Berneita Rice, who became dear friends. The Rices were like the Dilenas back in Long Island — good, solid, warm people with whom my parents could be themselves, and who had a deep love for God. Dr. Rice had a medical practice in a suburb east of Dallas, and, like my father, both he and Berneita were voracious readers, so Dad could talk with them about current events. But mostly my parents appreciated the Rices because they were salt of the earth people. Jack wore bib overalls on his property just like the rest of the farmers in Lindale, and Berneita's greatest joy was to give a tour of her canning room, where she'd put away the beans she'd grown.

As time passed in Lindale, Dad's godfather role expanded when young ministry leaders began showing up to pay him visits. He had come to be seen as a spiritual father in terms of innovative outreaches, and had befriended several progressive, adventuresome young leaders: Leland Paris of Youth with a Mission, Don Stephens of Mercy Ships, and Tony Salerno, Buddy Hicks, and Winkie Pratney of Agape Force. "They were all in their thirties, and they would come to Brother Dave for wisdom or prayer or counsel," Barb says. "Once they got here they would see the beauty of the countryside, and Brother Dave would encourage them to move. He even put them in touch with a realtor."

One by one, all of these ministries relocated to Lindale. Land was cheap, life was easy, and fellowship was ready-made. Soon word began to spread about the spiritual community forming in rural east Texas. Dallas Holm had formed a band, Praise, at Dad's suggestion, bringing a fuller sound to some of the ministry's outreaches, and now other musicians were also relocating — Silverwind, Keith Green, the Second Chapter of Acts. They all had their own property within miles of each other.

"There was never any big confab between them all," Barb recalls. "Each group had their own prayer meetings and Bible studies. But they all did visit, and they asked leaders in other ministries to come speak to theirs."

According to Barb, Keith Green frequently asked to meet with my dad. "It was always urgent," she says, " 'I've got to talk to Brother Dave, I'll be there at 3:15.' I'd call Brother Dave at his study, and he would come to the office. Sometimes Keith's excitement and his schedule collided, and he didn't show up. But Brother Dave loved him. He would say, 'I'll catch him next time.' "

Dad appreciated the zeal he saw in Keith Green — all out for Jesus, no compromise — but occasionally it could land Keith in a mess. I remember the fallout from Keith's concert at Oral Roberts University, where he called out students for drinking and partying, and was happy not to be invited back. I wasn't privy to Keith's conversations with my father, but from what I picked up, Dad's advice was, "Let's make sure this is all about Jesus. The repentance message is good, but it can't just be repent, repent, repent. We could rail against sin all day, but what good is it if we don't invite people to the Lamb of God?"

Keith's next article in his own ministry newsletter was titled "Just Because I'm Obnoxious Doesn't Make Me a Prophet."

Another figure relocated to Lindale who would serve as a great friend to my dad: Leonard Ravenhill. Since the early days at Teen Challenge, Leonard had made immense contributions to the body of Christ, especially in his study of revival. In the next few years, he would become as close to a mentor as my father would ever have.

Like my dad, Leonard became a respected elder statesman in the community. Young leaders paid him visits, thinking, "What a treasure to get a few minutes with this man." Three to four hours later, those guys would leave exhausted from the deepest, most intense spiritual challenge they'd ever had. Leonard was loving and respectful, but he could come across as hard. "You needed to have your ducks in a row pretty quickly," Craig Smith remembers with a grin, "because the sword could come out, and suddenly it's 'off with your head!' "

"How much do you pray?" Leonard would ask some young mentee.

"Two hours a day," the guy would answer. "Then you must pray three." Yet the emphasis was never on something measurable; Leonard was always addressing a person's passion for Christ. He was a tremendous scholar on the cross and on the sufficiency of Christ, so the things he offered weren't legalistic; they were reverent. And there was an authority in what he said, because it came from his own passionate devotion. In that sense, he and my dad were cut from the same cloth.

Yet my father revered Leonard for another reason. In his friend, Dad saw what generations of his family had looked for but never found. Leonard embodied the holiness values that my dad's parents had held dear, only without the legalism. He had a sober seriousness about life in God that attracted my father, but he also laughed and had joy.

My father ended up seeking out Leonard the way young guys sought Dad. "I need to go ask Leonard about this," he would say, grabbing his car keys, or, "I want to find out what Leonard's studying." It was a rare thing for my dad to be the mentee rather than the mentor, but he knew Leonard was a bit farther up the road in some important ways.

<hr />

ALTOGETHER, IT WAS AN UNUSUAL community by any standard — creative, innovative, passionate, and eclectic. The humble country churches in the area couldn't possibly feed the spiritual needs of all the young Christian progressives flooding into the area. Some ended up going to First Baptist nearby, whose pastor had become friends with my father. Then Dad started holding his own services for the crusade ministry staff, purposely scheduling them on Thursday nights so they wouldn't conflict with local churches. Leonard started a Friday night prayer meeting, where Keith Green came to play piano. As word spread about these spiritual gatherings, people drove from as far away as Dallas to attend.

Finally, someone in the community suggested, "Let's start a church," and almost overnight Lindale Community Church was birthed. "You walked in and there was Leonard Ravenhill," says Jerry Nance. "You might sit down next to Keith Green or talk to somebody in Silverwind. Next thing you know, Dallas Holm steps up and says, 'Here's a new song I wrote. I was in prayer the other night, and the Lord gave me this.'"

"At that first service, there may have been five hundred people," recalls Craig Smith. "They would just sit back and listen to the musicians whose records they owned and hear all the speakers whose books they'd read."

But Lindale Community Church didn't last long, at least in that form. Everyone in the community was a road warrior, having to travel for their own ministries. Besides, the church wasn't to everyone's taste. Not surprisingly, Keith Green had tired of it quickly. "Man, that was a circus," he told one musician friend. When someone asked Leonard Ravenhill for his assessment, he answered, "Too much salt." Craig Smith, who is a pastor today, saw Leonard's reasoning. "All these big hitters with wonderful giftings were gathered in one place," he says. "It was difficult to have what would actually be called a 'community church.'"

But it was a community nonetheless, one formed not in Nashville or Los Angeles or New York but in Lindale, Texas, of all places. "There were so many musicians who lived in that area, it was just crazy," Craig says. "Those are relationships I never would have had if it weren't for Brother Dave."

Jerry Nance, a recent Bible college graduate, soaked it up as it happened. "You went to a racquetball court and found yourself playing with Buck Herring," he says, referring to the Christian record producer. "You were hanging out with some of the fathers of contemporary Christian music. It was a pretty radical thing going on." Jerry learned something important from it all. "Everybody was traveling all over the world, and they'd come back to this little one-horse town," he says. "You just never dream of having a community like that. As a young man I had my blinders taken off. I had a chance to see world-scale ministry, to develop a world vision and not be afraid of it. I learned not to be intimidated by whatever the call of God involves."

The lesson served him well. Today Jerry travels worldwide as president of Global Teen Challenge, overseeing centers on five continents and making ministry decisions as boldly as his former boss did.

━━━

THE COMMUNITY'S REPUTATION — and the expanding influence of my dad's newsletters — grew such that Lindale became a kind of mecca in some people's minds. By this time his messages were being mailed to more than a million homes.

"People showed up all the time who felt led by God to come to work for Brother Dave," says Paul Annan. Paul had just become my dad's art director, literally crossing the street after having worked for Agape Force. He had been a major contributor to the design of that ministry's *Bullfrogs and Butterflies* children's albums, recorded by Barry McGuire and others.

"I'll never forget one family who looked just like the Beverly Hillbillies," Paul says. "They pulled up with all their stuff tied on top of the car. They'd felt led by God to come to work for Brother Dave's ministry." How my dad treated that family told Paul everything about his new boss. "Any other ministry would have told them, 'Sorry, we didn't ask you to come,' and shown them the door," he says. "Brother Dave talked to them. He told them, 'I wish you'd have called first, because I didn't hear God speak the same thing to my heart. I share your zeal, but we don't really have a place for you.' He explained how God usually speaks to both parties. Then he gave them five hundred dollars to help them on their way."

Other, more eccentric figures appeared. Staffers remember when three young "prophets" asked to prophesy over Dad and anoint his head with oil. Whether out of kindness or curiosity, Dad submitted, leading them to the kitchen in the ministry offices, where the cooking oil was kept. He sat in a chair, closed his eyes, and listened as the young men began praying. Soon streams of oil were dripping from his head, streaking down his cheeks, running past his chin, and pooling on his leather jacket. He realized they had emptied the entire contents of the jar.

Other visitors weren't as sincere or well-meaning. A local guy — very eccentric — parked a bus outside the ministry property and shouted through a bullhorn that Dad's ministry was diabolical. One day he was found rummaging through the garbage, looking for evidence of something damning. The ministry finally had to get a restraining order against him.

Any work with the scope of my father's is likely to attract eccentrics, but that's partly because the connection they sense is real. "Brother Dave's readers often felt he was talking directly to them," Barb says. "We received so many letters from people saying, 'It's like you're reading my mind. This message is exactly what I needed today.' He identified with their angst, their brokenness, their heartaches, their pain. The cover letters that accompanied his newsletter sermons became very pastoral, filled with grace and compassion. He shared his own battles, and people could identify with him."

Dad was the same way in his preaching. "He was self-disclosing in his sermons," Bob Rogers says. "When he preached on marriage, he talked about his own shortcomings, even about Gwen's struggles. He would tell the truth. When he did that, he was aces."

Vulnerable sermons like those, however, could be a mixed bag for our family. Sometimes when Dad preached, we heard something about ourselves for the first time — in front of thousands of people. "Whoa," we thought, "that happened in my parents' marriage, and I never knew about it?"

Some readers experienced Dad's newsletters as harsh and severe, bordering on legalistic. Uncle Don explains that effect: "He couldn't understand why people wouldn't choose a course of righteousness when given the opportunity. It just didn't compute to him, because life with God was good. Why choose sin? That was the energy behind his fire-and-brimstone messages. It also explains why he had compassion whenever somebody turned around."

Leonard Ravenhill's son David, who worked for Dad in the early days of Teen Challenge, reflects, "He didn't mingle much with the rest of the body of Christ. He was so singularly focused that I think he could be critical of things he didn't understand. He had a problem with people involved in the prophetic movement, for example. I did too, with certain aspects, but I think at times he threw the baby out with the bathwater."

"He wound up writing articles for Jimmy Swaggart that were anti-charismatic and anti-Catholic," historian Vinson Synan says. "He would help to start a movement but then would fight it as an archconservative, old-line Pentecostal. Renewal is so much greater than any of the weird excesses. Those happen in every religious movement; they just come with the territory. Dave Wilkerson was passionate and sincere, but at times he wasn't seeing the big picture."

Dad even publicly questioned Pat Boone, wondering if he had compromised his faith by being part of the Hollywood system. Dad made this statement during a rare appearance on a Christian talk show, calling out both Pat and Johnny Cash. When Pat heard about it, he respected Dad enough to call him in private. "Dave took my call right away and he was a little sheepish," Pat says. "He admitted, 'The Lord's been dealing with me about that, Pat. I'm sorry I said it. Your and Johnny's hearts are good, but young people think they can follow in your footsteps, and it's too dangerous.' I told him, 'Dave, how could I have played you if I weren't in the entertainment business?'" Their friendship remained solid, but the incident pointed to a deep discontent that had begun stirring in my dad.

———

IT'S POSSIBLE MY FATHER HAD his most profound impact through his responses to letters that people wrote to him. The ministry received letters by the thousands, and many were heartbreaking. A lot of hurting people evidently thought, "I'll write to David Wilkerson. He'll understand."

"People bared their souls," Barb says, "and no subject was taboo. When you're dealing with people honestly, you have to receive them honestly. He got a picture of how people's lives were being ravaged — physically, mentally, sexually, emotionally, financially — just every imaginable thing. A pastor writes because his son is on death row, no question about his guilt. How does he face it? Someone writes, 'My spouse is in a mental hospital. What does God say to me?' Elderly people wrote in, 'My husband pastored faithfully for forty years. Now he's gone through a long illness, and we have no money left.' People in need always weighed on his heart. Often he would call them on the phone with a comforting word."

Dad didn't hedge when he didn't have an answer, and he never offered false comfort. In those times, another gift emerged in him. "Brother Dave had a gift of saying the right word at the right time to encourage people," says Roger Jonker, Debi's husband. "He was a gifted, precise writer. Even in a card, he would say something very concisely and directly, and it ministered to people. I'm amazed how he could say so much in so few words."

"He wouldn't go into theological mysteries," Barb says. "He didn't know why some people were healed and others weren't. He preached a simple message, and he spoke to people in very basic terms. His bottom line was always, 'No sin is too awful to be forgiven,' and, 'Keep your eyes on Jesus. He holds you in his hand, and he will see you through.'"

There had to be an authority in those types of responses, and Dad's authority came from his own suffering. "He came across strong, but he was really very frail," Bob Rogers says. "I was a lot younger, so I wasn't the guy he would confide in at first, but in later years he was willing to. We spent evenings when he cried over Gwen's sickness and her depression and their struggles. One night in Pittsburgh he told me, 'I can't take it anymore.' He reached a point of brokenness, and he honestly was contemplating not going home. Yet he also knew that in the earlier years he was away from home all the time, not being a husband or a hands-on father. Brother Dave wasn't just frail physically; he was frail emotionally. That's why he would come across as harsh at times. I believe it was a defense mechanism, to hold people at a distance."

Barb had as close a perspective as anyone outside of our family. "Leaving Gwen for a crusade trip when she was sick and struggling was always difficult for him," she says. "Even in the midst of deadlines for books and newsletters and his busy ministry schedule, Gwen was always on his heart and mind. I don't know how he did it all."

When we think of spiritual callings, we rarely think of the one the apostle Paul received from God: "You get to suffer." Paul wrote again and again of the cities where he was privileged to suffer for the cross. I wonder: how many of us say no to a calling because it requires suffering?

After a certain period in my dad's life, at any point he could have hung it up. He could have sat back, written books, and taken it easy. At the very least he could have gone for a lot more comfort and a lot less sacrifice. But the suffering that God called him to is captured in a phrase that Dad used from time to time: "anguish of soul." One of his most enduring books came out of this period. *Have You Felt Like Giving Up Lately?* is still in print, offering solace from grocery store racks and airport kiosks.

Dad's own anguish of soul is why he kept reading those mountains of letters, kept subjecting himself to the crushing travails of a broken world in need of help, comfort, consolation, anything to remind people there is a God who cares. It's why he kept dictating all those responses to Barb; why he was compelled to pick up the phone and call a stranger who had written to him; why he ordered a check to be sent to an elderly couple or a single mother or a zealous young student. He understood. And he chose to say yes.

12
—

THE MAKING
OF A MAN OF GOD

Today we hear so much talk about success and how people obtained it. Success in biblical terms is vastly different. As we consider those whom God uses to stir their generations, we discover that the elements he used to shape them were torment, pain, sorrow, and failure.

Consider godly Job. Here was a man who failed in his motives. Job was proud of his own goodness, saying, "I have never harmed anyone. I have lived righteously." Indeed, as we read through this book, we wonder how God could have such high regard for such a proud man. Even though Job was godly, avoiding evil, he was clearly convinced of his own righteousness.

Next, consider David. Here was a man who failed in his morals, yet he still became a great man of God. Generations have been baffled by David's actions. How could a man so bold in godliness fail in such blatant immorality? This king ended up groveling in the dust. How could someone who fell so far end up, as Scripture says, "a man after God's own heart"?

Finally, consider Peter. Here was a man who failed in his mission. Peter had a vision and a calling; indeed, he was the one person Christ entrusted with the keys to his kingdom. Yet this same man ended up weeping on a hillside, having cursed and rejected the Christ he loved. In spite of so great a failure, Peter became a reconstructed man who served as God's spokesman at Pentecost, the birthing of the New Testament church.

What are the forces that go into the making of a man or woman of God? What do all followers of Jesus have in common? If we want God's touch in our lives, what inner struggles do we all face? And what are the forces and pressures that God uses to produce righteousness in us? We dare not pray, "Use me, Jesus," or, "Lord, put your hand on me," unless we are willing to face what will surely come.

— FROM THE SERMON "THE MAKING OF A MAN OF GOD"

STEVE HILL WAS THOUGHT TO be dying in a Dallas hospital when he received the news of my father's death in April 2011. By then, Steve had battled melanoma for almost four years. Facing round after grinding round of chemotherapy, his body had absorbed the toxic effects. Now his organs were shutting down, and he was told he had only days to live.

Steve didn't know what year it was. He couldn't remember his wife's name. He didn't understand what anyone in the room was saying to him. Then, when someone gave him the news about my father, he understood. "I cried my eyes out," Steve says.

Steve Hill lived for three more years. I received the news of his passing on the day I was editing this very paragraph, in March 2014. You may recognize Steve's name as coleader of the Brownsville Revival, the phenomenon that took place in an Assemblies of God church in Pensacola, Florida, from 1995 to 2000. During those five years, Steve preached on most nights at the Brownsville gatherings, where some two hundred thousand people gave their lives to Christ.

"I wanted to carry his mantle," Steve says of my dad. "I wanted to win people to Jesus. As students, we would travel with him in the crusades — to high school auditoriums, big arenas, you name it. Every time he stood up, he had something to say, and he said it with authority. I wanted that passion — to tell it like it is, no matter what anybody thinks.

I'd stand there watching him and say, 'Jesus, would you let me do that one day?'"

Revival was a subject on which my father and his good friend Leonard Ravenhill did not share a bond. Dad questioned the worth of most revivals. "They usually last two to five years, and then they're gone," he said. And what is left? What is the quality of commitment by those who have chosen to follow Jesus? What condition are churches left in? Does the fruit of the experience last? Has it been a work worthy of God's name, or a temporal spectacle? "I don't want a visitation," Dad often said, "I want a habitation."

Dad did not endorse the Brownsville Revival, but he did endorse Steve Hill. "I support people, not projects," he would say. He may have had reservations about what took place in Pensacola, but he never had any reservations about Steve Hill. It's because he trained him himself in a ministry program he founded called Twin Oaks Leadership Academy.

"I loved that school," says Roger Hayslip. Like Steve Hill, Roger was a graduate of the yearlong training program Dad started in 1976 for graduates of Teen Challenge. That year, farmers driving along Highway 16 near Lindale began to see buildings being constructed between the well-spaced hills of the ranch: a dormitory, a gymnasium, another dormitory. My dad had announced the program in his newsletter: twenty-five women and twenty-five men would be selected from across the country, young leaders who showed promise for ministry, whether for Teen Challenge, evangelism, or missions.

"Twin Oaks was spot on for what it purported to do," Roger Hayslip says, "which was to teach people how to work with others who have life-controlling problems. I don't think anyone else could have done that kind of specialized training in drug addiction, alcoholism, depression. Maybe from a professional standpoint, but from a ministry standpoint, nobody ever did as good a job as Brother Dave in reaching out to people from that background and lifestyle."

Everyone who walked through the doors of Twin Oaks Leadership Academy came from "that background and lifestyle." When fall arrived that year, the ranch property was crawling with fifty former addicts who had seen more than their share of life's underside. "It scared Lindale to death," Barb Mackery remembers. "People were told, 'This man is bringing drug addicts to your community.'"

It's true that Twin Oaks students weren't standard-issue college enrollees. "You have to be smart to be a drug addict," Uncle Don has always maintained. "That's why former addicts make such good leaders." As an addict, you have to be alert, to be able to read people, to know your surroundings, to bring in funds.

That kind of mind would respond to a clear-eyed truth-teller like my dad. "One thing those people always liked about Brother Dave is that he told it like it is," Roger Hayslip says, "and he really didn't care what the pope or the president had to say about it. A lot of people say you have to come from that background to be able to relate to it and understand it, and there's some truth to that. But Brother Dave never drank a drop of liquor in his life, and yet he connected with the people always."

❙━❙

TWIN OAKS LEADERSHIP ACADEMY BEGAN just in time for my uncle Don. He had been dealing with a growing problem in Teen Challenge: graduates who showed potential in ministry were leaving the program one day and being thrust into leadership roles the next. Most weren't mature enough to handle it. Dad's dream of a leadership academy was the perfect answer. He hired Charles Snow, who later became Dean of Doctoral Studies at Oral Roberts University, as director and academic dean. The faculty included twenty-one-year-old Jerry Nance and Roger Jonker, who had just married my sister Debi. Both men were fresh out of college. "I was the gym teacher," laughs Roger, who also was dean of students. "I was in charge of recreational activities. We put together some pretty competitive games with the other ministries in the area."

"We trained them in many areas," Barb Mackery says. "Bible, evangelism, music, counseling, business. This was before we had computers in our office, so we even had a typing class."

Dad had a row of offices built in storefront style with a boardwalk, and he enlisted Paul Annan to design it with a western motif in keeping with the ranch theme. "We had a barbershop where Gwen cut the students' hair," Roger Jonker says. "And Dr. Rice held a weekly clinic."

With fifty students on-site, the school had to hire a full-time cook. A catfish pond was on the property when Dad bought it, so it was put to use to supply meals. "You could throw your line into the center of a floating styrofoam square and just pull them in," Roger Jonker says. "In a short time you had enough catfish to feed fifty students."

Jerry Nance, fresh out of Bible college, remembers walking into the classroom that fall to teach his first Bible course. "Every student was older than I was, and they'd had lots of experiences I'd never even heard of," he says. "But the spiritual climate was amazing. Here were fifty people from all different backgrounds — blacks, Hispanics, whites, all learning and growing together. It was the most culturally warm setting."

It provided a lot of fun for me. By day, I was a student at Lindale High, mingling with sweet-natured classmates, but after school, I was a ranch crew chief supervising a dozen street-smart city guys. After three years in the country, I knew my way around ranch life. People were asking me to kill snakes, repair the tractor, or show them a hay-baling technique that wouldn't kill them in hundred-degree heat. But heading up a crew of these guys was a different kind of challenge. They were always plotting, scheming, playing tricks on each other. One minute I was rolling on the ground laughing at their jokes and the next I was breaking up a fistfight. It all must have looked a little weird to the locals driving by.

The environment became even richer when Agape Force staff and YWAM kids came to the campus gym to play basketball. The competition was intense and the fellowship was great, benefits that hopefully made up for the cultural nightmare some of the Twin Oaks students experienced. They had come from LA, New York, Boston, all kinds of urban areas to a town with one blinking intersection light.

As one of their assignments, the students had to preach at area churches. One student's New England accent was so thick the locals thought he was from a foreign country. Others had to restrain themselves from raising their hands and crying out to Jesus during worship, out of respect for the small, country church congregations. Dad brought in Tim and LaDonna Johnson, a musical couple who played in Tammy Wynette's band, to help teach the students to sing. "They would take the students into these little churches, which could make for some funny situations," Jerry Nance says. "But the next thing you knew, those same students were onstage in a big coliseum singing 'Rise Again' with Dallas Holm."

———•

MY DAD KNEW HIS STRENGTHS, and discipling was a role he left to others. Since the days of Nicky Cruz, a lot of guys had looked to my dad as a spiritual father, but he wasn't one to sit down and teach anybody about sanctification. Basically, he gave you direction, prayed for you, and left the rest up to the Holy Spirit.

When I began to seriously explore God's ways as a teenager, I patterned myself after my dad. He'd told me stories of going into the woods to meet with the Lord, so that's what I thought I was supposed to do. After school, I would load a little wooden crate with my Bible, a notebook, and some Navigators course books and set out for the woods near our house. I'd use the crate as a chair and spend an hour or two trying to learn about the Lord.

But I benefited most from my time with others. One mentor was Bob Rogers, who had given me the Navigators books and was a great guy to meet with one-on-one. Paul Annan and his wife, Miriam, opened up their home for youth meetings. It was a great advantage for us to have adults like those around who worked full time in youth ministry.

I'm sure Dad was grateful for the discipleship I received by others. His own attitude was, "I go to the Lord for everything. If I'm going to be a halfway decent father, he'll give me what I need for that." He was comfortable in his own skin, and he wanted us to be too. That's why he always told my siblings and me, "Be yourself." He didn't want us to be mini David Wilkersons who dressed like him or tried to be like him.

Hearing that from him was important to me, because I didn't like what I saw in a lot of other father-son relationships in evangelist families. Often the son was trying to look like some version of the father, as if he were being groomed as a successor. On the other hand, I knew a lot of evangelists' kids who couldn't stand their dads. "He's gone all the time," they said. "He can't relate to me." Some of them turned wild, running away from faith altogether.

If I was going to become a preacher, I didn't want to be forced into any image. I thought, "If that's the path, forget it. I'll work on a ranch." My dad was a dress-suit guy, and I was a jeans guy. He teased me about my wardrobe, but it was always good-natured; he never mandated anything like that for me. He was saying, in effect, "I believe in you, and you can do this by being yourself. You don't have to do it by trying to be like me."

I needed that encouragement. And I needed my dad's confidence because I'd been haunted by something ever since our childhood days in Long Island.

Dad had spent time in the mountains praying. "I've been seeking the Lord about all of you," he told us when he returned. He sat us down in a circle to tell us what God had shown him. I remember that Mom wasn't there. "Debi, you'll have a heart for missions, and you'll marry a man of God. Bonnie, you're going to have creative skills. Greg, God is going to use you in evangelism and speaking." Dad then turned to me and put his hand on my shoulder. "Gary, you're going to make it through."

Wait a minute, what? I thought. *Time out! What does that mean?* Dad didn't explain himself, and I was crushed. Was this all that my Abrahamic blessing amounted to — surviving?

That experience didn't just hurt. It made success in ministry my idol for many years.

———

EVERY ADOLESCENT HAS TO PUT to death the notion of his parents' being perfect. My siblings and I were long past that by the time we were in Lindale, but it helped when my dad took me aside to pointedly help me with the issue. "Right now you see me as a man who's made a good impact on the world," he said. "But if you haven't already, you're going to see many failures in me. Don't be surprised at that."

As a parent myself, I know now why he was telling me this. No parent wants to disappoint his or her kids, but it's inevitable. You can try to prepare them, but they're never fully ready to experience your shortcomings.

When I had played basketball as a kid in Long Island, I made an all-star team, and everyone seemed to think I showed promise. But for some reason, my dad never came to any of my games. That puzzled me because

I knew he liked basketball. In Lindale, I would bring home some of my high school teammates, and Dad would play with us. He had a great outside shot — in fact, he had to be guarded out to twenty feet — but he still never came to any of my games, not one. I never asked him why.

As I think about the times I felt shortchanged by him, I suspect he knew something that I didn't. It was as if he didn't want to encourage me in an area where he knew I was going to be disappointed. That happened once when Dallas Holm invited me to come over and play guitar with him. Talk about being excited! But when I told Dad about it, his response was, "Music is a tough career. You don't really like music that much, do you? It's a hard field to break into." I wasn't thinking in terms of a career; I just felt privileged to play with Dallas. But the truth is Dad never seemed excited about any of the things I was interested in.

By the same token, Dad didn't get too concerned over things such as bad grades. I wasn't a great student, but then he hadn't been a great one either. When I brought home a D on a report card, his attitude was, "Don't worry about it. You're not doing great at this right now, but you're going to be okay." I was always relieved to hear that, but it would have been nicer if he had helped me with my homework.

At a certain point, people began asking me what it was like to grow up in David Wilkerson's home. I was asked that probably a thousand times as a teenager. I answered, "I don't know. It's the only home I've grown up in." The question was an emotionally mixed bag for me. "Yes, he really is the man you think he is," I wanted to say. "He really does love God the way the books portray, and it's great that God can use him like that. But I wish God would use him a little bit more in my life."

When it came to hearing God's call on our lives, my dad and I couldn't have been more different. To him, you almost had to have an angelic visitation and hear trumpets blowing. It didn't happen that way for me. Maybe my calling was projected onto me, because people always asked me, "Tell me about your ministry calling." But I definitely felt one, and I told my dad about it.

He didn't exactly do backflips, but he didn't make it into a heavy moment either. He didn't ask questions such as, "Son, do you know what you're getting into?" Or, "Do you realize the gravity of this?" Honestly, I had no idea what was going on inside his head as I sat across from him at that pivotal moment in my life. Was he doubtful? Was he looking down the long road, wondering what kind of preacher I would be? Was he worried about how I could weather the ups and downs?

He just listened, and he quietly asked me a few questions. "Are you sure you heard from the Lord? That's good, son." It was a very brief exchange. Finally he told me, "Okay, I'll pray for you. We're going to support what God has called you to do." Those would be his roles in my calling as a minster of Christ's gospel. He didn't say, "Let's sit together once a week so I can share with you about life in ministry." Yet what he did was very characteristic: he took action. He scheduled me to deliver a sermon at the ministry staff's Thursday night church service. In short, I was being thrown into the deep end of the pool.

There were probably a hundred or so people there that night, mostly ministry staff and Twin Oaks students, along with a few people from the community. As my dad introduced me, I reviewed my sermon notes. I wanted to do well, but I was only slightly nervous; mostly I was confident. Bob Rogers had shown me how to put together a three-point sermon, and I was going to preach on the three friends of Job.

"This is my son, Gary," I heard Dad say. He then repeated something that he said every time he introduced me: "He's never given me a day of trouble in his life." That had gotten to be annoying. He always complimented me on my gentle spirit, too, but that was never what I wanted to hear. *Don't call me gentle*, I thought. *I'm bold and strong! Call my sisters gentle, not me.*

I can honestly say I was myself in the pulpit that night, and it felt good. Afterward, a sweet, older woman was the very first person to tell me something I would hear for years: "You sure don't preach like your dad."

"Thank you," I answered.

She looked a little surprised.

"My dad has always taught me to be myself — not to try to be like him or Billy Graham or anyone else, just myself."

Dad offered his own take on my sermon. "That was great," he told me. "Good job." But the most helpful thing I got from him came weeks afterward, when I overheard him telling his friends, "I'd never seen that particular insight on Job before." More than anything else, that comment set my heart in motion for ministry.

My sister Bonnie had felt a call to ministry too. She had gotten a job as children's minister at a church in Fort Worth where she met her future husband, Roger Hayslip. Bonnie threw herself into ministry full force, and if you know my sister, that's quite a bit of force.

Everyone knows that Bonnie is close to my dad in temperament, more so than the rest of us kids. That may be one reason why our dad's emotional reticence cut more deeply with her than with me. "I told some of my best friends that my dad never praised me," Bonnie says. "They said, 'Sure he does. We hear him praise you all the time.' But it was never to me personally. I just wanted him to be proud."

ONE WORD WE ALL USED to describe our dad was *patriarchal*, because his "Christian godfather" style extended to us kids. In certain areas, Dad was very directive — too directive, in fact — and we grew to depend on him for it. On the one hand, he was just trying to be helpful; he took his mantle as our father seriously. On the other hand, that trait ran counter to the reliance on God he knew we needed for ourselves.

I've compared notes with my siblings on this, and our dad often spoke with a very real authority — God's authority, drawn from that "other conversation" — so we learned to listen to him rather than listen to the Lord for ourselves. We couldn't argue with his intuition or rationale because it was usually right on. But we were always left wondering, "Did I just hear from God, or from my dad?"

As we matured, we grew to discern better when the "switch" was on — when Dad heard something in his spirit that was indeed from God. Suddenly the atmosphere changed and we knew we were on holy ground. Those moments were all too real, and yet it was still all too easy for us to let Dad make decisions for us because he always knew what to do.

When Roger Jonker was still a college student just beginning to date Debi, he encountered my Dad's directive nature right away. "After dinner we were all sitting in the living room," Roger says. "He stood up, pointed to Debi and me, and said, 'I want to talk to you two.'"

Dad led them into the bedroom he used as his office, where they all sat cross-legged on the floor. Roger recalls, "His first question was, 'What are your intentions with my daughter?' Then, 'Do you love her?' I was nervous as it was, but now I got really nervous. My mind was racing and my voice went up about eight octaves. I said, 'Well, I've only known her three weeks.' I told him I was going to finish my schooling, get going in a career, and then think about getting married. I thought he'd be impressed. Instead, he said, 'Why wait so long?'"

Dad told us he liked Roger because he didn't try to impress him. "The truth is I was nervous around him," Roger says. "All the other guys Debi brought home were fascinated by him and would ignore her. I was the opposite; I didn't want to be around him." Even more unnerving was that Dad had called Roger's pastor. "He did his homework," Roger says. "He knew my pastor and talked with him."

The same thing happened with my sister Bonnie. "I don't know how he did it, but every guy I dated, he always knew the background," she says. "I was embarrassed because he would be shaking the guy's hand for the first time, saying, 'Oh yes, you play football, you do this, you do that.' I was shocked, thinking, 'Where did you get that information?'"

———

EVER SINCE THE SIXTIES, DAD'S ministry staff had urged him to find a hobby. He had a kind of hobby in his real estate pursuits, but Dad finally found his true outlet in classic cars. He spent his personal income on what he'd fixated on since childhood: antique and collectible cars. Dad could get outright giddy over them.

"He told me about buying that Messerschmitt back in the fifties in Philipsburg," Bob Rogers says. "Talk about somebody vicariously living a moment of glee. His eyes lit up. It was materialism in a way you don't normally think of. He wasn't obsessed with impressing you by having a great car; he was just fascinated with the crafting and the uniqueness of them."

"He was definitely a car guy," says Barry Meguiar, the auto products mogul from California. Barry hosts *Car Crazy*, a TV program that showcases the kind of cars Dad loved. "The funny thing was, Dave never wanted to admit he was a car guy. He didn't want to think of himself as a materialist. He was so hard on himself."

On the bus, I would find buried underneath Dad's Bible and books a copy of *Motor Trend* magazine. I thought, "Why hide it, Dad? Come on, relax, enjoy this." But I respected that he didn't want to live for himself. I also knew that whatever car he bought, he would eventually either sell it and give the money toward missions, or he would give the car away to some person in need.

"He didn't lose money," Barry says. "He always got a car at the right price and he always sold it for more. He was extraordinary that way. God just blessed everything that went through his hands."

Still, Dad was never without guilt over his enthusiasm. When he bought a car, he always saw himself as having given in to temptation. Paul Annan remembers one purchase that didn't even make it home. "He bought the car in Dallas and had started for Lindale," Paul says. "But he felt horribly convicted, so he turned around and took the car back under some loophole. Well, on the way home, he drove by a different dealership, either BMW or Mercedes. The next thing you know, he's driving home in one, and this time he made it all the way home. But as soon as he got out of the car, he gave the car keys to a staff member and said, 'You take it back.'"

"He had a fascinating personal involvement with money," says Dad's old friend John Sherrill. "David and I spent a long time talking about it because at one time we were going to do a book together about money." John was visiting at Twin Oaks when Dad showed him the barn where he preserved the cars. "These were beautiful old classics, immaculately kept," John says. "David said, 'One day I'm going to sell these cars. It's not really the right place for me to put my money.' So he just off and sold them. That comes across as a rash decision, but I'm sure it was not. It came out of a spiritual foundation in him. David knew those cars had become a 'treasure' in his heart. He caught himself and said, 'I won't allow that.'

"I knew that David had a philosophy about money," John reflects. "That's what the book was going to be about. Money was not a 'thing' to him; it was a flow. If you hoarded it and kept it dammed up as a security against tomorrow, it would stagnate and become less useful. But if you kept it as a flow, so that as it came in, it went out very quickly, then it would be useful. I think what bothered him about the cars was that they were damming up things, not as security but as something personal. They had to go out."

Mostly, Dad wanted to keep his testimony clean. He didn't want even the appearance of taking ministry money to buy expensive things, when elderly people surviving on Social Security were sending ten-dollar checks to support the ministry. Dad sold the cars. "He wanted to squelch any rumor about his lifestyle," Paul Annan says. "It wasn't until years later, when I served on the board, that I discovered what he had done. He took all the profits and put them into a feeding program in Haiti."

———

AROUND THIS TIME, DAD BEGAN receiving offers of honorary doctorates from colleges in recognition of his ministry work. "He graciously declined them," Barb Mackery says.

"He laughed when Central Bible College named him alumnus of the year," Bob Rogers says. Dad's reaction revealed his low assessment of himself as a student of the Bible. "I don't think Brother Dave ever would have considered himself a scholar, but he was immersed in the Bible," David Patterson remembers. "From the time I began to travel with him in '67, I was impressed at what a strong and serious student of the Word he was. Right after Carol and I moved to New York, I got a look into the Bible he used as a pastor in Philipsburg. Literally every page from Genesis to Revelation was filled with underlined verses and notes in the margins."

When Dad spent time in the Scriptures, he wasn't looking to gain breadth of knowledge; he was searching to know the ways of God. That knowledge of God's character came across powerfully in his crusades. "Once we were in Columbia, South Carolina, and a Baptist pastor on the local crusade board got upset with Brother Dave," David Patterson recalls. "He told me, 'I've never heard anyone preach with less of the Word and yet see such great results.' I told him, 'There's a point of misunderstanding here. Brother Dave isn't quoting the King James verbatim.

He takes the Word and puts it into a contemporary story. But he's still sharing God's Word and biblical truth.' Hard-shell Baptists didn't find that comforting."

Dad received other invitations because of his notoriety, but he declined most of them. When Billy Graham invited him for a visit at his home in Montreat, North Carolina, I begged my father to go and take me with him. Dad wouldn't do it. He said, "Billy gets so many people coming to have their picture taken with him. He doesn't need one more day like that."

"Brother Dave shunned the idea of celebrity, including his own," Barb says. "He didn't want to be seen as playing into that. He had the highest respect for Billy Graham, but he had equally high respect for God's hidden treasures, those who labored for the Lord without public recognition."

One of those treasures was a Lutheran nun named Basilea Schlink, founder of the Evangelical Sisterhood of Mary in Darmstadt, Germany. Dad had been stirred by her compelling writings on Christ, and when he conducted crusades in Germany, he hired a van to take the team to Darmstadt to visit the sisters. He remained friends with Sister Basilea until her death in 2001. He also visited two of the sisterhood's other ministries, one on the Mount of Olives in Israel and one in Phoenix, Arizona. "They're prayer warriors," Barb says. "That's what they do — pray. He had great affection for these sacrificial women who were so in love with Jesus, who wept with the burden of God's heart over sin, and who reached out to broken humanity."

At the same time, Dad turned down invitations from presidents. The first came from Gerald Ford and the second from Jimmy Carter. "We knew these were public relations meetings," says Uncle Don, who went in Dad's stead. "David would avoid them for that reason. He didn't want to be seen in any way as political." This was at the height of political fervor among evangelicals. The Religious Right was just taking shape, and Uncle Don remembers meeting Jerry Falwell in President Carter's cabinet room. But Dad wanted no part of it. "He felt that a minister can't have a voice for the gospel if he's pigeonholed in any of that," Uncle Don says, "so David drew a line for himself."

Strangely enough, my uncle rarely heard my father mention politics. "He would read about it and keep up on it," Uncle Don says, "but he would see it the way a prophet does. He would speak out on certain issues, like homosexuality, but he would never make that his pulpit or platform. For him, judgment comes more because of the church's condition than because of what nonbelievers do. There are men and women of God who are meant to enter the political arena and make a difference, the Chuck Colsons. But the role of the pastor is to preach a biblical worldview, not a political one."

Barb may put it best about Dad: "Politics to him was a spiritual interruption," she says. "One person on staff was up in arms over a certain president's election, but Brother Dave told him, 'Don't go there. Don't let that get in your spirit.'"

As for homosexuality, my dad's view could be summed up pretty simply. He didn't see it as a category of sin all its own, the way some evangelicals do. He saw it as sexual sin strictly on biblical grounds. Yet overriding all of this was Dad's love for people. He wanted to preach a message that was redemptive and reconciling to God, that wouldn't keep anyone away from the church. Dating back to his books in the midsixties, Dad described his moving encounters with lesbians and gay men long before there was a political issue surrounding it all.

I saw him demonstrate amazing love whenever we did street outreaches in San Francisco's Polk and Castro districts. Sometimes gays brought signs to our rallies accusing Dad of bigotry and hatred, but he remained full of grace. Over the years when he wrote about the rise of militant homosexuality, he noted it as a sign of the times, never as a sign that God didn't love gay people.

When he himself failed to love, he owned up to it. He was in Boston once to preach for Rodney Hart, director of Teen Challenge in New England, who started a church in a poor, mostly African American and Hispanic neighborhood. The gay community had begun to move in, and they gave Rodney a hard time, often yelling at him to go home. When Dad arrived to preach, a gauntlet of gays and lesbians had lined up at the fence around the church. They yelled at Dad, calling him all kinds of names, and Rodney saw my dad turn visibly angry. When he reached the door of the church, Dad turned around red-faced and shouted, "You should come to the meeting tonight. I'm preaching a special message for people like you."

It was not my father's finest hour. Once inside, he buried his face in his hands and told Rodney, "I can't believe I did that. I'm miserable."

Some of the gay protesters came to the service that night. Dad preached a message of compassion, reconciliation, and brokenness — notably his own. He even told what had happened. "Earlier today I was being harassed, and I reacted wrongly," he confessed. "I said things I shouldn't have said, and I apologize for that. I came here to show the love of Christ, not my own anger."

How he owned up that night was a consistent trait in my father, according to Barb Mackery. "If he did something wrong publicly, he apologized for it publicly," she says.

———

WHEN THINGS WERE GOING WELL for my father — when he was not enduring pain of some kind and he was immersed in ministry activity — he was prone to having dry spells. "With so many irons in the fire and God's blessing on his ministry, his passion for intimate prayer waned," Barb explains. "He grew weary of the busyness that robbed that." In those times, Dad stopped to reassess. "Sometimes his thought was, 'Retreat for prayer,'" Barb says. "At other times it was, 'Look for property for a prayer retreat.' He longed for times when he would pour out his heart to the Lord and hear his voice." Next to suffering, dryness was Dad's most compelling catalyst for prayer.

"I'll never forget his graduation message to us," said Steve Hill. "Twin Oaks was Harvard to us, and we were ready to receive our charge. We were a bunch of ex-druggies ready to be sent out like Elijah and John the Baptist." Also receiving Dad's charge were Bill Lenz, who became pastor of Christ the Rock Church, a megachurch in Appleton, Wisconsin; and Rick Hagans, whose Harvest Evangelism ministry in Opelika, Alabama, made him a candidate for one of the state's high political offices.

"We were all in the cafeteria, which was the chapel area, in our graduation robes," Steve said. "Brother Dave pointed at us and said, 'Thou shalt have spells.' That was his message to us. He spoke about all the hard times we were going to go through. 'There will be times when you don't feel the presence of God. There will be times when you stand behind the pulpit and he is not there. There will be times when you go to your quiet place to seek him and you can't sense his presence anymore. You're going to have spells. I'm telling you to fight through them in faith.'

"I lapped that up like a thirsty dog," Steve said. "Look at me now — six years of melanoma. The most important thing David Wilkerson ever did for me was when he spoke on 'Thou Shalt Have Spells.' I needed to hear all of it, because I've leaned on that message. Thirty years later, I'm going through the hardest trial of my life. Brother Dave is gone now, but it's as if he's sitting here with his arms around me, saying, 'Son, you're going to make it.'"

Dad had spoken that message with very real authority. Around that time, my sister Debi was diagnosed with cancer as serious as my mother's had been. Part of Debi's stomach had to be removed as a result of the treatment. "He agonized," Barb says of Dad's reaction to the news. "He just wanted to hold and protect her." Our family had been handed another cup of pain.

———

To every true man or woman of God there will come a cup of pain. Consider Christ's prayer in the garden: "O my Father, if it be possible, let this cup pass from me: nevertheless not as I will, but as thou wilt" (Matt. 26:39). Jesus' entire ministry was about doing the will of his Father. Now, at Gethsemane, whatever was in the cup Jesus drank caused him to sweat great drops of blood. He cried out, "Oh, God, if it is possible at all, relieve me of this burden. It's too heavy for me. I would rather let it pass...."

So, you want to be a man or woman of God? You want the hand of the Lord on you? You are going to be served a cup of pain. You will lie in a bed of tears. You'll weep not so much at physical pain but at something much worse than that. I'm speaking of the pain of being bruised and rejected by friends. It is the pain of parents when children trample their hearts and become strangers to them. It is the pain between a husband and wife when brick walls are built up between them. The tragic turmoil that comes, the restless, sleepless nights — knowing that God is real, that you are walking in his Spirit, that you are loving Jesus with all that is in you … and yet you are forced to drink a cup of pain.

Yet we cannot run from this cup. Peter tried to drive away affliction in his flesh. He wielded a sword at Gethsemane, telling Jesus in effect, "Master, you don't have to go through this. I'll keep them at bay while you make your escape." Many Christians today have the same attitude. They take sword in hand to try to turn away afflictions, saying, "I don't have to face this. My God is a good God!"

I believe God is faithful. But Jesus tells us we cannot run from our cup of pain. He commanded Peter, "Put up your sword. That is not my Father's way. Live by your sword and you will die by it." Then he stated, "The cup which my Father hath given me, shall I not drink it?" (John 18:11).

When you trust the One who is serving you this cup — when you see his purpose behind your suffering — then you are able to drink it. It may burn, sear, and scar you, but don't be afraid, for your Father holds the cup. You are not drinking death but life.

— FROM "THE MAKING OF A MAN OF GOD"

Part Six

REPENTANCE

Men give advice; God gives guidance.

— *Leonard Ravenhill*

13
—
SHUTTING DOWN

Dad never escaped the thought that he was going to die young. In 1982 he began writing a manuscript he intended to publish, presenting a rather urgent revelation of his. Its working title was *I Renounce This World*, and he dedicated it to us, his children, and to his grandchildren.

Dad's exhortation to us read in part, "Don't live for the world. Live every waking hour as if it were your last. The true revelation of Christ belongs to those who live as pilgrims here on earth." Then he penned the following entry, all in longhand:

> I've often wondered what a person does when he knows death is coming. I've asked people who were about to die what difference it made in their lives. Did they pray more? Did they live out each hour with more reality? Did they change their lifestyle? Did material things lose their value? Did love mean more or less? Did Christ become more real? What changes took place? And now, I will learn from firsthand experience.
>
> I was praying late at night, secluded in my prayer hideaway in Hot Springs, Arkansas. For months God has been stripping me down, taking me lower and lower, trying to bring me to a place of total surrender to his will.
>
> The ranch at Lindale was now gone. Most of my staff was gone. My crusade schedule stopped, my future plans all shelved. All I

had was an inner hunger to spend time alone with my Lord.

I spent the day reading the Word. Fasting: about midnight I prostrated myself on the floor, calling on God to lead me deeper into a revelation of Christ. My soul cried out for a spirit of wisdom and understanding in the knowledge of Christ.

A powerful, relaxing spirit began to descend on me. I could feel the warmth, the ecstasy, and yes — an awesome fear. The presence of the Lord was being manifested. It was so still — so relaxing. And then the still, small voice.

"David. Fear not, but rejoice. You will not live to see your fifty-fifth birthday. You have less than three years of ministry left. You will have your eyes opened to eternal values. All that is material, earthly has no meaning whatsoever. All material things are unreal.

"You will live as a dying man, but you will enter into the rest of eternal life. Make each day count. Waste no time. Judge yourself that you be not judged. Sustain your spiritual vision with the knowledge that you must stand before the judgment seat of Christ and give an account of all you say and do. Rejoice — because as you near the time of departure, you will yearn to go. It will not be difficult. You will lose your fear of death. It will be but a passage into the presence of the Lord. You will not be afraid. Nothing will hold you. All earthly, temporal things will lose their value. Record your journey and all the Spirit says to you. Your living and dying will bring glory to his name."

Dad wrote this entry on August 19. It's possible to read his subsequent entry, on September 1, through a lens of humor: "I may have made a mistake. I told of my divine summons in my sermon in Winnipeg a few nights ago. It was just a few sentences, but it caused a lot of concern.... My wife is in turmoil.... She cannot comprehend why I did not keep this to myself.... I see now how it could be a source of pride."

My dad was utterly sincere about this notion of dying early. He filled fifty pages in his notebook, writing almost daily over the next two months. My mom was equally sincere in her reaction to it of frustration and confusion. It's fair to say she spoke for all of us in the family.

"It was just one more thing to be depressed about," Bonnie says. "I remember sitting in a service when he was preaching, thinking, 'He's going to die in three years?' I thought it was baloney, and I told him."

Dad actually gathered his sons and sons-in-law to tell us. "He was convinced, and it was a serious conversation," says Roger Hayslip. "He was preparing us, saying, 'You're going to have to carry on this ministry.' We all just kind of rolled our eyes. He had also just told us Gary Hart was going to be the next president."

It's not hard to see where this was coming from with Dad. He had just turned fifty-one years old, and as Bonnie says, "Grandpa died early, so he always thought he was going to." Some attributed this conviction to Dad's naturally gloomy outlook. But then Uncle Don, who's sunny by comparison, began having the same fears for himself. He started voicing his fears to Aunt Cindy, telling her he thought he was going to die as he approached his fiftieth birthday. Finally she asked him, "Didn't your dad die just past fifty?"

"Yes," Uncle Don mused. And with that realization, his fear vanished. As soon as it was brought to light from his subconscious, it lost its power.

In his own way, Dad was also trying to deal with his persistent thoughts of death by bringing them to light. The problem was, he spiritualized those thoughts — and then preached about them!

———

YOU MIGHT HAVE NOTICED IN his journal entry that Dad mentions the ranch had been sold. "Twin Oaks strained him," Bob Rogers says. "It was one of the few times when he had to get serious about fundraising. The academy was on a whole different level of funding than he was prepared for. He never wanted to be a hard-sell fundraiser, but he was forced into that role, and he didn't like it."

Evidently, one of Dad's first solutions to saving money was to disband Dallas Holm's band, Praise. Dad wanted Dallas to go back to opening for him solo. But Dallas didn't feel right about it; he felt a deep loyalty to the band members, so he told Dad no. My father didn't like hearing no, and this time Dallas's no wasn't a boardroom joke. Dallas is circumspect today about the details of that volatile meeting with Dad, but the upshot of it was that after ten years, he and my father parted ways.

"That left a great void in Brother Dave's heart," Bob Roger says. "Dallas was as close to being a son to him as any non-family member could be. His heart was connected to him. But Brother Dave could not bend Dallas, and the truth is he shouldn't have."

Other winds of change had been blowing. When the crusade bus pulled up to one venue, the marquee read "Dallas Holm and Praise," and on the line below it, in smaller letters, "with David Wilkerson." The team also had begun noticing people trickling out of the auditoriums after the band finished their segment. "How can that not affect you if you're Brother Dave?" Bob says.

Yet other forces were at work beyond anyone's ability to control. "Crusade culture in America was dying," Bob says. Over fifteen years, David Wilkerson Youth Crusades had seen its audiences change from despairing, on-the-brink teenagers to families on the other side of the Jesus Movement. The latter audiences were mainly adults looking to be reinforced in biblical convictions they already held.

Meanwhile, Christian television was on the rise. The Trinity Broadcasting Network and PTL Television Network with Jim and Tammy Faye Bakker had joined the ranks of CBN, Pat Robertson's cable network. Suddenly there were three times as many TV guest slots as before, offering platforms to anyone who had a worthwhile message to share.

"Naturally, it was in my mind to keep Brother Dave in front of more than two thousand people a night, but he wouldn't go on TV," says Bob Rogers. "It drove me crazy because of all the opportunities. TBN would have taken him twice a month if he would have gone. PTL would have taken him as many times as he wanted. But I was asking him to do things he wasn't supposed to do. He told me, 'God gave me a national pulpit. If he wants me to sustain it, he'll have to do it. I won't lift a finger.' That's why I loved and respected him. But the stream of his popularity had already passed."

After Dallas Holm left, Dad hired Craig Smith. Craig was an established artist from the pioneer days of Jesus music, with celebrated albums and top ten songs. But when Dad approached him, Craig was eager to use his music in direct, person-to-person ministry like my dad's. And to fresh eyes like Craig's, the crusade ministry was as powerful as ever. "I don't think *mesmerized* is too strong a word," he says of the first audience he saw Dad preach to. "We did a three-day crusade in Atlanta, and there was wonderful fruit. He was such a powerful speaker and delivered with such passion and authority. What astounded me were the altar calls — to see those people come forward in those kinds of numbers, for repentance and for first-time salvation. I'd been in festivals and at larger churches for concerts and services, but never where there was somebody as powerful as David Wilkerson."

In the pulpit, Dad remained fully himself, but outside of it, he was making decisions that in retrospect seem panicky. For example, Dad decided to form a backup band for Craig. It left some in the ministry wondering why Dad had let Dallas and Praise go in the first place.

Yet when Dad conducted street meetings, Craig and the band saw the same amazing fruit that the crusades produced. "Night after night we set up on Avenue D down on the Lower East Side of New York," Bob says. "The police rolled up and said, 'You guys are crazy to be here. This is the most dangerous part of the city. We can't be responsible for your safety.'"

"We were right across from what used to be called shooting galleries," Craig says. "The cops told us, 'Once you guys start, you're on your own.' It was a very tough place. Everyone we saw was either a pimp, a prostitute, a dealer, or a user, except for the smallest children.

"We started playing something from one of my albums, and nobody was listening. So Brother Dave sent Bob to tell us, 'It's not working. You guys have to do something to draw in the audience.' I was thinking, 'No pressure for a twentysomething guy who has to produce immediately for David Wilkerson.' So I turned to the band and said, 'Let's do a blues thing.' I start wailing on a harmonica and making up lyrics, and they were playing blues chords. Now people were streaming out of the buildings. There may have been a thousand people crowding up to the stage. As soon as they were there, we rushed off and Brother Dave got up. He said — and this is pretty close to accurate — 'You're pimps, you're drug addicts, you're prostitutes....' It was direct and no nonsense, and yet it was from a heart of compassion. I watched all those people listening — he had such an anointing. I turned to a guy in the band and whispered, 'If I had said that to these people, I wouldn't be alive right now.'"

Craig marveled at Dad's same gift outside of the pulpit. In Minneapolis, he saw a prostitute approach the bus after a crusade service. "She told David, 'I gave my heart to Jesus last year when you were here, but I failed. I've gone back into prostitution. I'm no longer a Christian.' David looked her in the eye and said, 'Did you mean what you said last year? If you did, you're a Christian. Jesus is in your heart. Now, walk like he's in your heart.' He counseled her on having to change habits in order not to fall again.

"At that same crusade, a very big man came to the bus to talk to David about a ministry he was running. He said he needed money. Suddenly I saw little David Wilkerson back this big guy up against the bus and poke his finger in his chest repeatedly. He said, 'You're lying to me. You're in adultery, and you're just trying to get money.' I thought, 'If I had done that, there would have been one dead musician lying on the ground.' But Brother Dave had the fabric to do it."

Jerry Nance saw the same authority at work in a street meeting in New York's Union Square Park. "There were people using drugs, smoking, drinking, gang members, but they were listening," he says. "Brother Dave spoke straight into their lives, getting right in their business. Suddenly he pointed to a woman in front of him and said, 'Ma'am, you have a son who's eighteen years old. He's a heroin addict.' He was just reading this lady's mail. She kept looking around, saying, 'How does he know this? How does he know?' Brother Dave said, 'God is telling me this. You need to ask Jesus into your life, and you need to get your son into Teen Challenge.' She just dropped to her knees, weeping like a baby, and we prayed with her."

The full scope of how people were responding finally registered with Bob Rogers. "We were in Greenwich Village after that," Bob says. "Washington Square is a big park, and there didn't seem to be a lot of interest in what we were doing. As David preached, there were no more than thirty or forty people in front of the stage. But when he got to the end and gave the altar call, hundreds of people started coming out of the apartment buildings. Then more people came from the sidewalks. Two hundred and fifty people gave their lives to Christ. We were filming all of this. The next day in Spanish Harlem, the same thing happened. Nearly five hundred people there came out of the buildings for the altar call."

It struck Bob as if for the first time. "I thought, 'Nobody does this. I've preached on the streets, and this just doesn't happen.' It was the gift of faith for souls. His heart had been uniquely tuned to believe for the salvation of people. He could call some people to the cross by faith when no one else could. It was not normal faith; it was a gift of faith for that particular purpose, and it was clearly empowered by the Holy Spirit."

Bob says it changed his life. "My wife, Becky, and I have often said, had we not had that season in our lives, nothing else would have worked. It was my spiritual education. I went to Bible college, I did all the normal stuff, but none of that prepared me. The walk of faith, the listening to God, the recognition of when God is at work—it has marked my life."

———

THOSE CRUSADE TOURS WERE THE beginning of a last hurrah. "We had started noticing the difference by the smaller crowds," Craig says. "And there were more questions on the bus, like, 'How were the offerings?'—comments I hadn't heard when I first came on board. I could see there was great concern."

"Brother Dave was restless," says Jerry Nance, who was now assistant crusade director under Bob Rogers. "We all knew it. That's when things started to change."

"When you've got a stack of invitations, it's easy," Bob says. "What Brother Dave didn't know was that for three years we had almost no invitations. I spent those three years calling people: 'Would you help us? We've been there before, could we do this again?' I never would have told him that because it would have humiliated him. I tried everything I knew, but he wouldn't say yes to opportunities like TV. He didn't write a book for two years. We hadn't put out a film in years. He would do nothing to sustain it. But he wasn't wrong; he was right."

During this time, people noticed a slight shift in my dad's newsletter messages. One month the message seemed hard, bordering on legalistic, and the next month it focused almost exclusively on grace. "A newsletter would be so hard-core repentance that you'd think, 'I'm dead, there's no use going on tomorrow," Craig says. "Then he would share a message on God's grace that made you wonder if he was hanging out with John Calvin the night before."

There was a primary influence behind this duality: Leonard Ravenhill.

I was on the bus with the crusade team one day when Dad boarded, his shoulders slumped. As he signaled for the driver to start moving, we all saw Leonard's car shimmy up the drive. "Lenny," Dad sighed. "He wants to talk to me about revival again. Or awakening. Oh, Lenny," he said, forcing a chuckle. It wasn't like my father to dread seeing his friend. Dad had been down for months, and we all knew it. He was facing yet another trip — touring nine cities in twelve days — and he felt like he had nothing to say. My father knew he needed something, but whatever that might be, he wasn't up for a discussion of revival at the moment.

Leonard emerged from his car, hoisting a sack, and Dad met him at the bus door. "David, I have something for you to read," Leonard intoned. "This is your future. Read it and it will change your life."

Dad may or may not have thanked Leonard. He may have thought to ask him for prayer. In any case, once Leonard's car was out of sight, Dad turned toward the back of the bus and slung the bag of books with force. It landed with a thud.

Yet during the course of that trip, I saw my dad's spirits lift. Instead of writing, he read the books Leonard gave him, mostly classics written by Puritan ministers. Dad was barely able to crack one without being struck to his core. "Lord," he prayed, "I don't know you the way these men do."

It dawned on my father there was a reason those books had endured over centuries. They had spoken to different churches of different cultures with different people throughout time. Those writers weren't just parsing abstract theological subjects. Their works spoke to all of life. When they wrote about the cross, they told of its beauty — not in lofty terms but so that common readers could grasp it. The writers weren't evasive on theological subjects; they were very direct, each sentence freighted with meaning and conviction. They cut to the chase, and that appealed to my father.

Over time *Puritan* has come to mean something dour to society. We've been conditioned to think of Puritans as gray-faced people in a movement that could be summed up in the word no. That did happen later, as the movement grew stale, which all movements do, but in their prime, the opposite was true of the Puritans. They were the fashion leaders of their day, encouraging colorful styles. To them, God was at the center of life — all of life — and, contrary to Dad's upbringing, no part of life was shut off from God's concern.

I could sense the world opening up before my dad through those books. It was a world full of God, and thus one of beauty. He read and read and read, and when he stepped off the bus after that twelve-day trip, he had a new determination in his eyes. Soon everyone in the ministry offices was being handed tomes with ancient-sounding titles and told, "This is the best book you'll ever read." Every time a volume struck a nerve with him, he bought cases at a time and handed them out.

The eye-opening truths Dad gained from the Puritans involved the breadth, depth, and unfathomable scope of the work of Christ — and that Jesus' work is all-sufficient for us. For a hyperresponsible man like my father, this teaching contained a powerful revelation: true faith means resting in Christ's finished work. Yet the effect on my dad was paradoxical: the more he entered into God's holy rest, the more compelled he was to action. The revelation of rest reignited his passion for souls.

Jerry Nance remembers Dad trying out his new thoughts on the crusade bus. "He would unload all this theology and say, 'Guys, what do you think about this?'" Jerry remembers. "It would be kind of quiet for a minute, and finally Bob would say, 'Brother Dave, I'm going to have to think about that.' I think Brother Dave got the message. He'd say, 'Okay,' and go back and wrestle with those things some more."

But Jerry's respect for Dad increased during those days. "I would see Judd Stephens, our driver, hauling boxes of books onto the bus," he says. "Brother Dave was going to read all those as we traveled across America to the crusades. I thought to myself, 'What a disciplined person.' When he got home, Brother Dave would say hello to his kids, but about ten or eleven every night he would go into his study to pray and start reading."

Dad's reading was no longer just fuel for ministry. He realized he needed something for his own soul — a sense of awe at what Christ had done — and the Puritans supplied it. I would peek into a book on my dad's desk, and almost every sentence was underlined with a phrase written in the margins: "This is the key!" The key he was discovering was, "My Father loves me! He accepts me, and I am pleasing to him."

This was a radically new perspective for Dad. It caused him to reflect deeply on how he'd lived up to that point.

<hr/>

"I'VE WASTED TWENTY YEARS of my life," my father told David Patterson.

"Those were his exact words to me," David says. He almost dropped his fork at the restaurant table. The crusade team had come to northern California, where the Pattersons now lived, and Dad had asked David to join him for breakfast.

"I've wasted my life doing these crusades," Dad explained. "I've just been running from city to city. What's the bottom line of it all?"

David knew that Dad could be extreme, but he also knew my father wasn't prone to making statements like this one.

"Brother Dave, you're wrong," David said. "Everywhere I go I meet people who've been saved in one of your meetings. Their lives were changed by God. I meet pastors who were called of the Lord at your crusades. That's not wasted time."

My father was adamant. "Don't tell anyone," he confided, "but I'm about ready to pull the plug on the crusades."

David thinks Dad may have been tired of the wear and tear of the road. "I think he would have tried to put a spiritual spin on that," he says. "But he was also questioning. He just thought it had not been a profitable time of his life."

"There was a transition coming," Craig Smith says, "but even he wasn't sure what it was. Everyone could feel it. Maybe a half dozen times Bob Rogers and I talked about how things didn't seem right, that they weren't unfolding as we thought they should."

One night Jerry Nance was working late at the crusade office when he finally decided to shut down. It must have been cloudy outside, he recalls, because after he locked the office door, he couldn't even see his car in the parking lot. He crept his way along the gravel path when suddenly he heard a voice whisper, "Jerry."

"I jumped out of my skin," Jerry recalls. The voice was my father's. He was on what we called a prayer walk.

"Wood, hay, and stubble," Dad said.

"Sir?" Jerry asked.

"Do you see all this?" Dad asked. Jerry could barely see my father, but he knew what he was pointing to — the bus, the warehouse, the buildings.

"Yes, sir," Jerry answered.

"It's all wood, hay, and stubble." Dad paused, as if pondering it all. "Do you know what really matters, Jerry?" he asked.

"What's that, Brother Dave?"

"That we know him," Dad said. "Jerry, if we're not comfortable in the Lord's presence down here, what makes us think we'll be comfortable in his presence up there?"

With that, Dad disappeared into the dark.

———

THE CRUSADE TEAM WAS FILING onto the bus for yet another trip when my dad stopped Craig Smith. "You need to have this," he said. He held out a hymnal with a tattered woven cover.

Craig wondered if the book was some castoff from the pile Dad was amassing at Leonard Ravenhill's suggestions. But in a quiet moment that afternoon, as the bus hummed along, Craig dipped into it. The hymnal was published by the Methodists and was well over a hundred years old. "Even in my upbringing as a Baptist, the hymns would have up to six or eight verses," Craig says. "But in this one, some of the hymns had ten, twelve, even eighteen verses. One of them had twenty-two. It was just phenomenal. I would read them and think, 'These are like miniature theology lessons.'"

Craig was so enamored with the hymns' beauty that he decided to try to record some of them. He approached the Star Song label, with whom he had an existing contract dating back to before his days with my dad. "I asked them if I could do a hymns album," he says. "This was in the early eighties, when nobody contemporary was doing that kind of record. It made no sense to them, but they let me do it."

When he had time off between crusade trips, Craig traveled to Houston to record with his musical partner Paul Mills. "We did it in a baroque kind of classical style," he says. The pair also recorded some of it in Nashville, adding strings on some tracks. When they finished it, Craig gave a copy to my dad.

I don't remember my father ever being excited over a record, but he insisted on listening to this one with the Ravenhills in the Smiths' home. "We were all sitting in my little living room — David and Gwen, Leonard and Martha, Dianna and me — listening to the album," Craig says. "It was a full LP, with two sides, and you know Brother Dave was not given to sitting down for any length of time. Each hymn was long, five to six minutes, because there were a lot of verses. At the end of every song, David would say, 'Wow.' He wasn't responding to me; he was responding to those songs and what it was like to hear them performed."

The listening party continued for almost forty minutes. Everyone — Dad, my mom, Leonard, and Martha — were crying.

"I'll remember that evening till the day I die," Craig says. "I was so moved, and so incredibly humbled. I had never seen Leonard Ravenhill weep, and I'd never seen David tear up. They all let their guard down and were having a moment. I think Leonard particularly was reliving something of his past, maybe experiencing some of his younger years, listening to songs by writers who loved God with all of their hearts."

I know what the experience did for my dad. He was immersed in the sheer beauty of God, apart from any works my father might have done in his name. The ubiquitous evangelist David Wilkerson sat still for almost an hour because he recognized God's Spirit dwelling at the very center of that beautiful evening — and he enjoyed the pure pleasure of it.

———

As crusade culture was slipping away, Bob Rogers remembered the success that the ministry had had at a previous crusade in Fort Myers. He persuaded the committee chairman there to let Dad do another crusade, over three nights. Bob hoped they would book the events in the same auditorium, which would have been the appropriate size. "Instead, they booked us in a convention center about fifteen miles outside of Fort Myers in the palmetto patches," Jerry Nance says. "It seated ten thousand people, and that really worried me. I kept calling all the committees I was working with — public relations, fundraising, prayer teams — and I could never get anyone on the phone. I kept telling Bob, 'This thing is going to crash.'"

It spelled disaster. "The first night of the crusade, we were in the bus parked behind that ten-thousand-seat convention center," Jerry says. "Brother Dave said to me, 'How's the crowd? I sent Judd in there thirty minutes ago, and he never came back.' So I went in and saw there were probably fifteen hundred people. This was twenty minutes before start time. Judd was afraid to tell him."

According to Jerry, when Dad preached that night, "he was embarrassed to death." The following night, Bob Rogers arranged for a curtain to be drawn across the arena, sectioning off the seating area to a capacity of about three thousand. But there were fewer people there than on the first night, and the third night was about the same.

Dad's bottom line was never about numbers. Everyone on the team knew he had as much purpose and passion preaching in Levant, Kansas, as in a major city. But that night, he was crushed — more shaken than angry — and afterward on the bus he dressed down Bob and Jerry. Craig remembers the heavy, anguished atmosphere as Dad collapsed into a seat and said, "I feel like my whole ministry is slipping through my hands."

Eventually, Dad viewed the experience through a spiritual lens. "Brother Dave took it somewhat as a sign from God," Jerry says. "It was the beginning of the end of the crusades. Within sixty days he fired Bob."

Everyone on the crusade team got a call from Barb Mackery. "Brother Dave wants you to meet him at his study," she said. That in itself was unusual. Once the guys arrived, my mom led them into Dad's bedroom. He was still in bed, in his pajamas. "Close the door," he said. They all knew the news was serious.

"I couldn't sleep last night," he told them. "I prayed, and the Lord is leading me to shut down the crusade ministry."

None of the guys was surprised. They had felt it coming for months.

"I'm going on a sabbatical to seek the Lord for what's next," Dad said. One by one he looked at the guys and said, "What's God saying to you?" Meaning, "What are you going to do next? Tell me in the next ten seconds."

Each one had some idea, because they had known this day was inevitable. As they answered, Dad assured each of them he would support them in their ministries. In fact, he told them specifically what they could expect from him.

I don't know what went through my dad's mind as the guys filed out. For the first time in almost twenty-five years, he had no idea what the next day held for him.

14

THE WORTHY SACRIFICE

EVERY FIELD OF ENDEAVOR HAS ITS TALES of leaders who isolate themselves from the daily grind so they can get back in touch with something they've lost. Before they can regain their bearings, they have to take a hard look within. For my dad, this meant one thing: shutting himself away to hear the voice of the Lord.

My father had always sought God's voice for direction, and he acted quickly once he heard that voice, a practice he followed for more than twenty-five years. But now he needed more than direction. What that might be, exactly, he didn't yet know. To find out required a shift that cut against his grain: less action and more prayer.

During his years in Lindale, Dad had spent his prayer time in a space built over the garage of their house. Now he spent every day there, and they were long days. "He was like a broken man," Barb Mackery says. "And yet he was endued with supernatural power. He would stay up there from late morning until well past midnight. He prayed for hours and hours, seeking the Lord and hearing his voice." Barb would call or knock only if there was pressing business for Dad; otherwise, she didn't bother him. Mom also had access to him, but no one else did. Sometimes Dad would come down for food; sometimes he wouldn't. Barb kept wondering, "How long can a man live like this?"

It was a repeat of his spartan days on Staten Island. Left to himself, my father had one focus — his ongoing conversation with the Lord, often to the neglect of everything else, including bodily sustenance. Sometimes he fasted; sometimes he simply forgot to eat. And with few exceptions, he didn't travel for all of 1985. "I sensed he was floundering," Barb says. "But I know what he felt during that time, because he told me. He said he felt like he'd been forsaken." Dad enumerated his losses to Barb: his crusade director was gone, his musicians were gone, his evangelistic ministry was gone, and yet he himself had been the one to bring them all to an end.

Several things were going on at once for my dad: He anguished over his ministry losses. He feared for my mom and for Debi, both of whom now lived under the specter of cancer. He suffered physically himself, with diverticulitis and colitis, which for years he tried to alleviate with rolls of Tums. He may still have had a lingering fear of death, though that seemed to have faded. "He had been in a hurry to get things accomplished because he didn't think he was going to live very long," Roger Jonker points out. Now, facing a void of any ministry beyond his newsletter, the prospect of dying seemed less of a pressing concern.

Knowing my dad, at some point during his year of isolation he probably questioned his comfortable, quiet life in the country. Uncle Don cautiously offers a take on that dimension of Dad's personality. "One of the things that made him so effective was all the afflictions he'd gone through," he says. "I don't think he could have written the way he did if he hadn't."

Indirectly, Dad's uneasiness with his own comfort became a subject in his newsletters. He wrote of "pillow prophets," ministers of God who were called to speak truth but who opted instead for comforting messages. He warned against apathy and complacency among preachers. He wrote of the dangers to self-satisfied Christians, going through the motions of a spiritual life that is meant to be dynamic, filled with a sense of God's presence.

He had a point. In very general terms, by the mideighties the church in America had begun making significant shifts. On the one hand, there was a move away from the grassroots edge the church had possessed in the seventies. Life in Christ to that generation had meant daily, personal evangelism and all-out passion for Jesus. Now the church was starting to take on the traits of a corporate approach, which would lead to the church-growth model. Within a few years, the term *megachurch* became common in the cultural lexicon. In turn, the increasing emphasis on church growth led naturally to a "seeker-sensitive" thrust in proclaiming the gospel. All of these were still a few years away, but their seeds were taking root.

Back in Philipsburg, my father had foregone TV to devote himself to prayer. Now, as he felt the need to isolate himself to hear God's voice clearly and discern the Lord's purpose for his life, he condemned watching television. TV must have been a severe distraction to him, because he became vehement about it, to the point that he destroyed his set. He urged his support staff to do the same. In his mind, this wasn't a matter of legalism; it was about eliminating distractions from a spiritual walk. Uncle Jerry told Dad he would take a pass. "I knew I would just have to buy another one later," he said. He had seen my dad go through phases similar to this one.

Inevitably, some of Dad's newsletter readers associated his pronouncements with legalism. Others identified it as a matter of spiritual urgency, seeing it as a call to personal holiness, to get serious about one's walk with Jesus in a time of church declension. To them, Dad was simply setting an example.

One of the things Dad said grieved him was "entertainment" in the church. He saw true worship being replaced by music as performance, professionals singing songs meant to put people at ease rather than draw them into God's holy presence. To Dad, substituting entertainment for worship was to step on something sacred, a spiritual matter akin to defiling the holy place in the temple. By extension, Dad had begun to criticize Christian rock. CCM — contemporary Christian music — had just begun its meteoric rise as a commercial enterprise beyond its grass roots as worship music during the Jesus Movement, and was generating income never seen by the pioneers of Jesus music a decade earlier. All of this troubled my father in ways he found himself unable to reconcile.

He voiced his grief that year in dramatic fashion. Other ministries in Lindale had begun to hold concerts and music festivals as part of their conferences for youth. One visiting musician who respected my dad knew about his sobering newsletter messages on Christian rock, and he took seriously what Dad was saying. This guy had been a successful rock musician before he came to Christ, and his own zeal for the gospel was genuine, so when he arrived with his band in Lindale for a concert, he made a point to visit with Dad. My father received him warmly, and they talked over the issues with open hearts. The musician invited my dad to the concert that night, hoping to relieve him of any concerns, and Dad agreed to go.

I don't think my father was prepared for how far Christian concerts had evolved by the mideighties. The band's opening songs were relatively gentle, but then came the centerpiece — a powerful rock song, accented by pulsating amps and a thumping rock atmosphere. It set off something in my dad. He was grieved, and he couldn't contain it. He began to groan. He rose up from his seat and found himself running down the aisle, waving his arms and shouting, "Ichabod! Ichabod!" — the glory of the Lord has departed!

Maybe some people in the audience understood why Dad did this. But to most in my generation, in their twenties or thirties, it wouldn't have made sense. Dad described the experience in his next newsletter, careful not to name the humble musician. But when he identified the song that set him off, younger readers knew who he was talking about. Dad's description of the experience didn't do the musician any favors. A few years later, he and the musician reconciled over the incident, sharing their respect and love for each other, but at the time, some of us kids were grieved at Dad. Roger Hayslip was compelled to talk to him about it. "Dad, you said you heard from God on this," Roger said. "Would you allow me to say I've heard from God too, but differently?"

"Periodically throughout his life, you'd see him question himself, 'What did I just do?' 'Why did I just say that?'" Roger says. "He had a dichotomy in almost every area of his life, trying to make something black-and-white when it really wasn't." Roger was hoping that would be the case over the concert incident, but Dad couldn't be dissuaded from what he felt. "In his heart of hearts, he felt it was from God, so he clung to it."

Soon after that incident, Dad met with the leaders of the ministry that had sponsored the concert. He loved and respected them, and he wanted to explain himself, but mostly he urged them to get their house in order and seek the Lord for purity of heart.

Barb characterizes that sabbatical year as one in which Dad was moving in a prophetic stream. He was writing a book, *Set the Trumpet to Thy Mouth*, that punctuated his grief. It hit just as hard as *The Vision* with its thrust of coming judgment, only its aim was different. This book was intended not for the world but for the church. If judgment was coming, it would "begin in the house of God," as Dad often quoted from Scripture.

•———•

IN AN ODD BUT WONDERFUL bit of timing, Uncle Don and Aunt Cindy moved to Lindale into one of the ministry-owned houses. My uncle was making a change in his own life, preparing to head up the global expansion of Teen Challenge, and Dad had invited him to relocate to Lindale. For various reasons the global project was temporarily diverted, but I'm grateful that it brought my aunt and uncle near to my dad. Aunt Cindy saw that her brother-in-law was much more relaxed in the country setting, and I think their presence may have added to that.

Uncle Don had picked up on some of the personal changes going on in Dad through the newsletters. "He was always a master at taking biblical truth and applying it to the average Christian," he says. Now he saw Dad doing the same with the Puritan theology that excited him. "He put it through his own sieve, his own heart and vision, and said it his own way."

One of the main things Dad was learning from those classic writers was an awe of God. For Dad, awe came from knowing God's holiness, but his view of holiness still carried seeds of the moralistic, behavioral kind he grew up with. As a result, some of his newsletters took on a tone more critical than usual. As Uncle Don says, "It's possible to push deeper and deeper into certain truths that cut you off from other truths. David got an overdose of some things. I heard him speak at a conference put on by another minister, and he was very hard."

Vinson Synan recalls this period in Dad's life from the view of a historian. "I've seen people who were so visionary and so prophetic that their ministry was stymied," he says. "They got obsessed with certain things. I think when David took on the prophet's role in that latter part of his life, he missed his calling."

That may be a fair assessment, but Dad also operated prophetically in the measured way God had commanded him back in Philipsburg — with some remarkable insight. For example, he and Uncle Don had had an unfortunate falling out with a minister friend. One day Dad called Uncle Don and said, "You need to take an olive branch to our friend. He's not going to be with us much longer."

"It blew my mind," Uncle Don says, "because sometime after that, the man was discovered to have a disease and passed away. It was just unbelievable to me. David had known it and said, 'Go and make peace.' I suspect he may have had words for other people like that, words he might not have spoken."

Dad did have words for others, including two of his most famous friends. The world wouldn't hear what those words were because Dad delivered them discreetly and compassionately, but they were not received.

———

THE TELEVANGELISM SCANDALS THAT BEGAN in 1987 rocked the church world, but they hadn't rocked my dad.

"He sent letters beforehand," Uncle Don says. "I saw them, and there was a lot of grace in them. David was clear in warning that if change did not take place, God would judge, and that happened. Then David would turn around and be compassionate, wanting to help and support them. He extended grace, yet even in the warnings, he made no threats. He just said, 'This is what the Lord is showing me.' It was an opportunity to repent."

Dad didn't write those letters out of the blue, and he didn't base them on hearsay. "He knew these men; they were his friends," Barb emphasizes. "He wrote with trepidation, yet with boldness, and above all, with love." Dad actually wrote at the invitation of one of the men, who wanted to hear what my father had to say. Dad followed up by writing, "This is one of the most difficult letters God has ever compelled me to write.... The Lord told me to prophesy to you — even if it cost me your respect and friendship...." He told his friend what God had revealed to him and offered the warning of judgment. He closed by saying, "I will always be your friend and fellow soldier of the cross." Dad's letter to the other man was similar. He closed with, "I am open for correction and rebuke, but I will sleep tonight knowing I have obeyed the Lord. With love to all of you."

Dad had known something was up with his two televangelist friends long before his sabbatical, when he was still conducting crusades. One day he called the team together as they boarded the bus for a trip, a moment Craig Smith remembers clearly: "He shared with us that some major Christian personalities were going to fall if there wasn't repentance. That was the word he used — 'fall.' He was very direct with us; he named names. He said if they didn't repent, they would lose their ministries."

His revelation left the team in silence. Once Dad left, the guys looked at one another and asked, "What does this mean? How's it going to affect the body of Christ?" When the scandals broke, many in the church wondered the same thing.

———

THE FIRST HALF OF MY dad's life had been all zeal, a consuming passion for souls. Now, as he looked to the second half, he seemed to realize, "I'm still consumed, still called to minister to the lost and hurting, but I know I'm not going to win the world. It's not up to me." It dawned on him that he could actually be more effective by striving less. He had always trusted God, but now that trust included resting in Christ's finished work. Of course, the nagging question, "Am I doing enough?" would always be with my dad, like a low-grade fever. It would come back for a season, at times making him soul-sick. But he had gained the wherewithal to respond, "No, that's not who I am in Christ. He has brought me into a place of rest."

I had never struggled the way my dad did with those issues, but I certainly wasn't at rest. With my father's help, I had started an inner-city church in Detroit. To bring in help, I enlisted my friend Tim Dilena, the son of Paul and Sonia, who shared his parents' wide-open, clear-eyed

New Yorker personality. I also called on one of the Twin Oaks guys who had become a good friend — Jimmy Lilley, a Philly native nicknamed "Nubs" because of a few missing fingers. But my real partner in ministry as well as family was my wife, Kelly, whom I had met in Texas at an Agape Force conference. As my dad had done, I dropped out of Bible college to marry my sweetheart and start a life in ministry.

At first I had resisted Dad's help, which is something any son of a famous minister goes through. We all want to make our own way with God as Father, not Grandfather. Years later, I identified somewhat with Franklin Graham's experience in his book *Rebel with a Cause*. Franklin was given good advice by Bob Pierce, the founder of World Vision, who said in essence, "You don't have to start from scratch to prove yourself. If you want to see God work, be willing to add to whatever your father has done. Take from him whatever he can offer and then add to it."

Franklin's story sums up my attitude toward my father at the time. Like Franklin, I wanted to know that God had called me, that I wasn't just following in my dad's footsteps. And I know Dad would have wanted it that way; he had already done everything he could to encourage me to be myself. So I was surprised by my reaction when he offered to financially support our ministry through the first year. It sent a shot of confidence through me, as if he were telling me again, "I believe in you. You can do this by yourself. You don't have to do it by trying to be like me."

He also encouraged me in another way. From time to time, since my first sermon as a teenager, he told me, "You say things about Scripture that open my eyes. When I was in my twenties, I didn't have nearly the revelation that you have."

Dad's tendency for most of his years had been to read a passage and resolve everything about it quickly. My approach was to examine it for everything, because frankly a lot of passages didn't make sense to me. So we ended up talking about Scripture quite a bit, and he admired that I was willing to look honestly at problematic things. On a few occasions he even said, "I'm glad we wrestled with that passage. If we hadn't, I would have kept it on a surface level."

I was going to need all of that encouragement from him. In Detroit, I was learning how right his words had been to me over the years: "You have name recognition around the world that will open doors for you. But once you walk through the door, it's all up to you. It's up to your dependency on God, your faithfulness as a man, and your skill as a minister."

It's strange to think now that while I was trying to find my way, Dad was trying to re-find his. Yet, thankfully, there were some very solid things about my father that never changed. In Detroit we held street evangelism rallies in some of the city's toughest areas, and we asked him to preach at one.

"I remember he was wearing Jordache jeans, white boots, a striped shirt, tinted sunglasses," Tim Dilena says. "In other words, he was doing everything you just don't do in an environment like that. A crowd was gathering, and people were going crazy — drunk, high, dancing, fights breaking out. It was just a wild scene."

Tim noticed Dad pacing behind the stage we had set up on the street — back and forth, arms folded, one hand on his chin, uttering prayers. "They had turned the street into a dance floor, but he wasn't concerned about what was going on," Tim says. "He was worried whether he would have a word from the Lord." Then Tim saw my father do what he had done for years. "He stepped up, grabbed the mike, and started preaching, and that crazy crowd went quiet under his voice of authority. I've never seen anything like it. They came under the authority of the Word of God."

Dad preached as he always had, a simple, short, direct message, and a great hush fell over the crowd. Then he gave the altar call "and it was jam packed," Tim says. People poured forward in every state of consciousness. "They were actually becoming sober as he prayed for them. God supernaturally touched them." Tim shakes his head at the memory. "It struck me — this was nearly thirty years after he started Teen Challenge, and it still was happening with authority and power."

The streets had never left Dad, and the impossible never stopped being possible.

———

THE NEXT FORMAL EVENT DAD held was in Texas, and it was an unusual one in Roger Jonker's memory. "He called the whole ministry staff together for prayer at a lodge where we used to have our Christmas banquets," Roger says. "It was about what the next step was going to be. His emphasis was, 'Let's make sure our house is in order.' He didn't call it a repentance conference, but that's what it amounted to."

Repentance was on Dad's mind — repentance at home, repentance in the church, repentance in the nation. Just prior to this, he had begun publishing a magazine with Leonard Ravenhill, which Dad advertised to his mailing list. They called it *The Refiner's Fire*, and it was comprised of articles by both men as well as reprinted works by Puritans and other writers of classic stature.

All of this was building up to something, and it involved two men my dad had met in recent years. The first was Reverend Bob Phillips, a shy man with a Baptist background who had been baptized in the Holy Spirit and preached in charismatic circles. Bob was disaffected by some charismatic trends, such as the hyperprosperity movement, and he had begun preaching on deeper issues of the Christian life. One of his topics was God's covenant with man and man's frequent willingness to break it.

Someone gave my father copies of Bob's teaching cassettes, and as Dad listened, he heard a certain "sound" that drew him. To Bob's surprise, Dad called and invited him to Tyler for a weekend, to discuss the subjects Bob was preaching on. At first Bob was intimidated by the man he considered a hero, but their hearts connected quickly.

"We spent three days together at the Ramada Inn in Tyler going through the Scriptures," Bob says. "There's a passage in Ezekiel 44 that's a pretty hard one. It talks about God's people breaking covenant with him. I'd been preaching from that chapter in a lot of my messages, and David wanted me to share my insights with him." In the passage, God allows his priests to preach the wrong message so the people would be fed the unholy things they clamored for.

As Bob spoke about the passage, my dad grew quiet. They were sitting at a small table in Dad's hotel room. Suddenly, my father slid out of his chair and onto the floor. "He just fell over," Bob says. "He curled up in a fetal position and began to weep and weep and weep. He was feeling the consequences of that passage of Scripture, and he was crying for the nation."

Bob was dumbstruck. "As I looked at David, I was still upright. All I could think was, 'I've been preaching this message for a while, but it has never affected me the way it's affecting this man right now.' I remember having this thought: 'He's feeling what God feels — and I want that.' I saw a man who not only carried the burden of God but was deeply impacted by it. That was David's tenderness. He was thinking and feeling with God's heart."

The other man Dad had recently met was Jim Cymbala, pastor of The Brooklyn Tabernacle. A former all-city basketball player, Jim pastored a church with a world-famous choir — not just because it sang gloriously but because it was made up of former drug addicts and street people. That won my dad's respect right away. Dad got to know Jim on a trip to New York and invited him to take part in what he envisioned as a series of repentance conferences. Based on his own burning conviction, Dad had developed a desire to challenge ministers to return to biblical truth and preach it to the nation. "His eyes were on national repentance," Bob Phillips says. Uncle Don adds, "David had been looking to develop a deeper message, and he did that over several years. Now he sought a pulpit where he could preach it." My father scheduled a three-day conference on biblical repentance at a hotel in Dallas and announced it in his newsletter. The speakers joining him were Jim Cymbala, Bob Phillips, Leonard Ravenhill, and Uncle Don.

I had decided to go myself, along with hundreds of pastors and lay-people, but after the first day, I wished I hadn't. The messages weren't just heavy, as the subject called for; they were cutting, piercing, soul-razing, though none so much as my dad's and Leonard's. Every sermon text was drawn from the Old Testament, except for Jim Cymbala's. He won't talk about this himself, but Jim was furious at what he saw being presented as Christ's gospel during the conference. When his turn came, he preached unabashedly an opposite message — on the transfiguration, in which Moses and Elijah appear and meet with Jesus.

"Here you have Moses and Elijah next to Jesus," Jim said. "God takes away the law, represented in Moses. And he takes away the prophets, embodied in Elijah. So here is Jesus. We need to look to Jesus, not to the law and the prophets." Jim was saying, basically, "What you're hearing in this conference is Moses and Elijah. You won't be able to survive if you try to live by that."

Afterward, Jim and my dad had a warm, respectful conversation in which they basically agreed to disagree. They genuinely loved each other, so neither wrote off the other. In fact, maybe over time they inched a bit closer to the other's view — my dad seeing Christ as central to the law and the prophets; Jim seeing the law and the prophets' roles were to reveal sin, with Christ as the remedy.

I wish I could have been in on that conversation, because I left the conference in abject misery. I had been shaken to my core and was convinced, "I can't do ministry anymore. I don't even know if I'm a Christian." I canceled every meeting I had for the next two weeks so Kelly and I could take a vacation. She was alarmed by how inconsolable I was. I couldn't stop thinking, "I'm so unholy, I don't know how to go on living. Being a Christian is so far beyond my capacity. What should I do?" I couldn't even read my Bible. All I could do was pray.

If I hadn't heard Jim's message, I would have given up hope. When I got back home, I talked to Dad about it, and he was astonished at how much I had fallen apart. "Wow," he said, "is this really how it's impacting you?"

The second conference didn't have quite the same heavy tone. Dad continued to press into the repentance message, but he corrected himself immediately when he felt he was stepping overboard. This happened most prominently in Poland in 1986, during what would be Dad's very last citywide crusade. He told Jim Cymbala the story, who later confirmed it with the Polish hosts. Dad was preaching to a large audience when the Holy Spirit stopped him midsermon. His message was on Old Testament sacrifices, emphasizing that only a lamb without blemish was a worthy sacrifice for a holy God. "Bring only a holy heart to God," he urged the people. "Don't bring him a heart that's sinful and expect it to be acceptable to him." But now Dad was ashen. He turned to the interpreter and admonished him to speak exactly what he said after that. "Everything I have just said to you is wrong," Dad preached. "You don't have to bring anything to God. Nothing you have is of any merit. Bring your sin, your brokenness, your pitifulness to the Lord." My father didn't get a chance to give an altar call. People thundered forward bringing their broken lives to God.

———

"HE WENT BACK TO NEW YORK that summer of '86 for the annual street meetings," Barb notes. The summer evangelism outreaches had continued for more than twenty-five years, since the days of Mike Zello and Harvey Kuflik. True to form, whenever Dad went back for them, he never picked the moderately bad neighborhoods. He picked those that were the most troubled, impoverished, and dangerous. Then he would ask which block in the neighborhood was the worst, and then which end of the block was worse. That's where he would set up.

I went back for the rallies that year and watched Dad as he strolled the streets prayerfully. Certain people knew him by name, and he knew their names. He would stop and chat with them, and they called him Pastor because they knew he cared for them. It was as if the skinny, serious, tender man who had come to the Fort Greene Housing Projects twenty-five years earlier had never left.

"I didn't see it, really, until we got there," Bob Phillips says. "New York City had never left his heart. It had always been a part of him."

I grin now at the thought that just five years earlier, my dad was convinced he wouldn't live to see this day. And I am awed by what proceeded from that summer. According to Barb, nobody knew what was coming next except my mother. My parents were staying in a hotel in the city when Dad came through the door and called for my mom. "Gwen," he said, "the Lord has been speaking to me. I need to talk to you."

She smiled at him and said, "We're moving back here, aren't we?"

Part Seven

RETURN

I was not disobedient unto the heavenly vision.

—*Acts 26:19*

15

A REMNANT IN BABYLON

"I'VE GOT THE STUFF THAT killed Len Bias!"

The crack dealer's cry snapped my head around. It was a sticky June afternoon, and I was counseling forlorn people at a street rally near Times Square. Dad's sermon had pierced the heavy air along the block, but now this drug dealer's claim shot through me like nausea.

Len Bias's tragic death was still fresh in the national consciousness. The previous week he had been the second pick in the NBA draft and was by all accounts a wonderful young man with a solid home life. Two days after his selection, after a celebration with family and friends, he decided to try cocaine for the first time. He overdosed and died.

"Dad," I waved, "over here. Listen to this guy."

My father heard the dealer's appeal and walked up to him calmly. "Why are you doing this?" he asked forthrightly. There was tenderness in his voice, but underneath were outrage and heartbreak.

To my dad, the cruel cry of Len Bias's name was a shot fired over the bow. Times Square in 1986 was a darkened shell of its glorious past. A block away, the Port Authority Bus Terminal spewed visitors onto the streets along with undeclared cargo. It had become what my dad and the Sherrills had predicted in *The Cross and the Switchblade*: an emptying point for international drug commerce. The effects of twenty-five years of constant drug traffic showed as dealers sold openly on the street, and the drug of choice in the eighties was crack cocaine. It joined the parade of other wares on 42nd Street, a vast row of peep shows, strip joints, and porn shops. Patrolling the space between the dealers were porn hawkers and prostitutes both male and female. To my dad, it was an extension of the Babylon he had first entered in 1958.

Many Christians thought Dad's decision to start a church in Times Square was bold. If they had followed the arc of his life, however, they would have seen it as normal, logical, even inevitable. His lifelong rush into the troubled areas of the world — and of the soul — encapsulates God's call on all of our lives. None of us gets to opt out of reaching out to the lost or caring for the poor. None of us gets to harden ourselves against compassion for the addicted or neglect God's mission in our community. My dad still saw the world as bent on darkness, yet he also had an accompanying sense of hope and a conviction that we could do something. He had always believed, "It's in the darkest places that God shows himself strongest."

Deep in his heart, my father had long been poised to move back to the city, though he might not have been aware of it himself. As Bob Rogers said so accurately, it was futile to ask my dad why he made the moves he did. All Dad knew for sure was that he had heard from God, and he had to obey his direction.

He put out the word that Times Square Church would hold its first service on the first Thursday in October 1987. It would take place in Manhattan's Town Hall, on 43rd Street just off Broadway, a national historic site seating fifteen hundred. When Dad and the ministry team arrived to open the doors, people were already waiting in line. "We placed announcements in the *New York Times*, plus there were a lot of New Yorkers on our mailing list," Barb Mackery says. "People in the city had been praying for a Spirit-filled church to open in the Times Square area." Jim Cymbala at The Brooklyn Tabernacle made sure his congregation knew. "Dave Wilkerson is coming back to New York to start a church," he announced. "I want some of you to go help him."

TOWN HALL'S MANAGEMENT WAS KIND to the ministry, allowing the church to schedule services there between its other bookings. Meanwhile, Barb says, "Brother Dave and I were beating down the doors of theater owners to find a place to open Times Square Church. At the eleventh hour, human nature says to panic, but I always saw him pretty much in control. And we were so grateful for the use of Town Hall."

Yet some New Yorkers were just as resistant to Dad's arrival as Lindale had been. The ministry had to deposit money for staff housing in a Manhattan apartment building. "The rental office 'lost' our deposit money," Barb says. "For six months they couldn't find it. Once we found other housing, suddenly the check turned up. Our attorney investigated and found out they were afraid we would bring drug addicts into their building."

Of all people, Roger Jonker, World Challenge's business manager, knew the financial stakes needed to open a church in New York City. Logic dictated waiting until the full amount could be raised, but that wasn't Dad's way. "If the Lord spoke to him to start a church in New York, he was not going to drag his feet," Roger says. That meant making unconventional business decisions, and Dad had already made plenty in Texas. A few years earlier, he had sold a huge portion of the Lindale property, including the Twin Oaks Leadership Academy buildings, to Youth with a Mission for less than ten cents on the dollar. "They're a godly ministry," he reasoned. "Let's help them." After that, he reduced what YWAM owed on the property.

Sacrificing to help another ministry was one thing; a move to New York City to start a new ministry from scratch was a major financial undertaking. "The business way would be, 'Let's not move until we can raise as many funds as we can,'" Roger says. "But his way was, 'I have a mandate to go to New York City, so I don't have two years.' That might look impulsive, but it was all logical thinking."

Uphill as it might seem, the decision to move made all the difference in my dad's energy. He came alive during his scouting trips, phoning his plans back to Barb in Texas. It was as if he already envisioned a church in Times Square, just as he had envisioned Twin Oaks Leadership Academy long before it came to pass. And he was resolute about fulfilling two of the church's missions: to do good to the city and to have a testimony for Christ at the crossroads of the world.

Yet this one decision to reach out again into the heart of New York City contained more burden, anxiety, stress, and responsibility than he had ever faced. At age fifty-six, he was returning to a city full of tough problems and tough-as-nails people. Financially, it demanded more faith than the sprawling Twin Oaks Leadership Academy had. "In New York nothing is business as usual," Barb says. "Most of the time you have to operate in crisis mode to get anything done."

All of these pressures awakened something in my dad. Suddenly he was free to fire on all cylinders. Right off the bat he had a clear idea of who he wanted on his pastoral team: Bob Phillips, the gifted, deeply thoughtful Bible teacher, and my uncle Don, whose talent for pastoring, as well as preaching and missions, had come to full bloom in his years with Teen Challenge.

In the church's first month, a galvanizing event took place. At the last minute, the Sunday evening service at Town Hall had to be moved to a hotel ballroom up the street. There, on October 18, 1987, my dad was in midsermon when he was compelled to stop.

"David was preaching a biblical message when all of a sudden he paused," Bob Phillips says. "He said, 'There's going to be a crisis on Wall Street tomorrow. It's going to crash in the morning.' He turned to me and said, 'Bob, I want you to go there with me.'"

My parents' faithful friends from California, Barry and Karen Meguiar, were in attendance that night. "We had seen these things happen with regularity," Barry says of Dad's prophetic insight. They joined the troupe that gathered the next day on the steps of the New York Stock Exchange, and what they saw unfold had the makings of a disaster movie.

"We went inside for the opening bell to observe the trading floor," Bob remembers. "We saw the chaos beginning to develop, and we knew it was happening. So we went back outside and watched as the traders came out." Bob was startled by the sight of grown men weeping hard. "Some of them sat on the steps with their heads between their knees. All the amounts of money lost, all the careers destroyed — it was devastating. You could feel the hopelessness. And we had just heard David say the night before that Wall Street was going to crash."

The group reached out to the brokers, offering to pray with them.

Some wanted prayer, while others waved it away. In the midst of all the chaos, Bob says, "I remember having a deep sense that our security is in the Lord. I recall feeling his sovereignty, that he is in charge of our lives, and that he had warned."

Bob also remembers my dad's compassion for the traders. "David was there for them," he says. "He wasn't weeping, but he wasn't just an observer. He didn't rejoice over this. His heart was to bring about change in people's lives, to bring the hope of Christ." The group stayed until well into the afternoon, praying with the distraught. They also prayed for the nation, which was about to feel the effects of the Black Monday crash.

▬▬

New York City seemed to be the audience my dad had prepared his whole life to pastor. New Yorkers appreciate directness, and my father's message was nothing if not direct. Yet Dad also knew that people wanted to hear what each of the pastors had to say. "David wanted that," Uncle Don says, "and people needed all three types of messages. Somebody once put it to me this way: 'David operates on me; he slices me open. Bob looks in and describes the problems in my internal organs. And Don sews me up.' People saw it as David's church, which it was, but he went out of his way to present Bob and me as being on his level."

Within a few months, the church found a more stable home renting the Nederlander Theater in Times Square, on 41st Street and Seventh Avenue. The Nederlanders, a famous family of Broadway producers, were gracious in dealing with the ministry. And though Dad was up front with them about the cross section of people his church would draw, they still must have been astonished by a typical gathering on Sunday morning. Several things distinguished the services in those days, beginning with an announcement at the beginning of each service: "Ladies, don't set your purses beneath your seat. They'll be stolen before you reach down for them." This was usually followed by another announcement, along the lines of, "Whoever owns the gray Honda parked outside, it's being broken into." There was also an assault of smells from the homeless who had wandered in from the street, and an assault of sounds from the mentally ill, who were equally welcome.

At the end of the block was the church's first mercy ministry—the Upper Room, housed on the second floor of a building directly across from the Port Authority Bus Terminal. Known for its sidewalk out front glistening from hundreds of shattered crack vials, the Upper Room was the church's most direct expression of Christianity, its presence shouting in the shadow of Lady Liberty, "Give me your tired, your poor, your huddled masses ... the wretched ... the homeless." It had the appearance of a typical soup kitchen and evangelistic outreach, but the Upper Room was also a discipleship center that took seriously "the least of these." Many of the homeless, addicts, and prostitutes who showed up for a meal didn't leave after they were fed. They stayed for Bible studies and asked questions, and they were addressed as Christ's brothers and sisters because they *were* Christ's brothers and sisters. Some were even inspired to minister on the streets themselves, despite being homeless. Anyone seeking help was referred to social agencies, and a gifted woman named Charlotte Crump was a great aid to the church in that area. She also referred them to job sources or to stores willing to supply them with new clothes or to parishioners who could help them find a place to live. The Upper Room saw every level of human need, from the destitute poor, to the mentally challenged, to investment brokers who had lost everything to a crack habit. There was hardly a day when the place wasn't packed.

The Upper Room also made ministry lifers of some of its volunteers, who ranged from Teen Challenge graduates, to theater professionals, to businesspeople, to students, to professors, to retired grandparents. It was these sacrificial servants, in fact, who confirmed Dad's decision to finally give up his credentials with the Assemblies of God. He felt the Lord wanted him to open Times Square Church as an interdenominational body, without denominational ties or barriers. David Patterson was a little surprised when he got wind of this news. After the many highs and lows Dad had experienced with the denomination—from its faithful oversight of Teen Challenge to the agonies surrounding *The Vision*—why leave now? "I'm going to see a flow of young men and women coming to God," Dad told David. "If I stay in the Assemblies, I won't be able to ordain them all into ministry. I want to be able to do that."

Dad wasn't necessarily referring to the volunteers. He was also talking about the needy who came to the Upper Room and to the church for help. He had learned from the moment he met Nicky Cruz that everyone is a candidate for powerful service to Jesus. Sure enough, a decade after Times Square Church opened its doors, a homeless young African American man who had drifted in and out for more than a year gave his life to the Lord. Within a few short years, William Carrol was one of Times Square Church's main preaching pastors.

In sum, the Upper Room was an outgrowth of a credo Dad had learned from his parents, and he preached it over and over to his staff: "We can't help every poor person in the city, but we can help some. And for those we do help, we may not be able to do everything, but we can do something." There was philosophy behind the action, and love behind the philosophy.

Dad told me he needed that kind of ministry to keep his heart right. It was something he talked about a lot: To be able to offer life, he had to know what people's real needs were. And to know that, he had to be in touch with the truly brokenhearted.

———

FROM ITS EARLIEST DAYS Times Square Church drew a huge cross section of New Yorkers. It beckoned street people and those from Wall Street, hustlers and the highly educated, Spanish Pentecostals and theater professionals, Messianic Jews and relocated Midwesterners. One of my favorite sights one Sunday was of a weary homeless man resting his head on the shoulder of a high-ranking military officer in full dress.

The church also drew suburbanites of all generations from Connecticut, New Jersey, Long Island, Pennsylvania, and upstate New York towns as far away as five hours. Some were old-time New Yorkers who knew of my dad from *The Cross and the Switchblade* days. Some had come to Christ through his crusades in the sixties, seventies, and eighties. Some first learned of him through *The Vision*, while others were introduced to him through his newsletter messages. Some caught up with him through *The Refiner's Fire* and his republication of classic Christian writings. Others were simply Christians who were disaffected by the condition of the church in general and were looking to hear meaningful preaching.

Times Square Church had drawn together another group as well: our family. Dad called on me to lead the church's prayer services on Friday nights. My brother, Greg — who, like the rest of us, had married a Texan, Teresa — led the singles ministry. In a short while, Debi and Roger Jonker relocated so Roger could be on-site to oversee the church's business matters. Bonnie and Roger Hayslip came for a short time before leaving to have an outreach in El Paso. And, probably most meaningful to my dad, my mother was a pastor's wife again after twenty-six years. Her gift of hospitality revealed itself in the encouragement and warm hugs she gave the New Yorkers streaming through the doors. A few years down the road, even my aging grandmother Ann relocated from Texas; she couldn't wait. "There are no sinners in Texas," she complained. "They're all Baptists and going to heaven." She needed a mission field as much as my dad did.

It must have occurred to my father at some point that by having us around him, he was recreating — or maybe redoing — his parents' experience, having the whole family involved in church life. I know he was happy for reasons beyond this as well. Bob Phillips immediately recognized my dad's "purpose and passion for the city, and the city's significance to affect the nation and the world. That's the difference I noticed most in David. There was no change in him; he had just stepped into his element. You couldn't help seeing he was where he was supposed to be."

One might not think Dad's tough sermons would go over well with the famous or well-to-do people who attended. But on any Sunday, the congregation at Times Square Church could include a maverick inventor, a well-known politician, the famous CEO of a corporation, an auto manufacturer, a society matriarch, a Tony Award winner, a rock singer. I'm speaking here of specific people who came week after week, forming prayer circles with street people and addicts to intercede for each other's needs.

"One of the outstanding things at Times Square was that mixture of the congregation," Uncle Don says, "rich and poor, middle class, all nationalities. And there were always visitors from throughout the United States. I don't think there was anything like it in the nation, given the location, the pastoral mix, the type of people who came. Someone at church once asked me, 'How come we don't see signs and wonders any-more?' I answered, 'Look around. Look around.'"

———

DAD FELT TIMES SQUARE CHURCH needed a permanent home, and that meant buying a property. Stanley Waldshan had been Dad's accountant since 1959. The son of Jewish Polish immigrants, he was Teen Challenge's first accountant back on Clinton Avenue. "All the times David wanted to do something, I'd say, 'I don't know, I'd like to work some numbers out. Are you sure you'll be able to handle something like this?'" Stanley recounts. "He said, 'God will take care of it. If he's calling me to do this, I know the money will come.' And lo and behold, the money always came. It was miraculous. Buying property in Manhattan was an enormous undertaking, but he never flinched. He never had any doubts in his mind. If he felt he had a calling, he would tell me, and he would move ahead."

"The Nederlander Theater was meant to be only a temporary home, and it was no longer adequate," Barb says. So Robert Nederlander took Dad and a church board member to view the Mark Hellinger Theater on 51st Street. Built in 1930 as one of the nation's first movie palaces on Broadway, it's a historic structure where the musical *Jesus Christ Superstar* had its amazing run. "When Brother Dave took me to see the Hellinger, there was a rehearsal going on for the Tony Awards show, which was held there every year," Barb says. "*Legs Diamond* was slated to open there the following week. Bob Nederlander told us the theater would be available whenever that show ended its run."

Broadway had hit a low point in 1988, with fewer people willing to come to Times Square because of the dangers. Coupled with the sagging economy, that caused a lot of theaters to go dark, with no shows running. But *Legs Diamond* had been a smash hit in London's West End, and the same was expected for it on Broadway. Dad believed otherwise: he was convinced the Mark Hellinger was meant to house a church, and his intuition turned out to be right. *Legs Diamond* flopped, closing in less than two months. "The Hellinger was ours the next Sunday, as a rental," Barb says. Dad immediately started long, protracted negotiations with the Nederlanders to buy it, but the process had to be kept under wraps because of the Mark Hellinger's status in the arts community. If the media got wind of a pending deal, there would be an outcry from theater circles and the deal would never go through.

My dad and Bob Phillips had begun taking walks together through Times Square, and one day during the negotiating period, Dad stopped in his tracks. "Bob," he said out of the blue, "I need you to believe God with me on this. I don't know where the money is going to come from for this theater." Bob answered, "Okay, of course, I'll believe God with you."

They walked another block, and Dad stopped again. "Bob, I mean it," Dad said. "I really need you to believe with me on this. I need you to stand with me." "Okay, yes, I will," Bob answered. Dad did the same on the next block. "David," Bob finally told him, "I'd love to believe with you. I'll do everything I can to believe. But how can I believe for fifteen million dollars? I've never done that."

Bob remembers that Dad's face turned stern. "It was not hardness," he says, "it was resoluteness of purpose. David was that way in everything he did. He asked me, 'Have you ever believed for five dollars?' 'Yes.' 'What about five hundred dollars?' 'Absolutely, over the years I've had to believe God for five hundred dollars for ministry.' He said, 'That's the same faith you believe with for fifteen million. You believe it is in God's hands, and the amount is no problem for him.'"

Dad never appealed to his newsletter readers for those kinds of needs. "To me that was more impressive than anything he had said," Bob says. "The mailing list was not a means of raising money. His newsletter messages were for God's people, to encourage the church. He stewarded the newsletters in the eyes of God, and that spoke volumes to me."

Within two years, while Broadway was still in a downturn, the Nederlanders sold the Mark Hellinger to World Challenge for sixteen million dollars. The ministry had the cash to pay the full amount. Then, within a few months, Broadway began to thrive again. The musical *Miss Saigon*, which had been a hit in London, was scheduled for a run in New York, and its producers approached the church about buying the Hellinger Theater. "They made an offer of about ten million dollars more than we paid for it," Bob says. "Of course, it wasn't for sale. They even offered

David the theater across the street, but he didn't do that either. That said a lot to me. David's concern was not money; he was concerned about the purpose God had sent him there for. That was paramount to him."

Dad once disclosed to a friend the philosophy he had formed about money. "God will allow millions of dollars to flow through your hands if you will not close your fists around it," he said. "If you allow it to flow through your hands, God will use it for the cause of his kingdom."

During the first Sunday service at the Mark Hellinger, Dad made a point in his opening announcement. "There are no superstars here," he said. "There is only the Bright and Morning Star."

"It was one of the biggest stages on Broadway," Uncle Don says. "And there was no hype, only worship and God's Word."

———

BEING A PASTOR AGAIN CHANGED my father. "David not only told me that personally; he said it publicly in my church," Jim Cymbala says. "He said he could be harsh and judgmental, but when he became a pastor, all that had to go out the window."

Dad told Jim the change began when he had a particular encounter on the street. He was on his way to church when he saw a woman from the congregation and they began talking. She had bought a subway token to get to church but couldn't afford one to get home. "But God is faithful," she said with a smile. "I know being in church tonight will help me."

Dad immediately grew convicted. The message he had prepared to preach that night was a hard one. He told Jim, "How could I possibly lambast her in a sermon? How could I show her everything she's doing wrong, every area where she's failing God? You can't build a church on that."

He spoke about it with his friend Barry Meguiar. "He talked openly about how he preached judgment during his crusades and it filled the altars," Barry says. "But he said, 'As a pastor you have to live with people the next day and the next week and the next month, and you realize they're on a journey.' It became clear to him that their problems didn't go away just because he preached a judgment message. The next week they would have the same problems, the day-to-day struggles of living. Dave said, 'I was wrong. I have no right to preach judgment until I understand the grace of God.' That was a profound change for him."

At one point, Dad refused to listen to tapes of his past sermons. If someone in the office was playing one, he would say, "Please turn that off. I'm screaming there."

Nicky Cruz visited the church often and saw the change taking place in Dad. "Dave was hard on himself, and as a pastor you can't bring that to the people," he says. "You can't put doubts on obedient children, and at times he was hurting people more than helping. But because he was a man of prayer, he listened to the Holy Spirit, and he said, 'I'm going to change that.' "

Complicating Dad's struggle was his prophetic burden. "He felt the heartbreak of God," Bob Phillips says. "He didn't like having to carry the burden of the prophetic message. It was not something he chose; it was God's choice for him. And David did it faithfully and at great cost. He hurt deeply when people called him a false prophet, but I never saw him defend himself." What Dad's critics didn't see was that when he prophesied things that didn't come to pass, he agonized over it — sometimes to friends, always to God, and without fail, to himself.

"A lot of people saw him as hard because of his message," Bob says. "But David didn't like having to carry that message. He had a tremendous love for people, and he came into a stronger message of love at Times Square Church. But that was not a new revelation to him; it's who he already was."

Mostly my father was struggling to learn grace for himself — slowly, gradually, from the outside in. "I don't know how many times we heard him say, 'I never knew God until now,' " Roger Hayslip says. "I finally told him, 'Dad, please stop saying that. You've always walked with God! You've never not known him.' " My father laughed because he knew it was true.

———

I WAS IN MY THIRTIES, married for more than ten years, and like a lot of men at that age, issues had begun to show up in my life. At the center of them all was my relationship with my dad. I recognized that

I'd held him on kind of a pedestal, and living to please him had become an obstruction to God's glory. That recognition was the beginning of a major change in my life.

I had gained some distance, unconsciously or not, through a ministry move. In the fall of 1989 I left Times Square Church to start an outreach in London, England, and while there I read some books that began my serious examination of my relationship with Dad. I saw in my reading that I was on a misguided search for significance — that I wanted to be somebody, to make a mark on the world. There's nothing wrong with those things, but the energy behind them was a drive to make sure my dad thought I was great. It wasn't godly ambition; it was a need to prove something to my father.

A few years later, Kelly and I moved our young family back to the US and started a church in Denver. There I began seeing a counselor to talk through what I was discovering. I made clear to the therapist that I didn't blame my dad for anything; after all, he had tried to prepare me for the disappointments I ultimately experienced with him. Yet the counselor made clear to me I still had some areas to sort out in my relationship with Dad.

"You've become too dependent on him," the counselor said, and that was accurate. No matter what trouble I had — financial, marital, parental, ministerial — I turned to Dad for advice on everything. "He's not your Holy Spirit," said the counselor. "You've got to cut the apron strings. I don't mean he needs to set you loose. You need to set *him* loose."

I had to stifle a laugh at the image. Apron strings are usually associated with mothers, but in the unusual case of my father, it applied. The counselor was spot on about my need to set him loose from my needs. There was nothing in my dad's heart that wanted to keep me needy of him. It was I who had to do the cutting.

It would have been too awkward to address "cutting apron strings" with my father, so I never said anything; I just acted on it. I stopped calling as often and made decisions on my own when usually I would have turned to him for advice. He must have picked up on this, because when I called after a long interval, he said, "It's been a few weeks. I've wondered where you've been." He wasn't offended; he'd just gotten concerned. But the less I called on him, the clearer God's presence in my life became, and ministry became all the more refreshing.

———◄

AUNT JUANITA'S DEATH CAME QUICKLY. She had called her sister Ruth to let her know the doctors had found advanced cancer, and that treatment would not help. She was given a few months to live. When Uncle Don arrived at the hospital in Phoenix the next week, he was startled to realize she would likely die within days. He stayed with her until the end. At one point he asked his sister whether she had made peace with God. Through the haze of painkillers, my aunt nodded yes. A short while later, she closed her eyes and stopped breathing.

Juanita's sudden death must have shaken my father at some level, but it didn't compare with the news about my sister Bonnie. Roger Hayslip called to tell us she had been diagnosed with stage 4 cancer. My parents flew to El Paso to be with my sister in the hospital, and when they arrived, the oncologist took Dad and Roger aside. "It was like a final report," Roger says. "It was an aggressive cancer that had already spread to the lymph nodes." The doctor told them Bonnie had less than a thirty percent chance to live beyond two or three years.

Yet something inside Roger told him Bonnie was going to make it through. My brother-in-law isn't given to spiritual revelations, "but in this one instance in my life, I knew," he says. "I never shed a tear or felt the grip of fear. I knew she was going to be okay." Dad experienced the news differently. "It devastated him," Roger says. "He took it very hard. He was absolutely convinced she was going to die, so he tried to prepare me. 'Son, you need to get ready; God is going to take her home.' That was just him in his most human moment."

That was more than twenty years ago. Today Bonnie and Roger live in the Denver, Colorado, area in good health, a gift for which we're all grateful. Once again Dad could thank the Lord that his healing mercy had rescued one of his dear ones. But my father hadn't yet reached his capacity for suffering.

16

WHAT DO YOU SEE?

Sam Maloney was sitting in the Dunkin' Donuts on Broadway near the church, hunched over reading, when a pair of shoes appeared in his line of vision. "I looked up and it was Pastor Dave, in his casuals," Sam says, accent betraying his Barbados roots. "He moved so quietly!"

"Brother Sam," Dad said, "I've heard a lot about you." Sam wondered what his pastor had heard. "I'd like to talk with you. I want you to make an appointment with my secretary." With that, my father pivoted and slipped away.

"Oh no," Sam thought, "what have I done?" He grins at the memory of that encounter. "Never a lot of talk with Pastor Dave."

For years Sam's severely curved spine has caused such severe pain that he's unable to sleep. He has undergone three corrective surgeries but with little relief. For a while he took strong aspirin until he developed stomach ulcers. His doctor prescribed oxycodone and other medications, but they induced hallucinatory dreams that Sam didn't want. He eventually gave up medication altogether, and when he couldn't sleep, he opened his Bible and read. Absorbing the words of God's goodness became his balm; only then could he sleep soundly.

Today, Sam is seventy-nine years old. But in 1987 he was still in his fifties, just as my dad was, when Jim Cymbala urged his parishioners to help out my father with his new church in Times Square. Sam happily obliged, attending the first meetings at Town Hall, and soon he was assisting during services as an usher.

Dad had learned from my mother about Sam, who often sat next to her and my grandmother near the back of the church. Mom observed how Sam attended to people's needs during the services. "We're forming a board of elders," Dad told Sam in his office. "I want to know every need in the congregation — when someone can't pay a bill or is sick or suffering. I need you to be my eyes and ears."

Dad was also concerned about Sam's own spinal condition. Sam says, "He asked me, 'Who is seeing you? Who is calling you? I'm going to give you my number, and you call me anytime. If you don't call me, I'm going to call you.' And that's what he did. Always true to his word."

Sam told Dad about a man who had been in the hospital for more than three months because of his blood pressure. The man's only income was his Social Security check, most of which went toward medication; he didn't have enough left over to buy food. "Get me his name and phone number," Dad said.

"He loved the old people especially," Sam says. "He took care of them, and they never knew the source. I would ask them how they're doing, and they would say, 'Sam, someone paid my bill.' They never knew." Sam laughs. "That was his way. He takes care of the need and then he disappears. Very, very tender. And when old people died without anything, he took care of it all — the body, the coffin, the grave, the funeral service, everything. A humble gentleman, kind, loving, and caring."

After a while, Sam started receiving phone calls from my father concerning a different type of need. Dad would ask him, "Sam, what's the Lord saying to you?"

"He would ask me about certain things I was getting from the Word," Sam says. "Like the word God gave to Joshua, 'Be strong and courageous, for I am with you.' Joshua was weak and wobbly in the knees, and the Lord told him not to fear what the people would say. Pastor Dave would say, 'Hmm, that's from the Lord. I might preach on that.'"

When Bonnie and Roger were in town, they observed a clear connection between the two men in their suffering. "Elder Sam lives in excruciating, unbearable pain every day of his life," Roger says. "But he'll never tell you that. He's always bubbling, full of the joy of the Lord. Brother Dave highly respected him for how he handled the life he'd been given. Dad was going through his own issues, so he watched this guy and said, 'Wow, how does Sam do it?'"

In turn, Sam saw Dad bearing the burdens of the church heavily. "To me, his one great need was for the support of the people in prayer," Sam says. "This man was a lion of Judah. He was skinny but he was fierce in spirit. And he had more than a plateful — his sick wife, his sick daughters. He had his own problems, too, with his stomach, but he never moaned or complained. Once I said to him, 'Pastor, I like the way you handle stresses.' He said, 'You watch me, but I watch you.'"

———

IN 1994–95, WITHIN A PERIOD of a few months, Dad faced what he called the most stressful period of his life. Bob Phillips resigned and left the church over a confrontation with my dad. Within a few months, my uncle Don resigned over similar issues, independent of Bob. Shortly after that, a cherished group within the church staged a walkout over yet another conflict.

The issues that led to these breaks are not particularly illuminating. At issue with Dad's beloved fellow pastors was an untenable disagreement. At issue with the other group was, I believe, at heart a misunderstanding. Both were tragic and unfortunate, and I wonder if each might have been avoided had cooler heads and more open hearts prevailed.

"He said it was the greatest hurt of his life," recalls Denny Duron, the evangelist and former pro football player whom Dad invited to preach monthly at Times Square Church. To add to Dad's burdens, as these conflicts took place, my grandmother had grown frail and needed to move back to Texas. Even more stressful was Bonnie's medical checkup revealing lesions on her liver which appeared to be cancerous. With these things piling up on him, Dad called me, needing a listening ear, and I sensed right away his nerves were raw.

"How dare they accuse me of those things?" he said of the people departing Times Square Church. It was almost as if he were stating, "I'm a man of God; I'm above accusation." This was the posture he typically fell back on when he was in pure defensive mode. I knew that some of the perceptions about him were wrong, and told him so. But that didn't help much because the accusations had tapped into one of Dad's highly sensitive areas — his self-worth before God.

He was in no mood to handle even a hint of questioning. When I advocated for a middle party to help repair things, he blew up. "Are you siding with them too?" I realized then I had to back off. My father had always been respectful whenever I challenged him, but this wasn't even a challenge; it was just an inquiry. Yet he had spiritualized the conflicts, framing them in terms of good and evil. On the one hand, I was sad that my father was being unjustly vilified and his heart misread. On the other, I was sad for the good people who were in conflict with him, and who were being vilified in turn, their intentions labeled demonic.

It was a picture straight out of Dad's childhood, and a nightmare revisited. When his father, Kenneth, was assailed by his church members, little Davie put on a football helmet and took up a plastic sword to battle the accusers. He was eight years old then and saw those conflicts exacerbate his father's ulcers, heightening the family's fears.

Now, as my father endured his own church battles, this was the most troubled of soul I'd ever seen him, and the trouble didn't soon abate. Over the next several months, people trickled out of the church in an agonizing, protracted ordeal that brought Dad more pain than he seemed able to bear. His colitis doubled him over in pain. "It broke him to the core," Barb Mackery says. "He went on in the strength of the Lord as his physical strength wasted away, because in his eyes he had failed miserably. He said, 'I couldn't keep the leadership together. I couldn't even keep my own family together.'"

"He loved all of them, and he was not in relationship with them at that point," Denny Duron says. "But he told me, 'Brothers always make up. Don and I will be back together eventually.' He also shared how Pastor Conlon had stood with him, and how much he appreciated that." Carter Conlon had joined the pastoral team just before my uncle Don left. A Canadian very much in the mold of my father, he helped steer the ship at a time when my dad needed it most.

◾━━◾

JUST BEFORE THE CHURCH UPHEAVAL took place, my father had begun writing in his journal of a "fifth stirring." One journal entry refers to four earlier stirrings in his life, but it doesn't identify what those were. As for the fifth, he couldn't yet put his finger on what it might lead to.

"One of the passages that God impressed on David when he went back to New York was Psalm 25:14, 'I shall make you to know my covenant,'" Bob Phillips notes. Dad had remained fixated on the subject of covenant since his first encounter with Bob in Tyler. Dad's initial focus had been on the judgment aspects of God's covenant with man. Now, through his continued reading of the Puritans and others, Dad had slowly turned his gaze to the beneficial aspects.

The implications of covenant grace challenged his very moorings. He saw plainly that his prior notion of grace had been rooted in trying to please the Father by obeying his laws, doing more, occupying himself with responsibilities. My dad had never turned away from a single truth revealed in God's Word — especially if that truth convicted him — but now he was hesitant. He feared that a headlong dive into pure grace might make him relax, pulling him away from his passion for God.

Yet he knew there was nowhere to go other than forward. So how could he own this biblical doctrine for himself, practice it, and preach it? Just as he had done with the message of repentance, God's church would be his laboratory for applying covenant grace, and he would have to lead by example.

I was proud of how Dad attacked the subject. I remember seeing a stack of volumes by John Owen on the desk in his study. During that period, I thought of my father as being like the apostle Paul in Arabia, spending years in the desert discerning the ways and doctrines of God before preaching them. For my father, the process had begun with the books Leonard Ravenhill gave him during the crusade days. Ever since then he had immersed himself in a particular theological environment, with truths that were slowly transforming him in ways he couldn't have achieved on his own.

Carter Conlon remembers moments in the pulpit when the truths of covenant grace became clear to Dad: "If you start from tape one of that series, and follow it in sequence, you come to the point where he says, 'I've got it! I don't know about you, but I've got it!' I remember his hands going up in the air, 'Praise God!' when it finally hit him, 'I can't please God no matter what I do. I've already pleased him in Christ.' It was almost the difference between the old and the new covenants.

"He had grown up under a rigid Pentecost that produces almost an eggshell walk— 'Oh, God, I shouldn't have thought that.' He was very, very concerned about pleasing God; it was the core of his being. But when he finally realized he couldn't please God— that he was fully accepted, received, and cleansed in Christ, made fully a son, that he could not add to his stature in the sight of God— that's when there was a release."

Uncle Don saw the difference in my dad from a distance, by reading Dad's newsletters. "That teaching not only changed his message but changed his life," he says. "David understood the verse, 'My yoke is easy; my burden is light.' He really ministered to people then."

What I saw happen with Dad was an evolution from the ministry of condemnation to the ministry of reconciliation. He received letters from people whose lives were being changed by his messages on covenant grace. For years they had been shackled by guilt, laboring under a performance-driven faith, but now they wrote saying, "Thank you, I've been set free!" Other longtime newsletter readers had an opposite reaction, writing, "Are you getting soft? It's been awhile since you've given a correction or a rebuke. What happened to the preacher of 'no compromise'?"

The changes taking place in my father registered on deeper and deeper levels. At one point he was compelled to call fifteen people he had been estranged from and ask them to forgive him. These were people whose relationships with Dad had ended badly, some of them his fault and some of them not. Regardless, he owned up to his part in the breach and sought reconciliation in a spirit of love.

Several of the people he called wept. This was something they had hoped for over the years. Now Dad was able to catch up on their lives, asking if they were still in ministry, inquiring how he might help them. Doing this gave my father a peace he had never known.

———

As Dad grew in his newfound peace, he was handed one more cup of pain. Of all the cancers that our family had endured, one has left the deepest scar. In 2000, Debi and Roger's ten-year-old daughter, Tiffany, was diagnosed with a brain tumor — anaplastic oligodendroglioma. Dad was in a hotel room in Charlottesville, Virginia, where the Jonkers lived at the time, when he penned the following:

> Tomorrow they operate on Tiffany (brain tumor). I'm too numb to pray! But how do you question a God of love!? How do you ask Him to change His mind when He knows best? I can't beg or plead. What can I do but trust my Father? There is no alternative. It may be cancer — but still God is above even that. God has not once failed me. He has done the miraculous over and over again.
>
> I cannot depend on inner voices. My own desires and hopes could take voice. I am driven to His Word — to His promises that all things work together for good to those who love Him and are called according to His purpose. If it is life-threatening, then the Holy Spirit must supply for all of us comfort, peace, and rest in Him.
>
> I had to put Gwen in His hand. Then Debi. Then Bonnie — in all their cancer operations.
>
> Lord, I do hereby put Tiffany in Your loving hands. Your will be done.
>
> I will love and trust You no matter what.

The surgeons were able to remove the tumor, and Tiffany was cancer-free for two years. But when the cancer returned, it was inoperable. Debi and Roger were told their daughter had a few weeks to live.

Tiffany had already led an inspiring life, especially in the two years after that surgery. Her final weeks were even more so, as Debi describes in *Letters of Comfort*, a collection of caring messages people wrote to the Jonkers after Tiffany's death. Tiffany astounded everyone with her peaceful assuredness in those weeks. She even told her brother Matthew, a great encourager, "Don't pray for me to be healed. Jesus and I have had a talk!"

During that agonizing time, my brother-in-law Roger was being prepared in an unusual yet merciful way. "We knew outside of a miracle that Tiffany wasn't going to live," he says. "I would pray for her healing, with faith that God could perform it. But every time I did, I would have something like a vision of her funeral service. I could see Carter preaching; I knew what the song would be; Bonnie would put together pictures of Tiffany's life. I would fight this, because I was still believing God to heal her. But the Lord was preparing me for him to take her.

"That's not something you can share with just anybody. I talked to Brother Dave, and he listened — I knew he would. I was Tiffany's dad; I wanted her to be healed; I believed God could heal. But in his spirit, Brother Dave just sensed that God was speaking to me. He seemed to understand it was the Lord's way."

The Jonkers were at my parents' house in New Jersey during Tiffany's final weeks. Roger and Debi slept only for intervals because they had to regularly replace Tiffany's medicine patches. At one point Debi sensed someone else was in the room. It was our father, keeping vigil in prayer for his granddaughter.

After Tiffany's death, Barb Mackery recalls Dad as being somewhat withdrawn, but he remained busy. Occasionally he would say to his secretary, out of the blue, "I miss Tiffany."

"I think that's when the real change started happening for him, when Tiffany died," Roger Hayslip offers. "Maybe he wasn't as strong or persistent about things as before."

Elder Sam tried to offer comfort. "I once asked him, 'You ever thought about going on a cruise with Sister Gwen?'" Sam says. "But he never wanted that kind of stuff. His citizenship was not of this earth." Yet Tiffany's brother Matthew saw in his grandpa a grief that was very much of this earth. He overheard his grandfather weeping in prayer, "My Tiffany, oh my Tiffany, oh Jesus!"

———

WHEN I THINK OF HOW my father viewed Carter Conlon — the man who stood alongside him through the ups and downs that both our family and the church went through — the word *ballast* comes to mind. Carter preached like my dad, prayed like my dad, and dealt with problems the way Dad did. So for my father to step aside in 2000 and name

Carter senior pastor of Times Square Church was like doubling his own impact.

There never seemed to be a question for Dad about whether I would be involved in the future of Times Square Church. Still, it may have been hard for him not to consider me because he knew I loved pastoring. I preferred it even to my growing work in the missions department of World Challenge, an area of ministry dear to my heart. Yet Dad had the foresight to know what roles would be right for each of us, something the years have proven.

By then Dad had been a pastor for more than a decade. As he gradually turned over the reins of ministry at World Challenge and Times Square Church, he decided to act on the urgings of his friends to minister to other pastors. One day he instructed his staff, "There are pastors crying out from slums all over the world. Go and find them." Over a five-year span, Dad faced down his fear of flying to travel to sixty nations bringing a word of encouragement to struggling pastors.

"Some were countries where 'name' evangelists don't go," says Claude Houde, a French Canadian minister whom Dad had championed as a young man. Claude traveled with Dad to many of the pastors' conferences, often serving as his translator in French-speaking nations. Almost everywhere, Dad's reputation preceded him powerfully. Many bishops and church leaders who received him — in Africa, Australia, Eastern Europe, and Latin America — had become Christians through *The Cross and the Switchblade* or Teen Challenge.

When Dad asked me to begin traveling with him, I was pastoring a small church of a couple of hundred people in Denver. I realized pretty quickly I couldn't handle both ministries. Pastoring was my first love, but after praying I decided to travel with my dad, stepping fully into the role of World Challenge missions director. Kelly and I picked up our family and moved to New Jersey, where we found a house a few blocks away from my parents' home. My folks were thrilled to have their grandkids nearby, and I would walk over to spend time with Dad almost every day. We prayed for pastors and talked about ways to help them through their struggles, and during those sessions my father asked a lot of questions: "You're a young pastor. What discourages you about the ministry?"

He was up to something I wasn't aware of at the time, but that was clearly by design. He never said outright, "Why don't you spend five years with me, talking and traveling, and I'll pass the baton of World Challenge to you?" but that's exactly what he was doing. Those years with him turned out to be an internship I hadn't imagined.

During our travels, Dad was more relaxed than I'd ever seen him. This was different from the crusade years, when he prepared intensely for every sermon; I got the feeling that these pastors' conferences didn't have to be earth-shattering events. Afterward, he offered casual critiques of my preaching, telling me, for example, when I tapered off at the end of a sentence, leaving listeners hanging. He gently advised me not to compare myself with him in the pulpit — otherwise the pastors in the audience would too. He offered all of this gently and constructively.

And he always introduced me with honor. Dad opened every conference by saying, "My son and I are thrilled to be here, and in just a moment you'll hear from him. Wherever we travel, people always say, 'Brother Dave, we love your message — it challenges us and convicts us — but we can relate more to your son.'"

At first I thought this was just Dad's way of encouraging me — and it did encourage me. Week after week, month after month, as I heard those words, I sensed my father communicating to me, "It's important that you're here because these men can really relate to you." But then he added something more to the introductions: "I want you to pay attention to what my son says because he's been a pastor longer than I have." With that he was telling me, "You're a pastor, and I respect you as one."

—•—

THE MESSAGE OF COVENANT GRACE had genuinely changed my dad. No matter what country we were in, my father made a series of confessions to his pastor peers: "I was too hard on people. Don't be unapproachable. Don't let your pride stand in the way of somebody correcting you." He was also more open and reflective, and in our casual times together — sitting in a hotel lobby, walking through a park, having lunch in a cafe — he and I began to open up to each other on a level as never before.

Dad vulnerably confessed to me his worries about Mom's health. More than once I saw him step to a podium to address throngs of pastors after concluding a worrisome phone call with her. In between sessions, he would write love letters and fax them to her. In turn, I shared my heartbreak with Dad when I learned that two of my sons had been caught smoking pot. We were at a hotel in Uruguay when Kelly called, sobbing, saying they had been arrested. Fortunately, the boys weren't experienced with marijuana, which the police sensed when they caught them. But as a father helpless to do anything a continent away from home, I was devastated. When Dad came to my room, I broke down in tears. "My sons are doing drugs," I told him, and he sat and cried with me.

"I've been praying for you during this conference," Dad told me. "The Lord has told me you are to trust him. He has assured me everything is going to be okay. You won't suffer loss because God is going to bring them out."

With that, the whole atmosphere changed. In the time it took my father to speak those few words, I went from spiraling despair to a bracing realization: "God *is* in control. I have nothing to worry about." The peace I had was genuine.

After that incident, I realized what my dad had gone through for all those decades on the road. He had had to rely on God to get him through every worry about us and about Mom while he was continents away from us. Both of my sons are involved in ministry today, and both of them talk openly about that pot bust. God has used the experience to their good, and a parent couldn't ask for more than that.

•—•

DURING A TRIP TO LATVIA, Dad and I were strolling through a park when we took a brief rest on a bench. "I don't talk much about this," Dad said, "but I struggle terribly with something." He cleared his throat and said, "I wonder whether God loves me."

That was the first time I had heard my father express this. I was taken aback.

"Most of the time I know he loves me," he said. "But I still go through droughts. I feel I'm not pleasing God, that I'm not doing enough."

I brought up what immediately came to mind for me — Dad's preaching on the new covenant and the Lord's all-sufficient grace.

"Yes, I preach that," he answered. "I stand on the gospel of grace. But I still feel like I'm under the works of the law, like I'm trying to earn God's favor. I catch myself at it."

His vulnerability opened a door, and it led to some surprising conversations. I learned, for instance, that my mother had almost left him once — no wonder, given their many hills and valleys over the years. Dad also confessed to having occasional doubts about his salvation at various times in his life. He talked a bit about his parents and how he wished they could have had more joy in God. And he asked me questions about my marriage, which really took me by surprise. I thought, "Whoa, did I hear right? Did my father seriously just ask me for insights from my marriage?"

Those years of travel were a period of growth for him — baring his soul, reflecting on life, asking hard questions of both himself and God — and it revolutionized my faith. I hadn't realized this was happening until our travels finally ended after five years. I concluded that anyone who spent fifteen minutes with my dad would come away with stronger faith, because that had happened for me. I emerged from our time together with a sense that I could accomplish anything in God. This wasn't some nebulous feeling of "God is sovereign and can do anything he wants" but rather "God can use me, and he *wants* to use me. Therefore I can do this."

When I had pastored in Denver, I struggled the whole time, wondering, "Is this going to work or not?" Now, after five years of being around my father, I was ready to start another church, even though I hadn't learned any more about pastoring. I just *believed*. "This thing is going to work," I thought, "and I want God to use me to do it."

In all that time together, my father never taught me the role of president of a nonprofit. He never gave me the principles needed to lead an international organization. He simply modeled faith to me, and in doing that, he spoke faith into me. His faith had rubbed off in a way that could not have been taught otherwise. It had to be lived.

Sometime during our travels, I remembered an awkward moment from my childhood in Long Island, when Dad returned from a time of prayer on a mountain with a word for each of his children. "Dad, do you remember that time?" I asked. He said he did. "Do you remember you told me, 'Gary, you're going to make it through'? Well, that crushed me a little."

My father was flabbergasted. "What? No, no. I didn't mean it that way. I wanted you to know you're going to make it — just the way you have. The reason I didn't have a specific word for you was because I was already confident."

———

MY FATHER'S FAITH HAS RUBBED off on others as well, on a massive scale. Toward the end of those five years, when Dad lost stamina for international travel, Claude Houde and I fulfilled all the pastors' conferences my dad had scheduled, including one in Congo. "We told them for six months ahead of time that David Wilkerson was not coming," Claude says. We had organized the conference thinking a few thousand pastors might attend, but we really expected only a few hundred. Eleven thousand pastors showed up. "That's the impact of a man who had never set foot in that country," Claude points out. *The Cross and the Switchblade* had been circulating in Congo for years.

Dad was still traveling when we held a conference in Brazil, and on our day off I was prepared to lead him on a tour through the local *favelas*, or slums, to see how World Challenge might offer help. Dad wasn't feeling well that day, so he stayed in the hotel while the rest of our team went. "You guys go," he said. "Come back and tell me what you see."

It was a question he had begun to ask us more and more: "What do you see?" Was there a need for a school? A feeding program? A church? An orphanage? But more than that, he was asking, "Are you seeing what God wants you to see?"

Two long-term ministries of World Challenge emerged from Dad's final international travels. The first was Community Development. Instead of simply giving money or equipment to people in rural villages, or building structures that would fall into disrepair, we sent workers to train locals how to be self-sustaining, whether with farming techniques or machines or buildings. "That sounds like social work," Dad said initially, but when he saw how Christian-run farms could multiply their crops with just a little bit of training, and thereby feed an entire community, he was all for it. He saw the clear connection between that kind of program and his own lifelong mantra, "When you care for the poor, God will bless your ministry."

In turn, I absorbed some wise caution from Dad. I had grown excited over Jeffrey Sachs's book *The End of Poverty*, which shows a way for everyone to pitch in to help end worldwide poverty within a certain number of years. I was all for that, but Dad was healthily skeptical. He held that poverty will never be eradicated — that man is corrupt, and left to his own devices he'll destroy his fellow man if not for God's merciful intervention. Dad's approach to the world's problems had never been to end them; his vision had always been, "In the midst of chaos and tragedy, God will have a testimony of what he's capable of doing." So, for example, instead of trying to end the problem of street orphans in Zambia, World Challenge would support a Zambian pastor, who would start a feeding program for orphans, which would improve their health, get them off the streets, and give them hope for the future.

The second ministry that emerged from Dad's travels was Please Pass the Bread, a feeding outreach that targets the world's poorest areas. Within a few years, World Challenge started or supported feeding programs that provide more than two million meals annually to more than ten thousand malnourished people in thirteen countries.

The idea for Please Pass the Bread had come to my dad as clearly as when he was called to New York in 1958 — and it happened in much the same way. He had been praying, asking God what he wanted from Dad at that stage in life, when he could no longer travel. Just as in 1958, Dad was reading a magazine when he came across an article about a pastor ministering in a slum, and he heard God's voice say, "Feed the poor."

———

"Your name will open doors. The rest has to be up to you."

Dad's words stayed with me when Kelly, I, and a few other couples started a Bible study in the basement of a Colorado Springs home. Two years later, The Springs Church was thriving, with fifteen hundred people attending Sunday services and volunteering to reach the city's poor neighborhoods. In the course of our outreach, we discovered that this reputedly Christianized city has a major heroin problem. A year passed before the problem began surfacing in the news. This was my dad's DNA at work: we had been taught to search out the very worst problems, trusting the Holy Spirit to lead us to them, so that God could bring about change.

Some people visited The Springs Church because my name is Wilkerson, and a few came seeking the holiness message they associated with it. I can honestly say no one will get a stronger holiness message than we preach at The Springs Church. They'll have drilled into them the one source of all holiness: Jesus.

As I write this, our church has been through its honeymoon period and has now leveled off. We're no longer a cool new attraction in town, which is just as God would have it. So, what now? I learned how to pray from the very best: "God, we can't do this. We need you. If you don't move, nothing will happen. Show us where to go, whom to reach, how to do it, and that's what we'll do."

I am not just a pastor in need; I'm a father in need, a husband in need, and I learned from my dad how to walk faithfully within all of these realities. I've learned to pray, "Lord, my kids get into trouble; I struggle in my marriage; I'm full of doubt and pain. Thank you, Lord — I know all these things make me your top candidate for the job."

When Carter Conlon visited The Springs Church, he was more than encouraging. "Gary, this is your scene," he said. "You're walking in a season of phenomenal grace." When Dad visited, he was genuinely amazed. "This is of God," he said. "Do you understand how rare this is, when a man gets to be part of something that God is clearly doing?" His eyes told me he knew this was what I was meant to do since I was a child. He said, "This is it, isn't it?"

"Yes, it is," I said. "It absolutely is."

"The conferences were good, weren't they?" he asked. "But you're in your reality now, aren't you?" It had been a long time in coming, and I was grateful that my father got to see it.

———

"Gwen is my ministry now. I'm just going to enjoy your mother." Dad meant these words as he announced them to us, and he proved them, by giving up all ministry activities to attend to Mom and her needs. She had become nearly blind with macular degeneration, she had constant back pain, and she could barely hobble around. Now in her seventies, our mother was diagnosed as having post-traumatic stress from the battering her body had taken through so many cancer surgeries.

Dad's own steps had also begun to slow, so the two of them did simple things together, like going to a mall to watch families stroll by. It was as if Dad were telling Mom, "Your last days will not be with me traveling. I'm going to be beside you." And his heart was in it thoroughly. Roger Hayslip observes, "He started really reflecting then. He was looking at life in a whole new light, almost as if it were being taken from him."

As Dad removed himself more and more from the ministry, his conversations with me began to shift. Whenever he talked about my leading World Challenge, he began by saying, "When I'm gone ..." His main concerns were that the ministry continue taking care of people he had pledged to support — a dozen or so couples, mostly elderly, some of whom had ministered alongside him in the early days, and others who just needed his ongoing help.

Dad still had his beloved books — C. H. Spurgeon, William Bridge, Thomas Brooks, and especially John Owen, the Puritan writer who had captivated him for twenty years. Dad even read Henri Nouwen, the Catholic priest who had become influential among evangelicals. In his later years, Nouwen gave up a prestigious academic career to work at a home for the mentally challenged in Canada, which impressed my dad. He must have identified to some degree, thinking, "This guy was willing to leave behind his reputation and ministry to work with the needy."

Yet in all his reading, Dad was still searching restlessly for what continued to elude him. He had begun to doubt God's love again. Nothing mattered more now than to find this one thing.

———

Dad was never awed by dignitaries, but he seemed particularly nonplussed as Mayor Michael Bloomberg presented him with a plaque, proclaiming Teen Challenge Day in New York City. He and Mom were back at Times Square Church for the fiftieth anniversary of Teen Challenge, looking on as Nicky Cruz, Sonny Arguinzoni, and Israel Narvaez recounted how God used one man's faithful obedience to touch millions of others with the good news. Yet before the weekend celebration ended, Dad collapsed and had to be rushed to a hospital. The stress of taking care of our mother had taken its toll on him, and his ulcers had begun bleeding.

Our father was also burdened by a newer concern. He had worried aloud to Barb Mackery about the state of his mind. Dad was forgetting things, and for a man who had shouldered responsibility all his life, it was scary to think he wasn't fully in control of his thoughts. Whenever Barb saw him start to despair, she asked Jim Cymbala to call him. Grateful to be alerted, Jim was a great source of strength to Dad, but as both of our parents began to break down, Barb finally had to call in reinforcements.

Roger Hayslip flew to New Jersey to assess the situation, and I followed the next week. When I arrived, I had never seen my father so downcast. "I'm tired, I'm hurting, and my mind is confused," he told me. "I don't know what to do."

Roger filled me in on the conversation he had with Dad. "He asked me to stay with him that first night," Roger said, noting that Dad never requested this from anyone. My father had seemed beside himself, and it was clear to Roger he needed someone to open up to. "We were talking, and he just flat out asked me, 'What was your father like?'" my brother-in-law recalls. Roger described his relationship with his father, and then asked Dad about his family life. Was he ever held? Was he ever told he was loved?

"No," Dad answered simply. He wasn't able to cry over this, so Roger did it for him.

———

MY PARENTS MOVED IN WITH Bonnie and Roger at their home in Colorado in 2010. To the daughter who had always wanted to be like her dad, it was a difficult stage of my parents' lives to see. On the one hand, Bonnie was grateful to be able to give to them, but it was also a trial. Dad didn't eat well and his health had gotten worse. Even with the Hayslips' help, his focus on Mom was breaking him down physically.

I'll always be grateful to my sister and brother-in-law for doing that heavy lifting with our parents; also to my other siblings, Greg and his wife, Teresa, who made long drives from their Dallas home to visit them; and to Debi and Roger, who took Mom and Dad into their home near Tyler after several months. The Jonkers helped them as they prepared to move into an assisted living facility in a nearby town. Yet while Mom and Dad were still in Colorado, they got the Hayslip treatment, which was direct, in-your-face love.

Whenever Dad retreated to his Bible, Bonnie told him to close it and she popped in a DVD of *The Andy Griffith Show*, because she knew our father enjoyed Barney Fife. For his part, Roger encouraged Dad to call Elder Sam, which our father did almost daily. "Sam always had a word for him that was right on target," Bonnie says. "Dad usually had tears in his eyes."

Once a week or so I drove up to the Hayslips' house from Colorado Springs to visit my parents and take Dad out to lunch. He was having a tougher time than any of us expected. "My days are done," he told me shakily, though what he said next disturbed me more: "I didn't do enough."

"Whoa, Dad," I said, "we talked about this, remember?"

"I shouldn't have bought those cars. I — "

"Dad, come on. All of your life is under the grace of the cross," I repeated. "Nobody expected you to be the superhero of the faith. Your children didn't, and God didn't."

He nodded knowingly. "I know, I know. But I'm really getting it again."

My dad was like a lot of us, in that our theology and our hearts don't always match up. On paper he was able to convince himself, "I'm free; I'm victorious; I know I'm loved by God," but in his heart he had never been fully convinced.

Further immersion in the Puritans continued to help him, which is something we discussed in one of our last conversations. Dad had a sly grin as he pulled out a book and told me, "I'm even reading John Calvin.

I want to get as much of a sense of God's peace as I can." Dad would have been uncomfortable with people knowing he read Calvin, but for any Christian seeking a deep, inner knowing of God's grace, Calvin's writing on the subject engages it beautifully.

Dad told me he didn't believe "once saved always saved," a tenet ascribed to Calvin. Instead, he read Calvin for his profound understanding of the extent of grace and the sureness of Christ's work for us. Dad was consciously trying to rid himself of the inner voice that said, "I'm not good enough. God doesn't love me, and I've got to do more." He had always been able to escape that battle through more confidence, more sacrifice, more boldness, more abandonment to God's purposes on earth, but now those escape routes no longer existed for him. He had to find true grace, something that was beyond his mind and emotions to grasp.

I believe God's grace landed mercifully with Dad one day when his strength was failing. Roger Hayslip had to take him to a hospital, and my father had forgotten his shoes. As he padded around in his socks, a patient walking by stopped and said kindly, "Here, sir, take my shoes. I can get another pair."

Dad had given his whole life to helping others, which famously included giving up his shoes to a poor kid on the streets of New York City. Now, when Dad needed to hear it most, God seemed to be asking him to receive the same loving grace.

HE DID RECEIVE. In the last few years of my father's life, he reached out to people — no longer to give, but to receive. He actually became more of a people person in the process, enjoying others and even his need of them. He must have settled the fact that he had no more mountains to climb or flags to capture, so now he could share his heart openly with others, to the extent that he was able.

He began calling Uncle Don and Aunt Ruth regularly, listening and asking a lot of questions. "He would call just to talk, and he had never done that before," Uncle Don says. "He would ask about my arthritis, and I would ask how he was doing. I know he had some long phone conversations with Ruth."

Bonnie and Roger were even more determined to see Dad connect with his siblings, so they arranged for a mini family reunion, inviting everyone to their Colorado home for a long, relaxing weekend. Jerry and Eve couldn't make it, but Uncle Don and Aunt Ruth did. "It was so good to be able to sit and watch the Super Bowl with Dave Wilkerson," Uncle Don says, "but it took all those years to happen. He was totally retired, totally out of ministry, and we just talked."

They recounted the Turtle Creek days, with Dad being reminded that he had teased Uncle Don by saying he was adopted. Uncle Don also reminded my dad of something special: "You became my father figure when Dad died. Preaching with you at Times Square Church was one of the great experiences of my life."

Aunt Ruth recalled the times Dad had helped her financially or sent her money out of the blue. "Why did you do that?" she asked. "Because I love you, Ruth," Dad said.

My father had begun calling me quite a bit, too, yet these calls were a lot different from our conversations in the old days. Dad didn't offer advice the way he once had. On the rare occasion I asked for it now, he answered, "Just figure it out for yourself. I'm too tired, and I can't wrap my mind around it. Do what God tells you to do. You've got this. You're going to be okay." Those were words of pure love.

❧

WHEN MY PARENTS MADE THEIR final move to Texas, Roger Jonker noticed the tenderness my dad showed my mom. "It was almost like he was trying to make up for all the traveling, all those years of being away from her," Roger says. Dad was also grateful to the Jonkers for even small kindnesses, effusive over the simplest bowl of soup Debi served for lunch.

Those moments were gratifying to my sister. Like the rest of us, Debi carried a measure of sadness over the lost time with our dad, whether from his literal absences or the conversations always running in his head. She had never resented him for that. Perhaps more than the rest of us, Debi had sensed that when Dad had to be away, his mind was on us and Mom. She recalled a moment from childhood when our father returned late at night from traveling and crept into her bedroom carrying something dark and furry. At first she thought it was a stuffed monkey, but quickly realized it was a live poodle. That gift probably didn't make our mom too happy, but it said everything about how Dad wanted us to know he loved us.

Our father preached his final church sermon in Tyler, at Debi and Roger's church, at the invitation of their pastor. Dad's message was on how to get through trials. He had a grandchild on his mind that morning; our family had been rocked by news of stage 4 cancer in Brandon Hayslip. "Brother Dave was hurt, torn, deeply grieved," says Roger Hayslip. "And he knew he couldn't fix it. He had to leave it in God's hands."

As Dad preached, he referenced a familiar passage in Hebrews: "'Believe that God is a rewarder of those who trust Him before the sons of man,'" he read. "This is foundational. You have to be convinced that no matter what you're going through, you are loved."

As I picture my dad saying those words, I mentally hit the pause button. "You are loved." He had preached from this same passage in Hebrews many times at Times Square Church. No one could have known the struggle behind those three words — "You are loved" — as my dad spoke them now.

"The Lord loves you no matter what, no matter how many lies you hear from the enemy, no matter how deep and difficult your life is," he preached. "People have written to me about having 'eclipses of faith.' This is when you go through a period that's dark, and you can't see the light, and you sense that God isn't answering your prayers. You've prayed, you've done everything the Bible says you ought to do to get an answer, but the dark just goes on and on.

"I'm a grandfather. We have ten grandchildren and two great-grandchildren, and a lot of the terror, the difficulties of keeping peace of mind, come because of the pain of others, those near and dear to your heart. I want to assure you of something this morning: You are never more loved than when you're in a trial. The Bible says we're to know and to believe the love that God has for us. I am seventy-nine, and I've seen a lot and been through a lot, and the one thing I know, the thing that has kept me over all these years, is that no matter what is thrown at me, God loves me.

"I used to think, 'I'm trusting God because of who God is.' No, he is a *rewarder*, and he asks us to reach out for the miraculous and say, 'Lord, I want a token of your goodness.' The great goodnesses that flow out of his storehouse include strength, peace of mind, and spiritual blessings. These are not just something in heaven, what's laid up for us in glory. No, we're living *here*, and we have to have God's goodness *now*."

That was the statement of my dad's life. From the time he was a pastor in Philipsburg, my father needed God *now* — to save him from a life of routine churchgoing drudgery; to preserve his life as he went to the streets of New York City; to believe for the deliverance of addict after addict; to believe for the soul and calling of every young person he preached to; to believe for healing and strength through all of his family's cancers.

"When you pray tonight, look by faith for the next day or the next week to offer you some little token of good, some of the great goodness of God. You may say, 'That's pretty brash, you know, "God, you owe me."' No, he made the statement, he put it out there, and we have to lay hold of it — some token, some sign or hint that God is in our situation. A little something that could come from nowhere but God.

"If you've had too many bad days, maybe you need a good day when you just lay down your battles and the Holy Spirit comes to you. I promise you in the power of his Word, God will send you goodness. And he's going to see you through."

It was vintage Dad, and it was the last sermon he preached. With that, David the giant slayer laid down his sword for the last time.

———

ON MY LAST VISIT TO SEE MY FATHER, he was eager to show me what he was learning from an old Puritan writer. The book was by William Bridge, titled *A Lifting Up for the Downcast*. The title said everything I needed to know about what was on Dad's mind. Bridge was known for his writings on the comfort of the Holy Spirit to reinforce to us the security we have in Christ, that Jesus' work for us supersedes the tremors of our nerve endings.

"There's more here," Dad said, tapping the book as he handed it to me. He didn't say anything more, but his tone urged, "Don't neglect this.

You can save years for yourself, your kids." I marveled at a nearly eighty-year-old man who was as hungry for a revelation of Jesus as he had been at twenty-five — and as needful of that revelation as he had been at any point in his life.

More than any other book of my dad's, I loved the one he wrote when he first pastored Times Square Church, *Hungry for More of Jesus*. That title was the great answer to the question he had asked as a young minister: "Is there more?" When he asked this, he wondered, "Isn't there more that God can do in this world? Can't he save more? Can't he deliver more?" The answer then was yes, that the Lord reveals himself in loving, caring action. Now the book's title answered the one question my father was asking most needfully: "Is there more for me to understand of Christ's love, in what he has already done for me?"

The phrase "more of Jesus" had been sufficient for my father his whole life, at every stage, for every need. And yet now Dad was telling me there was even more: "There is more to know of God's nature, more to see of what he has done for us. And there is more to do to serve this hurting world. We have unfinished business. Don't neglect it."

I pored over Dad's margin notes in the William Bridge book on the flight home. With every page I turned I saw the evidence of his continuing hunger. Long passages were underlined emphatically in red; paper clips marked so many pages they almost doubled the book's thickness. In every book Dad liked, he had written, "This is the key," and no doubt he had tucked away in his heart every key that William Bridge offered.

Dad offered one of those keys to Barb Mackery while it was on his mind. In January 2011 she was in a Gap store in Manhattan when Dad called on her cell phone. He told Barb to read 1 Peter 1:6 – 9 and hide it in her heart. "He said I didn't need to get back to him with any comments," notes Barb, who had to ask the salesclerk for a pen to jot down the reference. "He told me just to hold on to those verses." Barb looked up the passage in the New Living Translation:

"So be truly glad. There is wonderful joy ahead, even though you have to endure many trials for a little while. These trials will show that your faith is genuine. It is being tested as fire tests and purifies gold — though your faith is far more precious than mere gold. So when your faith remains strong through many trials, it will bring you much praise and glory and honor on the day when Jesus Christ is revealed to the whole world. You love him even though you have never seen him. Though you do not see him now, you trust him; and you rejoice with a glorious, inexpressible joy. The reward for trusting him will be the salvation of your souls."

———

UNCLE DON WAS IN THE parking lot of the Teen Challenge Center in Brooklyn when his cell phone rang. It was his sister Ruth, calling with the news.

My cousin Kristy was working part time at the center. She looked out the office window and saw her dad sitting on the curb below, his shoulders heaving. She ran downstairs to find out what was wrong, and when he told her, she sat down beside her father, put her arms around him, and wept with him.

My parents had just been visiting with Debi and Roger at their home near Tyler when they decided to go for a drive. Dad had just gotten his license renewed, and as they drove along a two-lane highway not far from the Jonkers' home, the wreck took place. It happened as they crossed a bridge at the same time as an eighteen-wheeler, and their car drifted into the truck's lane. Miraculously, my mother survived. Dad did not.

All my life people had been eager to tell me what my father meant to them, and in the immediate outpouring on the web, I got a fuller picture — and it took my breath away. Two days after Dad's death, on April 29, only the Royal Wedding site and a handful of others received more hits than my dad's. I wish I could contain the outpouring of testimonies of how my father had touched lives deeply, but that would require volumes, and probably more than a lifetime to read.

———

ALONGSIDE OTHERS, I HAD THE privilege of eulogizing my father, and in doing so I didn't hesitate to mention Dad's doubts about God's love. Because my father held his cards so closely, it was news to virtually everybody. When Bob Phillips heard it, he was heartbroken.

All this time, my mother did not know the funeral was taking place.

She was still in the hospital, only slightly conscious after the accident. Mom recovered to live for another fourteen and a half months, alternating between the joy of life and grieving for my dad, pining to be with him. What a journey they'd had.

"When they got married and pastored a little church in Pennsylvania, I don't think either David or Gwen had a clue what was coming," Roger Hayslip says. "They were two normal people from this meager, country Pennsylvania lifestyle. When *The Cross and the Switchblade* exploded, all of a sudden they were in this weird fishbowl world. Put yourself in Brother Dave's shoes: 'I've got to figure this out as it goes, because I'm in it and I can't bail now.'"

The life my father lived never should have happened, not the way that it did. Any way you might try to plan it out, it wouldn't add up. He wasn't supposed to emerge from the hills to write a bestselling book, never having written more than a sermon. He wasn't supposed to break down racial barriers, but that happened in the earliest days of his ministry, before civil rights in America. He wasn't supposed to break down denominational barriers, coming from a strict Pentecostal-holiness background, and yet the worldwide ministry he started has known no boundaries.

Uncle Don recently went back to Pennsylvania to visit Philipsburg, Turtle Creek, and the Living Waters Campground. "What amazes me is how small the churches were, how small the towns were, how small our thinking was," he says. "To be able to look back and contrast where we came from — it really is a miracle. David, the shepherd boy — it's so biblical."

"He wasn't of great stature; he didn't overwhelm you in personality; he wasn't really a people person," Barry Meguiar says. "He didn't have great talent for doing much of anything. And yet he was one of the most powerful men who ever lived. How does that happen? God. It was just God. I traveled with him — I knew his flaws and his idiosyncrasies, and I knew how God used him. I am to this moment in awe of this man of God. He shaped my life; he shaped my family's life; he was a second dad to my kids. He was my great friend, but he was on another level from me. He was the real deal."

As a young convert, Winkie Pratney visited Central Bible Institute, where my dad attended for a year. "His professors said, 'We don't remember very much about David in terms of student life. He wasn't a great athlete, he wasn't a scholar, and he wasn't the main guy. But he was always present for noon prayer, and he was always out there on Saturday nights to evangelize.' I thought, 'What a wonderful summary of David's life.' He was the model of an evangelist. But even deeper than that, he was a man who wanted to see God show up again and again and again, to do the things that he knew God could do."

Even the secular world acknowledges as much. After Dad's death, MSNBC's Martin Bashir did a profile of him on the "Clear the Air" segment at the close of the broadcast. Without giving Dad's name, Bashir enumerated the amazing contributions of one of America's "most remarkable public servants." Only at the end of the segment did Bashir mention David Wilkerson, because he sensed Dad would have wanted it that way. Very simply, Bashir said in closing, "Let there be no doubt, America lost a saint."

———

"THE OVERALL PICTURE OF HIS life was one of great worldwide renewal," historian Vinson Synan says of my father. "It's a picture of changing the face of Christianity and of evangelizing the world." Fellow historian Stanley Burgess notes, "He had an impact all the way through his life, and it happened in different groups."

"I see David as having been no different from William Carey," Uncle Don says, referring to the pioneering missionary who transformed life for many in India. "I know how that might come across, saying it about my own brother, but in reality David broke ground in what I call 'the fourth world,' a particular subculture. Addicts are a whole people group — there are 225 million today, not including alcoholism — and they are the same all over the world, with the same traits, no matter what their race or nationality. David went to them with compassion when the world had written them off. If you read David's early tract *A Positive Cure for Drug Addiction*, it's just as relevant today as then. The message is, 'God is no respecter of persons. He has healed others, and he can do it for you.'"

"Our dream is to put hope within the reach of every addict," says Jerry Nance, president of Global Teen Challenge. As he speaks, he is packing to fly to Europe to celebrate twenty-five years of ministry on that continent. "We're in ninety-four countries already, and thirty-three more have asked us to come to their nation," Jerry says. "I just keep saying yes. I don't feel like I can stop pushing or give up. Teen Challenge leaders will give everything to build these ministries, and that's what Dave Wilkerson taught us. He drew out our gifts to do what God endowed us to do."

"There was something unique about his willingness to entrust to teenagers what he thought God wanted to do," says Dave Batty, who assembled an illustrated history of Teen Challenge for its fiftieth anniversary. "Rarely do I see teenagers from the church community being recruited today to be actively involved in ministry the way he recruited them."

"He was a folk hero," says Denny Duron. "*The Cross and the Switchblade* was the textbook for anybody who wanted to do something heroic for God. We were enamored of the man who boldly walked into Brooklyn and in the name of Jesus took on the whole gang culture."

"He was fearless," says Uncle Jerry.

"It was love," Aunt Eve says. "There was a love in him that came out, and everybody around him was touched by it. Dave was just different. It takes a different kind of guy to be up in New York City and go out at nighttime by yourself, among the street people to talk with them. He talked to everybody on the street, and it was God's love that drove him."

—■—

"VERY POSSIBLY, BROTHER DAVE'S MOST effective years of ministry were at the end, when he felt like he was doing the least," says Dallas Holm. "Some of his best sermons were those he preached at Times Square Church, the messages of a man who had learned an awful lot. Through all the times of testing, the great successes and accumulation of what he'd done, the trials of all the cancers, we could observe a testimony of faithfulness."

"How many people were fed through his newsletters?" Uncle Don asks. "How many have come up to me and said, 'Thank your brother; his messages have been lifesavers to me'?"

"He had the wisdom to recognize the difference between what was of God and what wasn't," Steve Hill said. "He didn't always get it right, but he would admit that. The bottom line was you knew he cared about you."

"To me, David Wilkerson was the conscience of America," says Tim Dilena, who now pastors under Jim Cymbala at The Brooklyn Tabernacle. "When the pendulum swung one way, he had the ability to speak with an authority to try to get the pendulum back to normal. The difference between him and others is he would warn of the consequences. I don't think warning is in the language of the American church today; we've lost the heart to do it. Brother Dave had that. He could warn a nation and warn God's bride, the church.

"I feel like we're salesmen today, and the reason for that is we don't pray. Everybody today is an echo. They go to a conference to hear what everybody else is saying, and then they repeat it. But Brother Dave was intimate with God, and that's what allowed him to be a voice."

Jim Cymbala concurs. "Very few people are lifting their voices," he says. "All the statistics prove that, by every measurable parameter, the Christian church is sinking. Part of the problem is what we've been fed for the last ten, fifteen, twenty years — the focus on church growth, on being user-friendly, seeker-sensitive. All that has opened the door to unbiblical teaching, just shallow nonsense. It's resulted in getting away from prayer, away from the gospel, away from loving all people of all races, away from dependence on the Holy Spirit. My editor asks, 'Where are the Tozers, the David Wilkersons who'll say, "In all love, that is wrong"?'

"We're not preaching the gospel. The Lord said, 'My house shall be called a house of prayer,' and there are no prayer meetings anymore. There's hardly any prayer at all. When I think of David Wilkerson's life, I think, 'God, I want more of your Spirit in my life.'"

"Nowadays, there is so much talk about 'taking a city,'" Uncle Don says. "They talk about finding the 'controlling demons' of that city and praying against them. Come on. Come into New York City and show me a city you took. That saddens me, because it's just pride." To both my father and my uncle, New York City was a humbling place. "Even with all our victories, when great things would happen, the need in New York always remained so massive," Uncle Don says. "We always felt like we were dipping a small bucket into the ocean, and that leveled us out. David never had triumphalism."

There was one area where my dad allowed himself to revel in the triumphant. It was in the sea of faces he saw when he visited a Teen Challenge center — joyful, worshipful faces, each representing a miracle. For Dad, ministry was about those faces, each one an infallible proof of Jesus' power to transform a life.

It had all started with faces, in fact — seven of them, staring back at my father from a pen-and-ink illustration in *Life* magazine, late one night in his study in Philipsburg, Pennsylvania. Seven lost boys who, despite his best efforts, my dad never got to meet. Yet therein lay the substance of my father's faith: he pressed forward on the evidence of things yet unseen, because he believed — and that belief shifted the world ever so slightly.

———

THE VERY IDEA OF A BOOK LIKE THIS would have been anathema to my dad. "He never would have allowed it," Roger Hayslip says. In our dad's eyes, his life was simply a picture of normal Christianity, of a man who was flawed but yielded. To me, that's the very reason his life is worth writing about. "We're all flawed," says Dr. Stanley Burgess, "but we're not all yielded."

My father never saw enough significance in his life to write about it, except in terms of sermon illustrations that might help others. Maybe he was too busy from day to day to notice anything more than the details. I doubt it. Every time my dad asked me, "What do you see?" I sensed he was getting the big picture, the world as seen through the eyes of Christ.

What do I see, Dad? No, the question is, What did *you* see?

You saw a violent, angry Puerto Rican gang leader transformed into a life-changing messenger for Jesus. You saw ghostly, tossed-away lives rescued from the world's dark corners. You saw miracles take place, one life at a time, in a humble house run by humble young people on Clinton Avenue. You saw families broken by addiction reconciled and restored. You saw purpose fill the hearts of thousands of young people night after night, in town after town, nation after nation. You saw the poor lifted up from despair in all the troubled places you traveled, bringing the hope of Christ. You saw downcast pastors in impoverished countries renewed in body and spirit. You saw hungry young leaders take inspiration from your life and change their world as you did. You saw the homeless resting on the shoulders of the powerful, brought together under one roof by Jesus' love. And you saw yourself change, slowly freed from inner bondages, through the revelation of God's glorious grace. In all these things you saw the impossible made possible — a glimpse of the day to come when the lion will lie down with the lamb — all because you believed.

▸━━◂

AS THIS BOOK WAS BEING finished, an email message came from Uncle Don. He was elated to send it:

> What a surprise message I got on Facebook today. It was from Katie Farmer, of the Farmer family whose 15-year-old son, Michael, was killed in 1957 by the Egyptian Dragon gang, who were then tried for murder. It was the murder of Michael Farmer as depicted in *Life* magazine that drew David to New York City. Michael would have been Katie's uncle. In researching her family's history, Katie came across the Teen Challenge story linked to Michael's death. Someone gave her *The Cross and the Switchblade* and told her about me. She now lives in Long Island, NY.
>
> I am going to have her visit Brooklyn Teen Challenge and perhaps go with her to where Michael lived in upper Manhattan. This is the first ever link to any family member of the gang murder and Farmer family. She is taken aback to learn all the good that came from their family's tragic death. I'll keep you posted.
>
> Thank you, Jesus. Do we have a story to tell her.

ACKNOWLEDGMENTS

AS I OFFER MY THANKS to everyone who helped to produce this book, I need to begin by acknowledging someone at the center of the story who died since I undertook its writing; her contributions are all the more appreciated now. Thanks to my mother, Gwendolyn Rose Wilkerson, who went to be with Jesus fourteen and a half months after my father died. I'm grateful, Mom, that I could draw on your 1978 memoir, *In His Strength*, for your insights into our family's history and into your marriage to Dad. I love you.

My thanks to everyone who graciously offered help through their time and resources. Hopefully these generous people will recognize the immense value of their contributions in the pages of this book:

To my coauthor, Scott Sawyer, an editor for my father and for World Challenge for many years. This book would not have been possible without his interviews, long hours of research, and drawing up the manuscript. Scott was the only one I even thought of to put all of this onto paper, and I believe he was the one on God's mind for this as well. He has a keen mind, a Christ-centered heart, a yeoman's work ethic, and a skilled pen. He made this process a true joy.

To my siblings, Debi, Bonnie, and Greg, whose hearts are embedded alongside mine in our dad's story and yet whose own stories with him are sacred, precious, and to be preserved as theirs alone; thank you for your contributions to my all-too-brief version of Dad's life here.

To the World Challenge executive team whose wise oversight and helpful encouragement guided this book to its publication: Barbara Mackery, my father's personal secretary for forty-two years, whose insights into Dad's day-to-day thinking are nonpareil; and Roger Jonker, my brother-in-law and chief operating officer of World Challenge, whose insights into my father's unusual business approaches and whose recounting of Twin Oaks' history were immensely helpful. Both Barb and Roger offered time and efforts beyond any reasonable expectation.

To John Sloan, a visionary editor whose generosity, confidence, and encouragement inspired the shaping of this account of my father's life, and whose patient, wise, and steady hand saw it through to completion; the Zondervan editorial team, who astutely navigated and sharpened the thematic tracks within the mountainous narrative we submitted to them; the art and design team of Curt Diepenhorst, Sarah Johnson, and Kim Tanner; Brian Phipps and the production team, whose keen perception and care were crucial in the final editorial stages; Alicia Kasen and the marketing team, whose enthusiastic labors have brought this book to your hands; and the Zondervan publishing board for faith in a story that new generations may now get to know.

To Don and Cindy Wilkerson, my aunt and uncle, for personal tours through Brooklyn, Philipsburg, Turtle Creek, Barnesboro, Cherry Tree, and Living Waters Camp in Pennsylvania, and for dozens of hours spent gazing into my father's life, offering stories the world had never heard; my aunt Ruth Harris, whose book *The Wilkerson Legacy* remains a remarkable document of our forebears and the particular faith that ignited and launched my father's life of service; my uncle Jerry and aunt Eve Wilkerson, for offering a window into my father's adolescent years unknown to the rest of us; my cousin Kristy Wilkerson, for her especially perceptive portrait of the relationship between our grandmother and our aunt Juanita; and my brother-in-law Roger Hayslip, whose observations as both son-in-law to my dad and fellow minister/missionary offer a one-of-a-kind perspective.

To David Patterson, a wise narrator and firsthand witness to an important period in my father's life, and whose help in pioneering a unique crusade ministry remains a special contribution to the work of God's kingdom; and Carol Patterson, who propped up my dad on the administrative end until her sister, Barb, arrived for the long haul. The Pattersons have remained valued editors of my father's work over the decades.

To Nicky Cruz and Sonny Arguinzoni, among the first to encounter my father's gift of faith on the streets of New York City, and whose memories and insights are especially noteworthy after their own decades of godly service through renowned ministries.

To the witnesses of those early days when bold outreaches like my father's were largely unknown in US domestic church ministry: Dr. Donald Argue, Winkie Pratney, Dick Simmons, Dr. John Kenzy, Mike Zello, Sonia Dilena, and David Ravenhill.

To John and Elizabeth Sherrill, venerable pioneers in their own field, whose memories of work with my father revealed new dimensions of *The Cross and the Switchblade*, named by *Christianity Today* one of the Top Fifty Books That Have Shaped Evangelicals.

To Pat Boone, whose enduring friendship with my father provided telling perspectives on two crucial eras in my dad's pursuit of God.

To Barry and Karen Meguiar and Dr. Jack and Berneita Rice, whose faithful friendships with my parents provided tender insights into my dad from a special vantage point; Barry and Dr. Rice continue to serve with me as board directors at World Challenge.

To Ralph and Allene Wilkerson, whose work with my father during the Jesus Movement remains a milestone in American church history as well as in the hearts of a generation still loving Jesus fifty years hence.

To the crusade team, ministry staff, and friends who made it all go under my dad's leadership, and whose memorable experiences with him enliven these pages: Dallas Holm, Bob Rogers, Richard Schulz, Jerry Nance, Craig Smith, Paul Annan, Don Haney, Ken Berg, Connie Granberry, Bettina Marayag, Sam Maloney, Alan Nunn, Steve Coke, David Batty, Stanley Waldshan, and a multitude of others who spent precious years alongside Dad supporting both his work and our family.

To ministry associates who walked alongside my father to bring many victories in far-reaching places: Carter Conlon, Claude Houde, Jim Cymbala, Tim Dilena, Denny Duron, Neil Rhodes, Bob Phillips, Steve Hill, and others too numerous to list here, including many faithful servants of Christ all over the world.

To my wife, Kelly, and our children, Ashley, Evan, Elliott, and Annie, some of whose stories I have included with their permission, and whose love and faith are my greatest treasures.

And to others close to home: Valene Stoda, my executive assistant, whose vigilant management kept us on track and who together with the talented David Rhody supplied creativity and midnight-hour diligence for the photo spread; Joy Sawyer, my coauthor's wife and creative partner, whose perceptive insights into my father's earliest books and writings became bricks in the pavement of this book's narrative; Erika Thomas, whose efforts with photos under the duress of childbirth deserves special mention; Mariah Tramonto, Teri Schaller, and the team at Mile High Transcription, for timely and thoroughly professional work; and to our stellar, hardworking agents, Madeleine Morel and Tamara Shannon.

My deepest thanks to the late John McCandlish Phillips, the standard-setting feature writer at the *New York Times*, who championed my father's ministry from its earliest days in New York City. John was among those unique friends of Dad's who shared his prophetic vision and whose very public devotion to seeing Christ's name exalted are treasured contributions in God's kingdom.

Finally, I'm indebted to the many sources, published and unpublished, that helpfully supplied so much information about my father's life. These include my dad's own journals, sermons, newsletters, and the forty books he wrote, most notably those with the Sherrills, *The Cross and the Switchblade* and *Beyond the Cross and the Switchblade*; John Sherrill's *They Speak with Other Tongues*; my aunt Ruth Wilkerson Harris's book, *The Wilkerson Legacy*; my uncle Don's many books with stories about Teen Challenge; my sister Debi's book, *Letters of Comfort*; Harrison Salisbury's book *The Shook-Up Generation*; Dr. Vinson Synan's magisterial church history, *The Holiness-Pentecostal Tradition: Charismatic Movements in the Twentieth Century*; Dr. Stanley Burgess's equally monumental history, *Christian Peoples of the Spirit: A Documentary History of Pentecostal Spirituality from the Early Church to the Present*; the amazing history *Teen Challenge: Fifty Years of Miracles*, assembled by David Batty and Ethan Campbell; the archives of Ken Berg; the website of the inspiring journalist Dan Wooding; Christine D. Johnson's interview with John and Elizabeth Sherrill on the *Christian Retailing* website; and the many personal notes, letters, and materials provided by other helpful contributors. Thank you all.